FACING ALZHEIMER'S

Family Caregivers Speak

Patricia Brown Coughlan

BALLANTINE BOOKS • NEW YORK

Copyright © 1993 by Patricia Brown Coughlan

All rights reserved under International and Pan-American Copyright Conventions. Published in the United States of America by Ballantine Books, a division of Random House, Inc., New York, and simultaneously in Canada by Random House of Canada Limited, Toronto.

Library of Congress Catalog Card Number: 93-90068

ISBN 0-345-37549-1

Manufactured in the United States of America

First Edition: May 1993

Praise for
FACING ALZHEIMER'S

"The caregiver plays one of the most significant roles in the life of an Alzheimer's patient, and certainly one of the most difficult. [Coughlan's] book provides guiding strength for those in a position to deliver care. I know [her] words will bring comfort and companionship to the many families across the country who are coping with this devastating disease."

MARK O. HATFIELD
United States Senator
Oregon

"These courageous tales of coping with Alzheimer's disease together with the important expert advice and resources included in the book will make readers who are doing the difficult job of caring for an Alzheimer's patient feel less isolated and more empowered to do this overwhelmingly difficult job."

ROBERT N. BUTLER, M.D.
Brookdale Professor of Geriatrics and Adult Development
Mt. Sinai Medical Center

"This book gives very direct insights into the problems and challenges faced by caregivers, *as caregivers themselves perceive those problems and challenges*. It is an important addition to the growing body of literature on an urgent topic."

DANIEL THURSZ
President
National Council on the Aging, Inc.

To Roger Alan Scott
1948–1969

TABLE OF CONTENTS

❧

ACKNOWLEDGMENTS

This book has grown from work that was originally undertaken in pursuit of my master of arts degree in Interdisciplinary Studies/ Gerontology at Sonoma State University. I wish to thank Susan Hillier Parks, director of the gerontology program at Sonoma State, for her wise and gentle counsel, her enthusiasm for this project, and her unflagging support. Susan Carney spent countless hours with me as a friend and mentor in two different internships. Pamela Street also served in an advisory capacity. These women gave unstintingly of their time and emotional energy, and I am deeply indebted to them.

Tom Rosin was a delight to work with. His insightful questions and challenges were always offered in a spirit of genuine intellectual curiosity, with an understanding of what I was trying to accomplish, and a respect for it. His willingness to help push this work closer to the light of day is much appreciated. Thanks are also due the students of his anthropology proseminar for their gratifying and thoughtful comments.

It's been my good fortune to have had fine teachers throughout my life. Special thanks reach over the years to my early sociology professors at the University of California at Santa Cruz, Arlie Hochschild and Mark Messer, for giving me such an enduringly interesting slant on things.

I have been inspired and motivated by many people I have met over the last several years, including all of the volunteers at four of the annual Alzheimer's respite weekends sponsored by the Sonoma County Alzheimer's Task Force, and the staff and volunteers of the Alzheimer's respite centers sponsored by Catholic Charities here in Sonoma County. Scott Hale, who generously agreed to be interviewed, has worked tirelessly on behalf of Alzheimer's families, along with Ann McGee, Katherine Yoder, and others. Support group leaders Sharon Lieberman and Jeanne Goff provided invaluable insights, and I cannot thank them enough. Susan Ziblatt and all of the volunteers at the

Sonoma County Ombudsman Program are models of dedication and caring, serving as advocates for nursing home residents and their families. These people have all provided me with a vision of what it really means to be part of a community.

Donna Ambrogi of the California Law Center for Long Term Care, Nancy Crowe of the Medi-Cal office in Santa Rosa, and Elizabeth Finn of the Sonoma County Ombudsman Program all made themselves available to me. They patiently explained and reexplained complex subjects, sharing my hope that I'd be able to write about them in a clear and understandable way. Peter B. Dunne, M.D., and Dr. Carolyn Ellis, both of the University of South Florida, read the manuscript and made valuable suggestions.

Nancy Powers-Stone, Cynthia Scarborough and the staff of the Redwood Caregiver Resource Center have been valued colleagues. Robert Lumpkins and Elenore Schoen helped me greatly by giving valuable background interviews, and Salli Rasberry helped to guide me through the uncharted waters of the publishing business. My friends John and Teresa Stafford, Barbara Heffel, Martha Boyd, Carolynn Ranch, Theresa McDowell, Marilyn Sommer, Assunta Martin, Barbara Gauger, Vicky Tidwell, Patricia Gonnella, Jonanne Wimmer, Winifred Kingsbury, and many others, have been a deep well of faith and support.

I'm forever grateful that Iris Bass of Ballantine Books, through her own experience of friendship and caring, recognized something in this work that made her willing to give it a chance.

I've been richly rewarded by the enthusiasm of my parents, Catharine and John Lott Brown, and my mother-in-law, Jeanette Coughlan. My sister, Judy Brown, provided valuable resource materials. My children, Georgia and Robert Coughlan, have kept me firmly grounded through thick and thin. My grandparents, Carol and Jim Brown, and all of the people like them, have been the guiding light of this entire project. My husband, Merritt Coughlan, has made all of it possible.

The members of the Alzheimer's support group, each in his or her own way, have been an inspiration. I thank every one of them, past and present, for continually helping me to renew my commitment to this work.

* * *

I am humbled by the willingness of Aileen, Angie, Bonnie, Edith, Helen, Irene, Mabel, and Mary to share their stories with me. It is not possible to imagine more inspiring voices speaking for the legions of our friends, relatives, and neighbors who give care. I can only hope that I do them justice here.

INTRODUCTION

Sixteen years ago, my grandmother drank a glass of wine. There was nothing unusual about that. What was unusual was that after she drank it she couldn't find her way to the bathroom. I have always remembered that incident as the first time I really thought there was something seriously wrong with her. Up until that day, there had been no compelling reason to think a problem existed.

Just the summer before, she and my grandfather had driven from their home in Ohio to visit friends and relatives all over the United States, finally arriving at my house in northern California. She had seemed more irritable than usual to me, but I hadn't been alarmed by that. After all, she was seventy-five years old, and the trip had been long and very tiring. When she told me about getting lost walking on the logging roads in the woods above my house, and how my dog, Myra, had led her back home, I didn't think much about that, either. Those dirt roads through the woods *were* confusing.

It was so easy, in hindsight, to pick out a number of minor incidents that all could have served as warnings of her deteriorating mental state: the way she panicked at her total inability to decide what to wear to an important social function, the time she held the end of the garden hose in her hand as she called my mother out of the house to ask her where the water faucet was, or the irate phone call she received from a friend of hers who was angry about a forgotten lunch date. None of those things, in and of themselves, was enough to sound the alarm. None of them, taken individually, was particularly alarming. All of them, taken as a whole, pointed in a very distressing direction.

Eventually, it became apparent that my grandmother was suffering from dementia. "Dementia" is not the name of a specific disease, but is a word used to describe the mental condition of a person whose memory is impaired, and whose problems with processing information are severe enough to interfere with his or her ability to function normally. It is generally understood to be a progressive condition, and is not considered by medical sources to be a result of the normal aging process.

Extensive medical tests were done on my grandmother, and treatable causes for her memory problems and reasoning difficulties were ruled out one by one. It was also determined that her condition had not been caused by any sort of stroke or vascular accident. And so she was given the diagnosis that people like her are given: senile dementia, Alzheimer's type.

The incidence of Alzheimer's disease is commonly given as 5 percent among people over the age of sixty-five, and 20 percent for people over eighty. Other conditions, such as recurrent small strokes and certain cases of Parkinson's disease, for example, can also interfere with thinking and memory functions.

What happened to my grandmother is happening to increasing numbers of people all the time. Modern medicine has made major advances in the last few decades in conquering infectious diseases and developing treatments, medications, and surgical remedies for conditions that were assumed to be fatal in the past. Our success at treating more and more medical conditions means that more and more people are living long enough to develop dementing illnesses, and long enough to require total care, sometimes for many years. My grandmother, a thirty-year cancer survivor, is herself a good example of this new reality.

As the age balance of our population continues to shift upward, the necessity of providing care for dementia patients and people with other debilitating, chronic conditions will continue to be a private tragedy for families, but will increasingly become an important social issue for everyone else as well.

What happened to my grandmother is what sparked my own personal interest in the problems of people who give care, and it is my hope that somehow something of value has resulted from the effort to understand those problems better.

In the majority of cases, one person, who may or may not receive help from other family members and friends, bears the major responsibility of providing care for the dementia patient, and that person is referred to here as the primary caregiver.

For married people, the caregiver is usually the spouse; given the fact that men tend to marry women younger than themselves, the burden of caregiving within marriages falls disproportionately upon wives. In cases where a parent requires care, daughters or daughters-in-law are normally the primary caregivers.

There are many men providing conscientious and loving care for their wives or their parents. I know this because my grandfather was one of them, and because I have been lucky enough to meet a number of others. Their dedication is inspiring, and it is certainly not my intention to slight their efforts. However, at the present time, caregiving is something that still falls most heavily upon women, and this book reflects that.

Dementia patients can be extremely difficult to care for. A chief feature of dementing illnesses, as opposed to other care-intensive chronic illnesses, is that appreciation and reciprocity on the part of the patient are often completely absent. The patient may even be accusatory and paranoid.

Caregivers of spouses must adjust not only to increased responsibilities and to heavy custodial demands, but also to the loss of their partners' emotional companionship as they have known it. Relationships that have endured for years are turned upside down, and the emotional balance is thrown out of kilter. Familiar and comfortable roles no longer work, and new ways of functioning as a couple must be found.

Achieving this new balance can be especially difficult for a woman who finds herself caring for a formerly competent and strong husband; a husband who may have handled all of the couple's business affairs and who played the role of protector and provider for decades; a husband who now shadows his wife around the house, or is combative, or who wanders away, or who does all of these things to different degrees.

Many women currently in the age group most likely to find themselves in this predicament typically have very little in their experience that prepares them for the complete shift in roles that caring for a demented husband requires. What's more, they are being asked to make that shift just at the time of life when they are likely to be experiencing additional stress from things such as health problems of their own.

People facing the specter of a dementing illness in their lives want to know what they can expect in the future, but the disease process does not come with a clear road map or timetable. The progression of mental impairment may be quite rapid, or agonizingly slow.

There are books and articles on the subject that outline the stages that such patients will go through. While their information may be useful in providing an overall understanding of the likely course of a dementing illness, the fact is that no two cases are alike, and whether or not any particular patient will move through all of the prescribed stages, or at what rate he will do so, if he does so at all, is something that cannot be known in advance.

What we *can* predict is that someone providing care for a demented person will move through a series of stages of her own as the disease progresses. Each stage places different demands on the caregiver, and each stage calls for a different set of responses. These stages evolve as follows:

1. Overcoming denial that something is seriously wrong.
2. Initiating the process of obtaining a medical diagnosis and becoming an informed consumer of medical care.
3. Learning to accept the reality of the patient's condition and dealing with the losses and new responsibilities that involves.
4. Becoming an advocate for a person who is increasingly unable to speak for himself.
5. Fashioning a life for oneself in the midst of a difficult situation.
6. Facing the fact that nursing home placement may eventually become necessary.
7. Continuing to give care and support to a person in a nursing home, and becoming effective at dealing with problems encountered there.
8. Making difficult decisions about life-and-death treatment options.
9. Adjusting to life after the death of the patient.

Numerous academic studies have been done about the stresses upon people who take care of dementia patients, with the aim of providing some insight into what, specifically, caregivers find burdensome about taking care of demented people. These studies prove conclusively that giving full-time care to a demented person can be 1) stressful, and 2) depressing. But does this revelation actually help to uncover some core of commonsense wisdom that could be of real use to people facing a sad and awful predicament?

What really makes the difference between a person who can survive a terrible ongoing situation, and someone who is defeated by it? Is it possible to "succeed" at living with a dementia patient? Reading one study after another, I became convinced that people in dire straits need role models, not more surveys.

Attending meetings of an Alzheimer's support group in Santa Rosa, California, in connection with my studies in gerontology at Sonoma State University, I was fortunate enough to meet a group of successful caregivers. As it happened, all of them were women, and all of them were, or had been, in the situation of caring for their memory-impaired husbands.

When I say they were successful, I mean that I, personally, was struck by their apparent emotional strength, overall psychological well-being, and generosity of spirit. They came to the support group meetings and passed out literature, softly-spoken advice, or Kleenex, as needed. It was obvious that they had not only survived the illnesses of their husbands, and their own difficulties, but that they were willing to offer their hard-won insights as a resource for other people facing the same situation.

Eight of them agreed to be interviewed. They gave generously of their time, and spoke into my tape recorder with a candor that humbled and amazed me. By delving deeply into this small number of cases, I hoped to gain a perspective that would provide as much emotional depth as possible. The challenge was to illuminate the personal traits and survival strategies that had enabled these women to deal effectively with a devastating life circumstance.

For the next two years, I continued to attend the meetings of the support group. It was only after attending for a long time that I came to see that the group itself had played a role in the development of personal effectiveness for many of its members. This realization came about as I watched many different people in many different circumstances move through the stages of development that were becoming recognizable to me as a result of the interview work.

Along the way, a wealth of practical as well as psychological information also emerged: information about such things as dealing with medical people, making decisions about nursing homes, and the importance of getting good financial and legal advice.

It would hardly be possible for anyone, even someone who doesn't have to deal with the problems of caring for a demented person on a daily basis, to be involved with such a group for that period of time and come away unchanged.

That has certainly been true in my own case, and whatever perspective I'm able to bring to all of this is a direct result of that experience.

My hope is that anyone caring for a demented person will find something of value here, whether the person being cared for is a husband, a wife, or a parent. People who have been called upon to become another person's caregiver, advocate, and protector have a vast responsibility in common. It really doesn't matter what specific conditions have led to the assumption of that responsibility. The depth and breadth and weight of that responsibility are what matter.

The words of the caregivers themselves form the backbone of this book. Those words have a clarity that awed me the first time I heard them and that awes me still.

I wanted to know so much more about these women. Had they always been so strong, or had their experiences made them that way? I wanted to hear their stories and understand what was unique about them as people, and what was universal about their lives. I wanted to learn what they had to teach.

CHAPTER ONE

Their Stories

I was tough, and I was practical.
I became more tough, and more practical.

—Mary

Aileen

Aileen's husband, Louie, a carpenter, was only fifty-two when he started showing the symptoms of Alzheimer's disease. Aileen and Louie were able to manage well at home for nine years, but then his condition worsened sharply after his mother was attacked in her apartment and then died of cancer just a few months later. Louie became agitated and combative, and Aileen was forced to place him in a nursing home after several months of caring for him in that condition.

Aileen went to the nursing home to feed and care for Louie virtually every day, and she became a strong and knowledgeable advocate for his care. At the time of my first talk with Aileen, her husband was sixty-five years old and had been in the nursing home for four years. Several months later, Louie died. We talked again two months after his death, and once more a year later.

Aileen now goes to nursing homes with support group members to help them work through any problems they are having there. She also makes herself available at all hours to talk with people who are feeling overwhelmed by the difficulties of caring for a demented relative.

Mary

Ira, a forty-eight-year-old career army man, was confused when he got home from a tour of duty in Korea. He had been found wandering around in a small village near Seoul, his wallet missing. The army shipped him home, with no diagnosis, or any acknowledgment that he was seriously unwell.

Mary, a mother of four young children, struggled with army functionaries over the next several years in an attempt to get Ira diagnosed properly, but was repeatedly told that his problems were simply the result of his inability to readjust to family life. An army psychiatrist diagnosed him as severely depressed, and ordered shock treatments, a common practice at that time. Mary attempted to get the treatments stopped until Ira could be evaluated more carefully, but she was unsuccessful.

Ira was given twenty-two shock treatments, which only increased his memory problems. He was never fully functional again. His decline was slow, marked by long "plateau" periods, each one leaving him at a lower level of functioning than the last. With the eventual development of the CAT scan, it was revealed that Ira's problems were the result of a head injury. He lived for many years, despite the additional chronic health problems of heart disease and diabetes. He was at home with Mary until his death in 1984.

Mary worked for years to secure her family's rightful benefits from the army. Along the way, she became an expert on veterans' affairs, and she has helped many people to gain access to medical services and benefits.

Bonnie

Bonnie's husband, Henry, was fifty-five in 1980, the year his chain of retail businesses collapsed. For three years after that, he seemed very depressed and was drinking heavily. His attempt to start a new career in insurance sales was unsuccessful, due to his inability to find his way to clients' homes, or to complete paperwork properly.

In 1985, Bonnie and Henry moved. In new surroundings, Henry's condition deteriorated rapidly, and he was diagnosed with Alzheimer's disease. Bonnie placed him in a nursing home four years later, after he became combative. He died at the age of sixty-five, after eight months in the facility.

Bonnie has been involved in hospital chaplaincy activities.

Helen

Helen's husband, Donald, was sixty-three in 1983, when he woke up one morning with his face in a distorted expression. Helen thought that Donald had suffered a stroke, but their doctor diagnosed Bell's palsy. At roughly the same time, Donald began to have memory problems.

In 1985, Helen and Donald moved. Like Bonnie's husband, Donald did not adjust well to the move, and seemed to be "going downhill." In 1986, while Helen and Donald were on vacation, Helen was hospitalized suddenly. A friend had to step in and make the changes in their travel plans, since Donald did not seem to grasp the seriousness of the situation, or to be able to handle any details. It was on the same trip that friends who hadn't seen the couple for a long time remarked on the changes that they noticed in Donald.

Donald has continued to deteriorate very slowly, and his doctor believes that he has Alzheimer's disease. Helen has trouble accepting the diagnosis, due to the unusual way Donald's problems began. She feels that she has never received a credible medical explanation for this. Helen is still well able to care for Donald, in spite of her own very serious health problems, which have included cancer and kidney disease. She fully intends to continue caring for him at home as long as she is physically able to do so.

In addition to caring for Donald, Helen is the mother of a severely retarded adult daughter. The couple has no other children. Helen has served as president of the parent advocates group at the nearby state developmental center where her daughter, Janie, resides.

Mabel

Mabel's husband, Roy, was seventy-four when he started becoming confused. Despite several neurological examinations, doctors could not determine what was wrong with him.

He was placed in a nursing home after a sudden, violent episode. It was only then that the diagnosis of Alzheimer's disease was made.

At that time, the early 1980s, Mabel found the available information about the disease sparse and inadequate. Her activism stems from the difficulties that she had in getting a diagnosis for her husband. She has campaigned for funding for medical research into dementing illnesses, has testified several times before the California state legislature on the funding needs of family relief programs, has helped to establish an adult day-care center in her town, and has been instrumental in helping local families secure autopsies for their relatives with Alzheimer's disease, sometimes expediting the paperwork for the procedure in the middle of the night.

Irene

Irene's husband, Jim, was in his late fifties when he began suffering from an apparent depression. At that time, the couple still had four children at home. Jim began having problems at his engineering job, and retired at the age of sixty-two.

By 1975, when he was sixty-three, Jim was no longer able to find his way around well enough to drive. At that point, he was diagnosed as a probable Alzheimer's patient. After several more years he was wandering and incontinent. For the last seven or eight years of his life, he required complete and total personal care. Over the years of caregiving, Irene developed strategies for handling things like dressing, bathing, etc., and she generously shared her knowledge with other people in the support group. Irene kept Jim at home until his death in 1985 at the age of seventy-three.

Edith

Richard was a sixty-eight-year-old bachelor with an apple orchard when he and Edith, a widow with grown children, were married in 1974. Only two years later, he began exhibiting changes in his behavior. Three years after that, there was no doubt in Edith's mind that something was seriously wrong. At that time, Richard was diagnosed with Alzheimer's disease. Edith kept him at home for six more years until he was placed in a nursing home after suffering a stroke. He was in the nursing home until his death in 1988.

Richard had been a client of a respite program before he entered the nursing home. Such programs provide day care and activities for dementia patients so that family members can have some relief from patient care. Edith became a valued volunteer at the respite center after Richard's death, and is now a member of the staff.

Angie

Angie's husband, Hugo, was in his mid-sixties when he was diagnosed with Parkinson's disease in 1982. Hugo was a highly successful businessman, with a strong sense of control over his own life, and the Parkinson's diagnosis itself seemed to have an adverse effect on his mental state. Signs of dementia started in 1984 and were steadily progressive.

For several years, Hugo could still be taken on outings to restaurants and on short walks, but then he became increasingly difficult to manage, due to his physical rigidity and intermittent combativeness. Angie had a live-in helper, Manny, for three years. Since she could no longer physically handle Hugo alone, she had to hire additional part-time aides so that Manny could have some time off.

In 1989, she discovered that one of the helpers had been stealing from her—forty thousand dollars' worth of coins and jewelry were missing. When she went to the police for help, they suggested that she "just fire everyone." Since she was unable to do that and keep Hugo at home, she set out to trap the thief herself.

In an act of desperation, Angie sat in her hall closet with an unloaded gun throughout one person's shift, listening for signs that the man was entering parts of the house he had no business in. Eliminating that person from suspicion, she repeated the operation several days later with another helper. This time, she heard the person rummaging in her office

awers and bedroom cabinet. For forty-five minutes (she
:pt time by counting to sixty and making pencil marks on
e wall), she listened to the thief going through her things
hile her husband was restrained in a kitchen chair.

Finally, she became convinced that the thief knew she was
the closet and decided that it was time for her to act. She
mped out of the closet and pointed the gun at the man,
lling him not to move. With one hand she held the gun,
d with the other she called 911. The man was arrested, con-
cted, and served time in jail.

My first interview with Angie took place only a few weeks
ter that incident. She was still taking care of Hugo at home,
d was dedicated to keeping him there as long as she pos-
bly could. Angie did eventually place Hugo in a nursing
me for eight months, but she was unhappy with the care
received, and brought him home six weeks before his
ath. This time she hired a married couple to live in and
lp care for him.

Angie and I talked again three months after Hugo's death
the spring of 1991.

CHAPTER TWO

❧

In the Beginning

> When we got this house, he let me do *all* the corre-
> sponding with the people who were selling it . . . The
> business end, and the title company, etc. He absolutely
> referred everything back to me. I couldn't believe it,
> because he wasn't that kind of a person. He expected
> me to do everything. I had to do everything. Anything
> that required any conversation, any dealing . . . I
> thought that was so funny. And I thought, maybe he
> realizes that, possibly, I'm going to have to do this
> some day, and he wants to get me into it. That was
> my thought, at the time. So he was slipping way back
> then, twenty years before he died.
>
> —Irene

The onset of symptoms in dementing illnesses can be so
gradual that most family members respond to questions about
when the disease process began by saying something like, "I
knew for certain that there was a problem five years ago, but
looking back, I realize now that things weren't right for a
long time before that." It often takes people a while before
they are able and willing to face up to the fact that a serious
problem exists. Typically, it is only when reasoning problems
and memory losses can no longer be ignored that medical
help is sought.

The obvious loss of memory is only one of many things
that can signal the onset of a dementing illness, and the sub-
tlety and diversity of other possible symptoms almost encourages people to rationalize away troubling signs; behavior
as seemingly innocuous as a gradual withdrawal from friends

social events, and activities. For example, a person may make excuses about why he doesn't want to go fishing with the friend he has fished with for thirty years. He may seem a little more irritable or anxious than usual, somewhat less energetic, or inattentive and distracted. Someone who was previously content to sit and watch television in the evening may begin walking around the house instead.

None of these things, by themselves, would usually be enough to cause a concerned relative to seek a medical evaluation, at least not at first. The time period in which symptoms occur is also very important in terms of when medical help is sought. The case of a person who becomes more restless, inattentive, and forgetful over a long period of time will not be perceived as problematic right away, because the people around him are slowly adjusting to his new behavior, maybe without even being aware of it themselves.

On the other hand, someone who wakes up one morning and starts pacing up and down, not responding to anything anyone says to him, will draw attention much more quickly.

The picture is also complicated by the fact that a person with dementia can often function fairly appropriately socially (nodding and smiling at the right moments in a conversation), even though he may not be able to understand all of what is going on.

The experience of most people is that the patient himself usually does not initiate a discussion about his need to be evaluated medically, but sometimes patients do show that on some level they are aware that something is wrong. Like any other early sign, this is something a family member may or may not pay attention to.

Irene: He used to kid about having a hole in his head, and we always thought it was a joke. He would say to people, "Oh well, I've got a hole in my head." And it was kidding. In a kidding way. And now, when I think back, I think he more or less meant it.

Warning Signs of Dementing Illnesses

If you are wondering whether someone you know may be developing a dementing illness, the following discussion of possible early indications is offered as a general guideline. Some of these things may seem to contradict each other; for example, "emotional lability" and "flatness of response." It is important to remember that none of these things, by themselves, proves that someone is demented; only careful tests of mental functioning, administered by a professional, can determine the extent of any individual's cognitive losses.

However, any person who exhibits an overall pattern of changes or behaviors similar to the ones on the following list is probably a worthy candidate for such testing. Keep in mind that even if a person is found to be suffering from dementia, that person will most likely not manifest every single symptom on the list.

The important question in terms of any single symptom is the *degree* of trouble it causes. Losing our car in a parking lot doesn't prove anything, but if it takes us two hours to find it, or if it happens every single time we go to the store, then we may have a problem. There is a difference between someone who has the unfortunate habit of repeating himself, and someone who asks the same question over and over until the nerves of everyone around him are frayed.

It is also important to note that individual strengths and weaknesses must be taken into account. The inability to cut boards so that they would fit together snugly was an important warning in the case of someone like Aileen's husband Louie, a skilled carpenter, but we wouldn't necessarily worry about the same deficit in someone who has never cut a board before and does it badly on his first try.

The reasoning difficulties of a patient with progressive dementia become more understandable if we keep in mind that he is increasingly unable to process new information. At the same time, he is losing the ability to retrieve and use information he has accumulated throughout his life. His behavior becomes more understandable, also, if we view his actions as those of a person who, on some level, feels profoundly insecure, and is trying to maintain some sense of control and security in his life.

The symptoms of early dementia fall into the following categories:

1) personality changes
2) loss of problem-solving skills
3) communication problems
4) disorientation
5) new and unfamiliar behaviors.

1. Personality Changes

• Frustration, Anger, and Irritability

It is not hard to recognize that anyone who is losing his ability to understand what is going on around him might very well feel stymied and overwhelmed by the tasks of daily living, and irritability and anger are logical outgrowths of that frustration. A person may not even be consciously aware that his mental capacities are slipping, but he still feels baffled or annoyed as a result of his deficiencies. Mabel describes her husband Roy's anger and confusion:

Mabel: It got to the point where he would grit his teeth and double up his fist and say, "I'm going to get this settled." He had no idea what he wanted to settle, but he was always going to settle something.

Irene's husband was still working when his illness began, and his ability to stay in control of himself became a problem:

Irene: He really did realize he was slipping mentally, but I don't think he realized he was sick, or that there was anything special wrong with him. But then, he did not get along on the job. Like I would call a child. Tantrums. Temper tantrums. But this was an adult doing this. On the job.

• Emotional Lability

This term describes the state of a person whose moods are unstable and changeable. A sense of solidity is missing, and the person overreacts to seemingly trifling, inconsequential events. Sudden crying spells or inappropriate laughter might also indicate emotional lability.

• Paranoia, Suspicion, and Jealousy

Paranoia arises when the person's sense of reality is under assault. We all know what it feels like to open a drawer and not find an item that we *know* we put there. If this sort of thing happens to someone many times a day, the person will very likely make an attempt to structure an explanation for it.

Edith: He'd made his living as a mechanic. He'd keep his tools in the shed. And he'd forget. And then he'd accuse somebody of taking [something], or say, "Somebody was here and stole that," whatever it was. Because he was forgetting.

Paranoia and suspicion go hand in hand. The person who can't make sense of a conversation may conclude that people are talking about him. If he is confused by a business transaction, he may decide that the businessperson is trying to cheat him. Someone who can no longer balance his own bank account or write checks to pay his bills may accuse the person who steps in to help of stealing his money. All of these feelings stem from the sense of a loss of control over one's life.

Someone who unconsciously realizes that he is becoming more and more dependent on his wife may become jealous of her, questioning her about her whereabouts when she is away from him, or may even make unjust accusations.

• Insensitivity to Others

It is often reported in the support group that patients seem to be unaware of other people's problems and feelings. For example, a man may ask his wife, who has just come home from the hospital after having surgery, why she is so tired, or when dinner will be ready. The ability to empathize with someone else is decreased.

• "Flat" Emotional Responses

This symptom can show itself as a generalized leveling out of emotional expressiveness. Speech patterns may become more monotonous, and someone who used to have a good sense of humor may no longer laugh easily.

The person's reactions to events are not what would normally be expected, and he may seem "coldhearted." Mabel was shocked to discover that her husband had his beloved hunting dog put to sleep without saying anything to her about it:

Mabel: I asked my friend, "Has Roy said anything to you about our dog?" And she said, "Don't you know?" I said, "Know what?" She said, "He had her put to sleep three or four days ago." And the reason he had put her to sleep, she was only eight years old, was he thought her hearing was bad, and she was getting lost all the time. And after that it was as if we'd never had a dog.

• Poor Judgment and Impulsiveness

One woman in the support group who had dimly suspected that something was wrong with her husband for a long time was finally convinced of it the day that a box full of vitamin supplements costing forty dollars came in the mail. While there is nothing inherently demented about ordering that many vitamins, this woman recognized that it was the sort of thing that her husband, a frugal man, would never, ever, have done before.

This case illustrates the subjective nature of symptoms. While most of us would agree that walking in the middle of the highway shows poor judgment, the issue of what sorts of actions represent poor judgment in an individual case must take into account the individual's normal standards, beliefs, and values.

Lots of people try new things as they get older, and there is nothing wrong with that. The important point is that there is reason to be concerned about someone who begins behaving in a way that puts himself and others at unnecessary risk, or who starts squandering his money, or who generally seems to be acting impulsively in an inappropriate way.

• Loss of Inhibitions

The loss of inhibitions can take many forms. People may lose their "self-sensor" in terms of what acceptable behavior is—going outside or answering the door dressed only in underwear would be an example of this; making a blunt remark like, "My, you're ugly" to another person would be another.

That same lack of awareness can cause a loss of sensitivity to conversational appropriateness, and the person may cross beyond a boundary of social propriety in ways such as revealing the details of the family finances to casual acquaintances. One man told of the embarrassment he felt as his mother regaled his business associates with the story of how he had learned the facts of life.

• Fear of Being Alone

One of the things spouses often notice early is that the patient wants more togetherness than is comfortable for the other person, and clinging behavior may be in evidence. A wife may find that it becomes hard for her to go out of the house or pursue her own activities as her husband acts more and more forlorn whenever she leaves. It is not unusual for a woman in this situation to run over to the grocery store for a loaf of bread and be told by her husband upon her return that she has been "gone for hours."

2. Loss of Problem-Solving Skills

• Inability to do Familiar Tasks

People who start having difficulty doing things that were second nature to them, like the carpenter who couldn't figure out how to assemble a simple piece of cabinetwork, are displaying a serious warning sign. This happened to Edith's husband, who had been a mechanic all his life:

Edith: He lost stuff all the time. When he was fixing machinery, he would drop something and couldn't fix it. And sometimes he just couldn't remember what he'd taken apart. He couldn't remember what went back.

• Inability to Make Connections

The ability to see relationships between things, whether on the abstract or concrete level, is a critical component of problem solving. For a demented person, things are becoming disjointed. The connection between a hammer and a bag of nails lying next to each other on a workbench is no longer obvious or apparent. A demented person may pick up a familiar tool and be unable to determine what it is used for.

This loss of awareness of common associations makes it virtually impossible to figure anything out logically, or to use cues from the environment to gather usable information. My grandmother's inability to locate the water faucet by following the garden hose is an example of this.

• Inability to Make Decisions

Dementia patients lose the ability to think abstractly. They become increasingly focused on practical matters, and on things that are immediately visible to them. The sense of the relative significance of things is gradually being lost, so that small decisions take on an overwhelming importance in the person's mind. A woman in turmoil over which dress to wear has lost the idea that she is free to make her own choice. The very concept of "choice" itself is foreign to someone who is less and less capable of abstract thinking. Instead, she sees the question of which dress to put on in terms of determining which dress is the "right" one. Since there is no one right dress to wear, she is paralyzed with indecision. She has lost sight of the fact that in the grand scheme of things it really does not matter which dress she wears, anyway.

• Inability to Initiate or Complete a Project

The family of someone who displays this symptom will often mistakenly accuse the person of being lazy. What they don't realize at first is that even relatively simple jobs require doing things in a remembered sequence, or making decisions about how to carry out the job. In the case of washing a sink full of dishes, for example, a person must decide how much water and soap to use, how hot the water should be, whether to use the sponge or the scouring pad, which dish he should pick up first, etc. It is possible for him to be derailed by any one of those decisions.

Bonnie describes her frustrations at trying to get her husband Henry to help her pack boxes for a move:

> *Bonnie:* In trying to move, I just almost went crazy with Henry, because he couldn't follow directions. I'd say, "Let's pack this room. We'll start at the top, and then we'll pack it." If I left him for a moment, he could never finish what he'd started. If I'd yell at him, he'd say "Do it yourself!" and I'd be mad.

3. Communication Problems

• Problems Finding Words

Most of us know what it feels like to have a word or a name on the tip of our tongue, but not be able to retrieve it. For a dementia patient, the ability to recall or correctly apply the word he wants to use is often lost. If this experience becomes a regular occurrence, it can cause a great deal of embarrassment and frustration. Occasionally the person may say something like "Look out the mirror" when he means to say "Look out the window," or "I'd like something red to drink" instead of "I'd like something hot."

• Inability to Follow a Conversation

An impaired person who may still be able to communicate adequately in a one-to-one situation may have great difficulty functioning conversationally in a group. As the attention span becomes shorter, and the ability to focus and concentrate is gradually lost, following the thread of a conversation becomes more and more difficult. The higher noise level, interruptions, and cross talk that occur when more than two people are talking together are just too confusing.

Accordingly, withdrawal in a social situation is often a signal of a developing cognitive problem. Helen describes the way her husband, Donald, compensates for his inability to follow a conversation:

Helen: He doesn't talk much. He will be very gracious, the introduction and the first few words of conversation. But then he will not talk very much more, because he knows, I think, without question, that he may make a boo-boo. He's going to ask you something he's already asked you. Maybe twice already.

This withdrawal can be very subtle, and the spouse may be the only person who is aware of it at first.

Mabel: Pretty soon Roy was sitting there, not paying any attention to what was being said. He wasn't contributing to the conversation. The others couldn't see it. But I would notice.

Eventually, the person may try to avoid social encounters completely. Not everyone withdraws, however. Some people reveal their inability to comprehend what is going on by periodically interjecting a remark that has nothing to do with what the rest of the group is saying. Still others will deliver a monologue that allows no interruption. This "running commentary" strategy is adaptive in the sense that as long as the person himself is the one doing the talking, he will not be called upon to make any responses to anything anyone else has to say.

• Repeated Questioning

Someone who is not retaining information will not remember the answer to a question he asked an hour ago, or five minutes ago. A repeated question might not even be a real request for information, but rather for some kind of reassurance. For example, a repeated question like "When are we leaving?" can be interpreted as a bid for reassurance that the person will not be late for an appointment.

4. Disorientation

• Disorientation to Time

The sense of time; of how long it has been since breakfast, of what time of the day, day of the week, or year it is right now, or of how long it will be until dinner, is eventually lost in dementing illnesses, and the person also loses the ability to process information in a way that gives him clues about what time it is. Mabel's husband Roy woke up when it was dark outside, and the late-night news was on television, but neither of those pieces of evidence alerted him to the fact that it was still nighttime:

> **Mabel:** Roy would eat his dinner, we would do the dishes, and he'd go to bed. And I would be listening to the eleven o'clock news and the bedroom door would open, and he'd say, "What's the matter with you? You didn't come to bed last night."

The person's sense of time is increasingly fragmented, so that he can only grasp what is happening in the present moment, and concepts like "soon," or "recently," or "later on" become meaningless. This can be very anxiety-producing. In my observation, a large proportion of repeated questions have a strong "when?" element.

• Disorientation to Place

Disorientation can also be evident in terms of place or location. Getting lost in a familiar neighborhood, or along a route one has traveled for years, is often the first tangible, frightening thing that happens to dementia patients.

This disorientation is also sometimes evidenced by a near-total inability to absorb information about a new place. This is illustrated in the case of a person who has spent three days in a hotel, and still hesitates about which way to turn to get to the elevator from the door of his room.

• Disorientation to Person

The inability to recognize familiar individuals is an important warning sign. Mary describes an incident that happened one day after her husband Ira returned to their home in Seattle from his tour of duty in Korea:

Mary: The day after he came home, his brother came over. His brother and his wife. Ira's stepfather had just passed away and they wanted to go back to the funeral. They wanted Ira to go. I tried to explain to Dean that there was something wrong, that Ira was confused, but he said, "Naw, he's just tired." And I said, "We have orders to be in Virginia in ten days, and I have to finish up the final sale of the house, and get the paperwork cleared, and get us moved. We don't have the time." So anyway I said no, he couldn't go, and Ira wouldn't answer one way or the other. And as we were standing on the steps watching them drive away Ira turned around and looked at me and said, "Who was that guy?" So I knew that something was seriously wrong.

5. New and Unfamiliar Behaviors

• Neglect of Self and Property

A decline in someone's customary standards of maintenance can be a warning signal. A prizewinning gardener whose yard is full of weeds, or a formerly meticulous housekeeper whose house is dirty are each demonstrating an uncharacteristic neglect of his or her property.

It is important to distinguish the causes for this sort of neglect. A frail older man may no longer be able to push a heavy Rototiller, and declining vision may make it difficult to notice that dust is collecting on the venetian blinds. Therefore, what is significant here is not the actual state of the home, but whether or not the person seems to care, or even notice, that things have gone downhill. It is an attitude of disconnectedness and indifference to ordinary maintenance that may be indicative of a problem.

A decline in standards of personal hygiene and grooming is another common symptom of early dementia. The person's sense of smell may have declined, along with the awareness that it is time to bathe. Bathing or showering become daunting tasks to be avoided, especially if an impaired person has already had an experience like inadvertently flooding the bathroom, or if he has been scalded in the shower.

Inability to make decisions renders choices about what to wear overwhelmingly burdensome, and the person may wear the same outfit day after day, often putting it on directly over pajamas or nightgown. The person may have lost the ability to determine when clothes need to be laundered, or she may have forgotten how to operate the washing machine.

• Hoarding

Many people have a garage full of junk, or a big stack of magazines they intend to read someday, but some people cross over a fine line and reach a point where it becomes impossible for them to get rid of anything.

In the case of early dementia, this can be interpreted in two ways. First, objects represent security to some people, and dementia patients are nothing if not insecure. Second, throwing something away requires making a decision to throw it away. The person has lost the ability to distinguish between something of value and something that is worthless, and becomes fearful of discarding anything.

Having a cluttered, messy house certainly does not mean that someone is demented. However, if a junk collection gets so large that it starts taking over the house, or if it presents a fire or health hazard, it is not a good sign. If the person has a panicky reaction to any suggestion about "getting rid of some of this stuff," that can also indicate a problem.

The same insecurity that leads to hoarding behavior can also reveal itself in the form of painful anxiety about money matters, or in an apprehensive reaction whenever any money must be spent.

• Fixations

One woman in the support group described how her husband would get up early every morning and go around straightening the newspapers on the neighbors' lawns because he didn't like the way the paperboy threw them there. Another woman who asked a service station attendant to check the oil in her car when she and her husband were out for a drive reported that her husband fretted for weeks afterward about whether or not the car had any oil in it.

The elements in the list of early warning signs of dementing illness are not mutually exclusive. The man who angrily tells his wife that she has been gone for hours can be exhibiting his irritability, his fear of being alone, his jealousy, his paranoia, his faulty sense of time, or all of these things together. The woman who goes out to her mailbox in her underwear in December in Minnesota is displaying her loosened inhibitions *and* her poor judgment.

It is important to look at any particular case in terms of the total picture. A person can appear to be functioning adequately in some areas, but not in others. Bonnie describes how this was true in her husband's case:

> **Bonnie:** Hank took the test for insurance broker, and he passed. So when we talk about Alzheimer's, and the fact that it doesn't totally affect all of the brain, in my sense, at least for Hank's story, that was true. Whatever part of the brain that can function and take tests was still okay. Within a couple of months, even though he knew how to sell insurance, he didn't know how to find his way to the prospect's home.

Families of dementia patients may live with a growing sense of unease for months or even years while the evidence that something is wrong accumulates and becomes harder to deny. The prospect of dementing illness is frightening, and something from which people understandably shy away. To a limited degree, some initial denial can actually be a healthy response, insofar as it gives someone time to adjust gradually to a disturbing truth without being overwhelmed and paralyzed by it.

Denial can show itself in several ways. In some cases, there is a turning away from the signs and symptoms: "If I don't see it, it isn't true." Some people are able to live this way for a long time, but eventually it is just not possible to ignore the fact that *something* is wrong. At this point, people often develop their own explanations for the person's problems. Irene and Helen describe how they did this initially:

Irene: He was a very conscientious worker, and something went wrong on the job. Anyway, I heard about it through gossip and I thought, now, that's unusual for him. I always thought he was depressed, because of his work, because he had to take a cut in salary when there were no jobs on his level. I thought he was depressed over that. And physically, I thought he was going down a little too.

Helen: He retired, and he just seemed different to me. I kept saying to myself, "He's not adjusting to retirement." And I excused his change of personality to that, thinking, "He's not accepting this very well." I noticed he'd forget things, and then one evening a couple who were very good friends of ours were going to take us out to dinner, and about ten minutes before they were due, he said, "I'm going to take a walk." I said, "You can't go now, Betty and Johnny will be here." He said, "I'll just walk down the street. I'll leave my coat here." He left his coat, and they came within five minutes. I said, "Did you see Don outside?" They said no. And naturally I was very cross, thinking, why did he do this?

So they said, "You get in the car, and we'll bring his coat." So we did, and he was on the next street already. And I said, "Donald, what possessed you? You *knew* we were going." And it did not seem to reach him at all. But we all laughed, and went out for dinner, and that was the end of that. And then there were other little things that I couldn't understand his reaction to. So I kept saying to myself, "He had a stroke. A very slight stroke, with this Bell's palsy." That was the beginning.

One method that people sometimes use to avoid facing the implications of the situation is to become overly focused on one disturbing aspect of the person's new behavior. People are initially more comfortable focusing on their own immediate reactions to what a demented *patient* is doing or saying than on the fear and sadness that facing the terrible reality of the patient's *illness* is sure to produce. For example, the feelings that accompany the thought, "He's asked me that three times in the last half hour," though unpleasant, are more familiar and easier to deal with than the feelings that arise when one contemplates the image of one's husband as severely disabled, incontinent, or in a nursing home.

Mary speaks, from her years of support group experience, on this aspect of initial adjustment to a spouse's dementing illness:

Mary: Well, I think part of it is the enormity of the situation. You can't take this whole thing in at one time. It's impossible, especially in the early stages. Your own future, their future, the future of your whole family, it's all mixed in together. It's overwhelming.

So what do you concentrate on? Oftentimes, it's the trivia. Especially in the beginning. It's almost like, "Well, if I could solve *that* problem, the other problems would fall in line." Of course, they don't, but that's the way it is. Talking about the trivia to keep from talking about more serious matters.

Denial can be stripped away abruptly. It is not uncommon for the deficits of a patient who has functioned marginally well in his own environment to be exposed harshly when he is away from home and lacks familiar objects and routines to help orient himself with. This was true in Edith's case:

Edith: We went back to Kansas in '79, and that's when I decided he was really bad. From the time we started, it was "Where are we going? I want to go home. What are we here for?" On and on. Confused, I think. We celebrated his birthday at his sister's in Oklahoma. We got into town the day of his birthday. He didn't even remember that. He didn't even seem to know. He talked with everybody and everything, but he didn't seem to know his brother, his relatives, or anything.

Behavior patterns that have been viewed as minor eccentricities take on more ominous meanings when the person suddenly does or says something so bizarre that there is no way to rationalize it. Mabel recalls such an incident:

Mabel: He was left alone to cut the lawn, and it suddenly dawned on us that we had not heard the electric lawn mower going, and when we looked out, he had the edge-trimming shears, and he had cut the entire cord into about foot-length pieces. Why he wasn't electrocuted we'll never know. But he sat there and cut the cord.

Recognizing that things are not "business as usual," overcoming denial that something is wrong with her husband,

and facing the fact that he needs medical attention is often the first instance in the long unfolding of a dementing illness in which a wife realizes that it is up to her to take control of the situation. It is only when a woman finally acknowledges that her husband is no longer capable of making sound judgments about his own needs that she can begin the process of becoming an advocate for his care.

Irene had very gradually taken over more and more of the responsibilities in her marriage over a long period of time. She describes what happened the morning she was confronted with how serious the situation had become:

Irene: I more or less did the driving. On Sundays we went to church. And sometimes I'd drive, and sometimes I'd let him drive. And, this one Sunday I encouraged him to drive, and said, "You know the way to church, we go every week." Well, he couldn't. He couldn't find his way. I had to have him pull over, and I took the wheel, and I took him to church.

I got him out of the car, and he didn't want to go in, which was most unusual. And I said, "Come on, you can go in." And I helped him get up the stairs and in the church. And after I got him in there I realized: this is no way to treat him. I don't think he's together, something's wrong this morning. So I walked him right back out of the church, and down the steps of St. Eugene's, got him back in the car, and I headed for the hospital.

CHAPTER THREE

Patients, Caregivers, and Doctors

> They gave him a little pill. I used to know what the name of it was. It was supposed to help his memory. You take it the last thing before you go to bed at night. A little tiny green pill . . . Anyway, the doctor said, ''I'm not expecting anything from this. This is something to do. You want a pill, he wants a pill, this is a pill.''
>
> —Bonnie

Learning to function as someone else's advocate is something that comes easily for some people, and is a long, arduous process for others. It is usually in the arena of dealing with doctors and medical personnel that the wife of a dementia patient gets her first taste of what that role is like, and of the kinds of things that will be increasingly required of her as she attempts to fulfill it.

The wife, having come to the painful realization that medical help must be sought, now finds herself between her husband and the doctor in the unaccustomed role of interpreter of her husband's behavior. Before any diagnostic search can be started, she must convince the doctor to take her concerns seriously. In some cases, this can be a frustrating and invalidating experience for her.

As many caregivers soon learn, it is possible for patients to sustain severe memory loss and still appear superficially ''normal'' to people, including doctors, who do not know them well.

Helen: If you met him right now, if you were to talk to him, you would not think something was wrong. Unless you stayed long enough to find out that he did not remember what we had said twenty minutes earlier. But he does not know how to get to our garage anymore. I can understand why neurologists would be confused, because they only spend, at the very most, a half an hour with him.

The tactic of evading direct questions and fabricating answers is called "confabulation." It's very common in dementia patients, and some of them are quite convincing at it. For example, a patient who is asked his opinion of a current news story may reply, in a perfectly articulate sentence, that he has been much too busy to read the newspaper lately. He may answer other questions with elaborate, detailed replies that may or may not have any basis in fact. Only careful, systematic testing can fully reveal the scope of the person's cognitive deficits.

A physician may not be easily convinced that there is truly something wrong with a person whose social presentation is still appropriate and who is superficially pleasant and cooperative. Fortunately, as doctors' awareness of dementing diseases has increased, this problem is not as troublesome as it used to be. Mabel, whose husband was diagnosed in the early 1980s, and Mary, whose initial contacts with doctors were much earlier than that, describe their experiences:

Mabel: Nobody else could see it. The doctors couldn't. He was examined by six different doctors. This one doctor up in Santa Rosa that did the last scan before Roy went into the hospital said, "Oh, everything's within normal limits." And this was a neurologist. A very prominent one. We went up to the office, and Roy sat next to the doctor, and answered his questions reasonably well. Not all accurate, but reasonably well. We came out of the office and we got in the elevator, and Roy said, "Who the hell was that guy?" When we went out the front door to the parking lot, he stood there and looked around, and said, "Our car's gone." I said, "No, the blue one. Right here. That's our car." He said, "Never had a blue car in my life." But we rode home in that same blue car, and the doctor's report was "Everything within normal range." That was when I wondered if the poor man really *did* have a neurotic wife.

Mary: It's a favorite statement of mine, and I've noticed that quite a few other spouses say the same thing: "The first diagnosis you get when you take your spouse in to a psychiatrist because of the dementia, the first diagnosis is going to be that the patient is fine, it's the spouse who suffers from some kind of personality disorder." Invariably, that's what happened. Because the patient is bland and calm. The other thing is the spouse, by this time, is looking disheveled, harassed, and upset.

As Ira's dementia increased, I knew that he wasn't telling the truth when he talked to the doctors. He would maybe tell it as he saw it, but as he saw it when he was talking to the doctor wasn't the same as he saw it when he was talking to me. Trying to convince them that he was hale and hearty. And at the same time he was a hypochondriac. With me.

Incidents like these are exasperating exercises in learning to trust one's own perceptions. Just because a caregiver has recognized the necessity of taking the initiative in seeking a diagnosis, there is no guarantee that her efforts will provide her with any quick answers or gratifying results.

Uncovering the medical cause or causes of dementia in a given patient is not a simple task. Unfortunately, a surprising number of people still hold the mistaken belief that progressive forgetfulness is a normal part of the aging process for some unlucky individuals. In accordance with that belief, they may have trouble seeing the point in pursuing a time-consuming and possibly expensive medical workup, thinking that there is nothing to be done about the problem anyway. The older a patient is, the more likely he is to be victimized by this faulty thinking.

A thorough and methodical quest for as accurate a diagnosis as possible is absolutely essential, and there are a number of reasons why:

1. There are a wide variety of treatable, reversible causes for dementia, and these conditions affect a significant minority of cases, perhaps as many as 10 percent.

2. If symptoms are shown to be the result of multi-infarction dementia; repeated small strokes that have damaged small areas of the brain, the progression of the person's

impairments, though not reversible, may be slowed or halted by treatment with proper blood pressure medication, monitoring of salt intake, etc.

3. If dementing illness is found to be untreatable and progressive, it is in the best interests of the patient and his family to know this at a time when the patient is still functioning logically enough to participate in planning for the disposition of his affairs, sign necessary legal documents, and make known his wishes regarding his future care.

4. Family members can face the difficult days ahead with the reassurance that they have acted responsibly toward the patient, and that anything that can be done for him is being done.

Any doctor who tells a family that increasingly severe mental impairment is simply a result of the aging process is revealing him- or herself to be a highly dubious source of information and advice, at least on this subject. It may be necessary to seek out a neurologist, or a specialist in geriatric medicine.

One means of determining whether or not a doctor's diagnostic procedures will be thorough enough is to ask him, in the initial consultation, which tests he plans to administer, and what information he is hoping to gather from them.

The following list is intended to provide a general idea of some of the standard procedures in a good workup, and should give an indication of some of the various conditions the physician is looking for:

1. Detailed History

The purpose of this is to gather clues about the onset and course of the disease process so far. Have the symptoms been very gradual, appearing over time (characteristic of Alzheimer's disease), or have they been marked by drops in functioning followed by long ''plateaus'' (characteristic of multi-infarction dementia)? The more thorough the history is, the more information it will provide.

It is critically important to determine what drugs, if any, the patient has been taking. Different drugs, taken together, may cause adverse reactions in some people. Dehydration caused by the use of diuretic medications can also cause confusion. Dosages of drugs that have been taken with no apparent problems for years may need to be readjusted, and this is particularly true for older people. Drug toxicity has been known to cause dementialike symptoms in some individuals.

What is the person's nutritional status? A person suffering from chronic malnutrition will not be thinking clearly.

Depression in the elderly can present itself with symptoms closely resembling dementing illnesses, and this condition is known as "pseudodementia." However, one hallmark of depression, as opposed to Alzheimer's disease, for example, is that the person suffering from depression usually realizes that his memory is not what it should be and will verbalize that, whereas an Alzheimer's patient probably will not. Elderly people have often sustained many painful losses, such as the end of their careers and the deaths of friends. It is understandable that this could have a very depressing effect over time. Treatment of the depression can go a long way toward alleviating symptoms.

2. Mental Status Tests

Patients are asked a series of simple questions to determine whether or not they are oriented to time, place, and person. The examiner seeks to determine whether or not they are still able to perform simple calculations, and to memorize a short list of items. For example, is the person able to duplicate a pattern of colored blocks? If so, how long does it take him to do it? His language skills will be gauged by showing him pictures of familiar objects and asking him to name them.

The collected results of the various mental status tests provide a detailed picture of the nature and degree of the person's memory, language, and reasoning deficits.

3. Neurological Examination

Reflexes are checked, and patients are asked to do a number of simple things like touching the tips of their noses with their eyes closed, or balancing on one foot. The purpose of this is to determine whether problems exist in the functioning of the nervous system.

4. Computerized Axial Tomography

Commonly known as the CAT scan, this test provides a sort of map, or picture, of the brain. Evidence of conditions such as brain tumors, head injuries, strokes, and damaged areas caused by multi-infarction are revealed by this test. (Many people mistakenly believe that a CAT scan will provide a definitive diagnosis of Alzheimer's disease, but the results of the test are often within normal limits in Alzheimer's patients.)

When the ventricles, or cavities, inside the brain are enlarged, but the pressure of the cerebrospinal fluid inside them is normal, a condition known as normal-pressure hydrocephalus exists. This condition can occur spontaneously or as a result of an old head injury, and it is an important condition to look for, because a significant number of patients who suffer from it can be helped by surgery in which the excess ventricular fluid is shunted away from the brain.

5. Electroencephalogram

This test gives a reading of the electrical activity of the brain. An important reason for it is to see if any subtle form of seizure disorder exists.

6. Various Laboratory Tests

A complete blood count is administered to detect a deficiency of vitamin B_{12}, or any evidence of infection. Electrolyte levels are checked, and tests measuring the levels of kidney, liver, and thyroid functions are done. Tests measuring pulmonary efficiency, such as respiration rate tests and tests of blood gasses, are also performed. Untreated syphilis infection can cause dementia, and the test for it is called the VDRL.

7. Lumbar Puncture

Also known as a spinal tap, in this test spinal fluid is analyzed to rule out the possibility of an infectious disease of the central nervous system such as meningitis, encephalitis, or tuberculosis. Generally, this test is most likely to be done on people whose history reveals a very sudden onset of symptoms.

Alzheimer's disease can only be definitively diagnosed with a brain biopsy, or through autopsy studies of the brain. Researchers are hard at work trying to develop noninvasive radiological and biochemical tests for the disease. But until they succeed, microscopic study of brain tissue will be needed to determine whether that tissue displays the signs that distinguish the disease anatomically.

These signs are an increase in "plaques," lesions made up of amyloid proteins and degenerated cell fragments, and "tangles," collections of pairs of neurons whose filaments have become twisted together. There is some evidence to suggest that a deficiency in the neurotransmitter acetylcholine is also a factor in Alzheimer's disease.

Because brain biopsies are rarely performed, Alzheimer's disease is mostly a diagnosis of exclusion in living patients. It is the name given to a particular case of dementia after other causes for it have been ruled out. Cases occurring in people under the age of sixty-five are referred to as Alzheimer's disease or "presenile dementia." People over the age of sixty-five are said to have "senile dementia, Alzheimer's type."

It is now known that people diagnosed with Parkinson's disease are also at risk for developing dementia. In 1980, researcher Francois Boller set the number of such cases at 30 to 50 percent of Parkinsonians.

There are a variety of other degenerative diseases that cause dementia. Fortunately, these are rare. Among them are Pick's disease, Huntington's disease, and Creutzfeldt-Jakob disease.

Since there are so many causes of dementia, and so many

factors that can undermine a person's mental functioning, any particular case may have more than one contributing cause. None of the causes of dementia, reversible or not, are mutually exclusive. Treatable and untreatable conditions can certainly be evidenced in the same person, and if that turns out to be the case, then the person deserves to have any appropriate treatments pursued aggressively.

It is always worthwhile to do all that can be done to optimize an individual's level of functioning. Regardless of the person's diagnosis, it is important to maintain good nutrition, monitor drug intake carefully, see that he receives regular exercise, continue to monitor other aspects of his health, and see that his eyeglasses, hearing aid, and dentures fit properly, work the way they are supposed to, and are readily available to him.

Bonnie describes her painful feelings in the days just before her husband's Alzheimer's diagnosis:

Bonnie: Well, I was dealing with [his] alcoholism and depression. So the alcoholism was already diminishing. It was sort of like I'd almost gotten rid of that. Depression was something that perhaps you could handle with a pill, but also, it was very close to mental illness, and that wasn't going to be easy, or great, at all. And if that meant hospitalization or internment in an institution for mental illness, I was willing to look at that, and think about it. Thank God, it wasn't me. And how dreadful. Better than cancer, but at the same time, not really knowing. There was sort of like a black picture. Don't know what that's going to be. That's undetermined. Unknown.

When diagnoses of dementing illnesses were actually made, the doctors varied in the way they gave people the news, or in some cases, avoided giving them the news:

Aileen: We went to the neurologist in San Rafael and the neurologist sent him for a brain-wave test, and did a psychological evaluation, did a CAT scan, and he said he was sure that Louie had dementia. Alzheimer's. The doctor told him he had Alzheimer's. A lot of doctors don't tell people, which I don't agree with.

Helen: Dr. C. called me after Donald had been tested, and the first thing he told me was did I know, or understand, what dementia was? And he said, "Well, your husband has a form of dementia. And I believe that it is Alzheimer's." And I almost dropped the telephone. Donald was sitting right by me. We were having our dinner. So I hung up. Donald said, "What was that all about?" Well, of course I couldn't tell him. I could have, but I wasn't about to. We saw Dr. C. again in his office, and he asked me to step back in the office and Donald to wait outside, and he felt there was no question but that it was Alzheimer's. I would have liked it better if he had said to both of us, "I think we have here a case of Alzheimer's." And I've always regretted that he handled it that way. That, to me, would have been the way to do it.

Irene: I'm not going to tell the doctor that I suspect that it's Alzheimer's. I'm gonna wait for *him* to tell me what *he* thinks. Well, he never told me. He never came out . . . Whether he suspected it or not, I do not know. He never once said it to me. But he told me, "Don't bring him back. I can't help him." And I said, "Well, where do I go?" He didn't know. He shrugged his shoulders.

Edith: When I moved into town I started going to doctors. Well, I had talked to his doctor. I said, "His brother has Alzheimer's. We think his sister may have had it too. Maybe that's what he has." The doctor had never said anything about dementia or anything to me. Whether he didn't know, or didn't want to tell me, or what . . . I also had him to [another doctor], and he said, "Alzheimer's."

Bonnie: [The doctor] immediately antagonized both Hank and me. We both got real backed up with this guy. He's brusque. A bustler. And no nonsense. And he's giving you fifty minutes, and that's it. We'd gone in there maybe three times. And this was the third. They said, "With Alzheimer's you have three P's: Possible, Probable, and Positive. And positive is to take a bit of tissue from your brain, and examine it. Or an autopsy." And I said, "Well, I don't think we'd want to burr into his brain, take any tissue. If you feel that this is the illness he has, we'll accept that." Hearing bad news is always difficult. There's always a sense of shock, and a sense of "That isn't what I want to hear."

A medical label for dementia, even though it can provide a measure of relief from what has usually been months of doubt and uncertainty, does little to answer the question, "Where do we go from here?" Mabel's new career as an activist in the Alzheimer's movement was born when she discovered how little information about the disease was available to her:

Mabel: My anger was not gradual. No. No, the very minute we got the diagnosis, and couldn't find a word in all those medical books, I was furious! Why doesn't somebody know something about this? I'm going to find out! Of course, they all told me it's something that's going to be progressively worse, and there is no cure. And I started going to meetings. When I wanted to know something, I wanted to know.

Even though much more information has become available since the diagnosis of Mabel's husband, once a diagnosis of untreatable dementia has been received, the fact that there is nothing that can be done medically must still be faced.

Helen: I was hardly able to digest the fact that my husband had this very serious illness. In fact, I didn't accept it. I was sure it was wrong, and they didn't quite know what it was all about, and he'd had a slight stroke that had damaged the part of his brain that stored recent memory. His recall was just bad. I'm still, in my heart, not sure that isn't his problem.

I was very depressed thinking every door was shut. You think you're going to get some help, and the door is shut, or you don't get any kind of an answer that's worth anything. I couldn't have said, "So, whatever is wrong with him, that's going to be it." No, I think you have to do something. And that's one of the most difficult things about Alzheimer's, that you really, other than getting somebody to tell you what it is, you just have to live with it.

The realization that medical science can, as yet, offer no cure, marks a fundamental shift in the way that family members regard doctors. Most of us are used to thinking of doctors as people who prescribe medicine, perform surgeries, and otherwise make active interventions on our behalf when we're sick. Most of us don't have much experience with being told that there is nothing that can be done for us, or for someone we love. Caregivers must not only accept the truth of the situation, they are confronted with it every time they take the patient to the doctor.

Angie: I take Hugo to Dr. M., and he just looks him over, and takes his blood pressure. I ask him questions and he just says, "There isn't anything that you can do. He's just going to get progressively worse."

Accepting the reality of the disease, and accepting the patient's limitations, is one of the greatest challenges family members face. As difficult as that acceptance is, and in the absence of any real medical treatment, it is not surprising that some people whose relatives are newly diagnosed try various "retraining" programs in an attempt to preserve and bolster the patient's remaining skills. Bonnie describes what happened in her husband's case:

Bonnie: The doctor told me about a therapist, and a program she started, on cognitive retraining, or cognitive something. And what she intends to do is use different exercises. Mental exercises, and paper work. So he'd go home with homework. But during the time in her office, she would try to keep what ability he still has at this level going, with exercise, word exercises and so forth. There was a lot of homework. And he'd try to do the homework, and eventually we'd end up in a big fight.

After diagnostic tests have been completed, the issue of whether or not a particular dementia patient would benefit from taking certain drugs continues to engage the caregiver in interactions with the doctor. In cases of dementia, drugs can be prescribed to help calm sleepless, wandering people, or to quiet a feeling of panic. Sometimes the drugs work very well.

However, such drugs do nothing to treat the underlying confusion and in some cases can, paradoxically, make problem behaviors worse. There is no way of knowing how a particular drug will affect a particular patient, or whether the effects of the drug may change over a long period of time.

The search for pharmacological relief of distressing symptoms involves the caregiver just as much as the doctor, for it is she who must be the arbiter of whether or not the drugs are having the desired effect. It is *her* sleep, not the doctor's, that is interrupted by the patient's agitation. After his doctors had tried several different drugs on her husband, who suffered from Parkinson's dementia and was combative, Angie realized that she was on her own:

> *Angie:* Well, the medical profession hasn't . . . They've done tests on Hugo, and really didn't come up with too many answers. Hugo was at a neuropsychiatric hospital for six weeks, and they came up with less. They tried different drugs, and nothing worked at all. They finally sent him home with Ativan, and that was really destroying him, making him more combative, and just really wild. And so I just took the Ativan away. I couldn't handle that. And he's been better since he's been off the Ativan. There's Mellaril, and all those other "drill" things that they've tried, and nothing worked on him. The only thing that seems to be working is Xanax. But that wasn't the doctor's suggestion. I called the doctor about it, and he said, "Sure. Try it. Try anything you want."

Anyone who has previously thought that doctors have all the answers might find that opinion undermined after being told to "try anything you want." Angie found that the doctor's guidance about drug dosages was even less definitive than his advice about the drugs themselves:

> *Angie:* I called him. We were giving Hugo one pill, and we wondered if maybe we should increase it. I called the doctor and asked him, "What do you think? What would happen if I gave him two of those?" And he said, "Well, go ahead and give him two. If you want or need three, give him three." They leave it up to you. You become the doctor. And in many cases he said, "Well, try the Sinemet. If one works, if you think it's too much, cut it in half. Or if you think it's not enough, go ahead and give him more." How am I to know, you know, what is more or less for him? But also, I have to consider this: the doctor is not with him twenty-four hours a day. The doctor can't see him twenty-four hours a day. The times that Hugo goes in to see the doctor he looks pretty good.

When a wife acknowledges to herself that she, and not the doctor, is with her husband all the time, she is realizing that the doctor, at least in the case of her own husband, may not know more than she does or have a more solid basis for assessing what is best. She begins to have more faith in her own judgment. Even if that faith wavers, she comes to believe that her judgment is probably as good as anyone else's.

> **Helen:** I said to the doctor, "You know, for three years I've been on a yo-yo, almost, as to what's wrong with my husband. And yet," I said, "I think I could tell you more about what's wrong with him than you can tell me."

That belief will be very helpful to wives as they are called upon to make treatment decisions over the course of the disease. The experience of a woman in the support group provides a good illustration of the way in which caregivers must ultimately assume responsibility for choices concerning their impaired family members, even if they would prefer to leave those decisions in the hands of the doctors.

Mrs. Doe's husband was having great difficulty swallowing and had already inhaled food into his lungs several times. She was faced with the decision of whether or not to have a feeding tube inserted directly into his stomach. The doctor told her the reasons why the surgery was a good idea, and then gave her just as many reasons why the surgery was a bad idea. Still on the horns of a dilemma, she told the group, "That's not what I wanted to hear." Another group member asked her what she had, in fact, wanted to hear. She replied, "I wanted him to tell me, 'Do it, or don't do it.' "

In this case, the wife had to weigh different factors and make a difficult medical choice on the basis of her own good judgment. Mrs. Doe came back to the group a month later and announced that she had consented to the surgery, and that the results had not been particularly gratifying. However, she felt comfortable with her decision, confident that she had made the best choice she could with the information available to her.

Sometimes a new attitude of assertion is generated in the caregiver as a result of the logistics involved in escorting someone through a series of tests and appointments. Everyone knows what it is like to be kept waiting in a doctor's office, and we understand that sometimes it cannot be helped. But to be kept waiting for more than a few minutes with a confused, agitated person who asks questions like "What are we doing here?" "Why isn't the doctor here yet?" and "When are we going home?" over and over is another experience entirely.

Helen had an unpleasant interchange with a specialist who kept her and Donald waiting for over two hours, and then was unresponsive to Helen's questions about a procedure that had been very painful for Donald:

> **Helen:** Her whole attitude was, you are an imbecile. Just get out of here. I just felt so terribly put-upon. I just resented her attitude completely. I resent being talked to as if I don't know anything. True, I'm not a medical person, but I'm not stupid. Because she felt defeated or something, she just was not very nice to me, or wouldn't have been to anybody else in the same situation. But anyhow, I reported her. I did. I just thought, I didn't want anybody else to get that sort of treatment. I can remember thirty or forty years ago I would have been a whipped puppy with her attitude. Not anymore.

As Helen described the incident, she said, "I never had much of a temper before, but I've got a beauty now." Her use of the word "beauty" to describe her temper reveals her growing awareness that personal assertiveness is potentially a plus, and not a minus, in terms of her dealings with medical people.

Many elderly people with dementing illnesses have other health problems as well. Mary's husband Ira was a heart patient and a diabetic, in addition to suffering from normal-pressure hydrocephalus as a result of his head injury. She became aware that his overall care was not well coordinated, since he was being treated by different specialists for each problem, with no one physician overseeing his case. Only through educating herself was she able to address his needs:

> **Mary:** It was so frustrating trying to get anybody to look at the total person. In the meantime, I did have some medical back-

ground. I was a surgical technician, and had a fair amount of intelligence, and the ability to comprehend what I was reading. And I started becoming an expert on conditions that related to my husband, whether it was his heart or his diabetes or his mental problems. And also, on his medications.

In interactions of medications, I started finding problems. I became a thorn in the side of quite a few doctors, because they would prescribe more and more and I'd say, "Doctor, look at the amount of medication." I always kept a list and carried it with me. "Well, I think he should try this," they'd say. And I'd got a hold of a copy of *PDR* [*Physicians' Desk Reference*] and I'd look them up, to see if it was safe to give the two together. And several times, it wasn't. And I'd call and tell them, and their reaction was very negative, as a rule. By that time I had learned that it didn't make a damn bit of difference what the doctor thought of me because they think the worst, anyway. I had accepted that fact, by that time.

Mary's remarks illustrate that wives must do more than just gather information if they are to become effective health care advocates for their husbands. They must share that information with professional people when it seems necessary, and sometimes they must even be willing to engage in open, forthright questioning of a doctor's advice.

It is important to point out that Mary reached this point sooner than most people, and reached it more emphatically, because of her belief that her husband's problems had been made worse in the very beginning by what, in hindsight, was egregious medical mismanagement of his case. Fortunately, doctors have come a long way, and her story would not be typical today:

Mary: I get the word that they're going to give him shock treatment. And I tried, I got in my car and drove down. It was the first time I had driven in Washington, D.C., and I had to go all the way through to the Maryland side, to see if I couldn't get the shock treatment stopped until they had evaluated him more completely. But they were adamant. And at that time, an enlisted person could not refuse shock. An officer could, but an enlisted person couldn't. So, to add to the trauma of a previous head injury, they did say, before they gave him shock treatment, that he was suffering from dementia, aside from the depression itself.

But they were going to treat the depression. Which they proceeded to do. And he received about twenty-two treatments. Bilateral shock. On a forty-eight-year-old man. I mean, he wasn't a kid anymore. Well, the shock treatments did one thing. They taught him not to complain so much to authorities. He only did it to me.

Aileen "took the gloves off," so to speak, after her husband, Louie, had a bad reaction to the drug Haldol. Just before he was admitted to the nursing home, and during his early days there, Louie continued to be given the drug, over Aileen's protests that it was making him worse. After he had spent weeks with his head slumped onto his chest, the drug was finally discontinued, but then Louie required physical therapy to strengthen his neck muscles:

Aileen: Then I was getting charged four hundred and some dollars for the therapy, and I called the HMO [health maintenance organization] and said, "You caused this, this medication," and I said, "I'm not paying it." That's where I became assertive. That's when I thought, hey, I'm in charge, and it took me about four or five phone calls, and I just told them, I said, "I'm not paying this bill. You caused it." And they said, "You can't say that." And I said, "I don't care what you say, I say you caused it." And they ended up paying it, and he had four or five months of therapy, at four hundred and some dollars a month, and I didn't pay it.

My intention here is not to engage in physician-bashing, but rather to demonstrate how wives may develop a sense of personal control over their situations within the context of medical decision-making. As they became more knowledgeable, assumed more responsibility for their husbands' care, and no longer regarded doctors through the veil of mystique, the women I interviewed went through steadily evolving stages of becoming more confident and assertive.

There was consensus among these veteran caregivers that doctors have become better informed and more responsive over the last few years, and have made positive steps to improve care.

Mary: I think the doctors are getting better. There's been a good information campaign going around somewhere, because doctors are getting more alert as to the interactions of drugs, and something I see now that I didn't used to see, is that whenever you meet a new doctor now they sit down and insist that you list every medication that you take. They have that in their charting now, all current medical problems, which I consider a big improvement.

Even though doctors still have no real treatments to offer the families of dementia patients, many of them now recognize the importance of emotional support for families, and accept the responsibility of encouraging family members to seek it. There is still room for improvement, however:

Mary: Doctors still have a tendency to concentrate on their own patient, and not look at the patient within the family. They like nice, neat things, that here's this nice little problem way out here, and we'll do this and this and this. Problem solved. But unfortunately, the problems with dementia only get worse.

What is necessary for effective caregiving is not an adversarial relationship with medical personnel, but a recognition of the inherent limitations of available treatment. Sooner or later caregivers must realize that as hard as doctors may try, and as sincerely as they may wish to help, they can treat patients only on the basis of what is known scientifically at this time. Unfortunately, for people with dementing illnesses, they still do not know much.

Aileen: I always thought, like, the doctor is God. They know what they're doing, but they're human. I can't fault them, really. I really can't fault them because they don't know what medication to give an Alzheimer's patient. My nephew is a professor of pharmacology, and when he was down for Christmas, I asked him, "Have they come up with medication for Alzheimer's?" And he said, "No." So the doctor was trying to help, and I feel he just didn't know what to do, so I don't hold any bad feelings against him.

In a best-case scenario, informed and effective families act as partners, rather than adversaries, to concerned members of the medical profession. The search for a doctor who is sensitive and caring, as well as medically competent, will be richly rewarded if it is successful. Such a doctor can be an important support person in a caregiver's life. Unfortunately, not all families will be able to count on finding one.

CHAPTER FOUR

Gathering Losses

Have I ever had self-pity? The answer is yes. Yes, I felt cheated, and abused, and all the other unpleasant emotions. I've felt them all.

—Mary

The erosion of a patient's capabilities can show itself in innumerable subtle and overt ways, and the resulting emotional and social fallout has deeply wounding effects on his caregiver's life. Giving an account of what happens to a woman whose husband develops a dementing illness is like trying to list how many different types of losses a person could sustain: the losses of companionship, emotional support, social activities, personal freedom, and hope for the future are all examples.

The nature of dementing illness is such that adjustments must be made over and over again as the patient's cognitive and behavioral status changes. Demented people can behave very differently from day to day; something as simple as a head cold, lack of rest, or constipation can cause vacillations in behavior.

Mary: They don't fit into a niche and stay there. They keep popping out at odd times. You can't get a handle on it. Just because they seem rational right now doesn't mean they're going to be rational an hour from now. There's so much pain involved. I've made no bones about it from the word go.

Angie describes her inability to schedule activities, because her husband's condition varies so much:

Angie: I never know. I can't make plans for the day, because I don't know what he's going to be like. So, right now, I don't know. I can't look too far ahead. I just go from day to day. This morning he slept until about eight, and he very nicely took a shower, and did everything he was supposed to do, and had his breakfast. And yesterday morning he wouldn't eat. He wouldn't eat lunch, he wouldn't eat dinner. Nothing. Now today he'll be an altogether different person. So I don't know how to attribute it. I don't understand it.

It is safe to say that if we can't make plans because we don't know what someone is going to be like tomorrow, we certainly do not know what the situation will be like in six months, or in two years. Hopes and expectations for the future give way to a murky uncertainty.

It is not just a matter of learning to live with the situation as it is, though that is certainly difficult enough. It is a matter of learning to accept the fact that assumptions about the future, about the retirement years, and about what the rest of one's life is going to be like, all have to be reevaluated, and reevaluated in a profoundly disappointing way. Even the sense of how the present has flowed from the past is disrupted. Helen, whose family consists of herself, her husband, and a severely retarded institutionalized daughter, addresses this issue:

Helen: I have never, I can honestly say, been bitter about my life, or Janie's. Disappointed, yes. Heartbroken, yes. Devastated, yes. Not bitter. My husband was bitter about Janie. I am on the borderline of bitterness about my husband. I'm on the borderline. Because I don't know why it had to happen at the time of life when you think you've weathered the storm, and now you can just kind of sit back and enjoy. And you can't.

This new ominousness about the future goes deeper than the ruination of plans; it can have a profound impact on a person's whole identity. Angie relates the effect that receiving a diagnosis of degenerative disease had on Hugo himself:

Angie: The things that he had planned, this life that he had planned out . . . Hugo is, always was, a watcher. A clock-watcher. At ten o'clock we'd do this, and at eleven o'clock we'd do that. And so, he had planned his life. And to have something like that step in, and change his life, was devastating. And he didn't take it. I think that was part of the downward spiral. Definitely. It was.

Angie's words describe her husband's reaction to the vision of his own cruelly disrupted future, a future that no longer harmonized with his most basic conception of himself. If we are to understand the situation of caregivers like Angie, we must recognize that devastating illness disrupted her life every bit as much as it disrupted her husband's life. If Hugo's vision of his future self was destroyed by the specter of an incompetent man being pushed in a wheelchair, then Angie's vision of her future self was destroyed by the image of a woman pushing one.

After a diagnosis of dementing illness has been made, families are called upon to make some very difficult decisions as they begin adjusting to the newly defined realities of their lives. Can a person who lives alone continue to do so? Can a person who lives with other people be safely left alone at all? Families must attempt to make such decisions knowing that none of the available alternatives will be pleasant. Accepting the necessity of adopting a frankly protective posture toward a close family member, and of making arrangements for the person's constant supervision, can have serious implications for one's own freedom, too. Accordingly, many people have a rocky time fully accepting their new roles as caregivers.

For wives, perhaps no single issue is more symbolic, more important, or more emotionally wrenching than the issue of whether and how to prevent a demented husband from driving.

Some women, like Irene and Aileen, are fortunate enough to have had a relatively easy time with their husband's transitions from being drivers to being nondrivers. In Irene's case, her husband stopped driving on his own before he was diagnosed with Alzheimer's disease:

Irene: He was still driving. He would get lost, and then he couldn't find his way home. One day, I didn't realize he was lost. And so, this one time he lost his way home, and he came to me and said, "I couldn't find my way home. I guess I shouldn't drive." Thank God. I mean, most people have the other problem. They have to hide the keys and everything to keep them from driving, but he said, "I shouldn't drive."

Aileen never had to struggle with this issue, because her husband Louie readily accepted his doctor's orders to stop driving:

Aileen: When he would drive, he'd take the wrong turn. He'd turn off two roads before he was supposed to. Then the doctor, the doctor told him he shouldn't drive, so as we came out of the doctor's office, the type of man Louie was, he handed me the keys, and he never fussed about it, which most of them do. And so from then on, I did the driving.

Unfortunately, the cessation of driving is a much more difficult transition for many couples than it was for these two, as Irene and Aileen are both aware. It is one thing to recognize on a purely practical level that one's husband is no longer a safe driver, and that for the sake of his own well-being and that of the community he must no longer drive. It is quite another to be the enforcer of that prohibition, and to take away yet another powerful symbol of freedom and adulthood from somebody whose personal identity is already being assaulted every day. Bonnie's husband Hank was emotionally devastated at being told he could no longer drive, and his feelings affected her deeply, too:

Bonnie: The doctor said to me, "All right, the very first thing you have to do is take the car away from your husband. I don't want him out on the road in a car. His reflexes are such that he could kill a kid on a bike, or kill anybody. Starting right today. That's it." So he says, "Henry, did you hear me say that?" and Hank says, "Yea. Who the fuck are you to tell me I can't drive?" He says, "I'm a doctor who's knowing that your reflexes are gone. You cannot drive." And Hank cried. He cried for days. And then he never cried after that.

The certain knowledge that driving has become dangerous is countered by sorrow for the husband's losses, and these opposing feelings clash, resulting in a deep ambivalence. As one woman in the support group said simply and tearfully, "I feel mean about it." It is over this issue that wives are confronted most dramatically with the very nature of the role they find themselves thrust into.

Angie: When he found out he wasn't allowed to drive anymore, that was another thing that really sent him into a tailspin. And he insisted that he could drive. I went riding with him one day. He was going to take a driver's test. He scared the daylights out of me and I said, "Hugo, please don't take the test." But he was determined. He didn't know he wasn't driving well. And so finally, the doctor just told him, "Hugo, you are a menace on the road, and you must turn in your keys. You're not allowed to drive."

He still took the test, but he failed it. He took it two or three times. He made all kinds of errors on the driving test. He barely passed the eye test. He got through that. But when he took the driving test, it came up to the third time, and he failed it. So that's the only reason he didn't drive.

But that was a very hard thing for him to do, to give up the car keys. In fact, even to this day, he'll ask for a set of car keys, and we'll give him a set of keys, and he will carry them in his pocket. And that gives him the security that he does have a car. You wouldn't believe how many days we went round and round with that car. He'd back it out and sit in the driveway. One day, I watched him back it out, and at that time we were living on a steep hill. He came *that* close to going over the side of the hill. And I ran out.

So, I just took the car keys and put another set of keys on it that didn't fit any car. But he was very determined about the car. That was another thing that set him back, too, when the car keys were taken. It's just been a steady downhill. You just watch this person being eaten up by little tiny little pieces every single day. And that's what makes it tough.

Helen's husband, Donald, had become an increasingly unsafe driver when he almost had a serious accident. The incident convinced Helen that it was time to take action to insure that her husband would not drive again:

Helen: I took the key off his key chain, the ignition key, because a neighbor of ours had put some shelves in our garage, and he said when he finished putting in the shelves that he told Donald, "Well, I'll call Helen out and have her put the car back in the garage." And Donald said, "Oh, I can do it." And our friend said, "Oh, I don't think you'd better, Donald. Helen told me that she wanted to do it." And he said, "Well, I can do it." And Don got in the car and almost went through the end of the garage and Frank screamed at him, "Stop the car!" Frank told me it scared him, and he said, "Helen, you must take the keys, and you must do it today." So I did.

That was about a year and a half ago. That is the only time he has tried to drive, but he will offer. For instance, after church, when the parking lot is full of people and cars, as we approach our car he'll say, "Want me to drive?" And I'll say, "Oh no. Thanks a lot, Donald." And I just get in.

Each woman's experience was unique in terms of what she was called upon to deal with when her husband stopped driving. Yet in each case, the resolution of the issue represented a new phase in the course of the dementing illness, and a new phase in the life of the caregiving wife. What they all have in common is the tremendous amount of sadness they felt at finding themselves literally and figuratively in the driver's seat.

On a purely practical level, women are required to take over in areas that, in many cases, were the husband's domain. Sometimes they must do so alongside a husband who is emotionally unable to fully relinquish control himself, even though he is no longer capable of following through. This can be an extremely difficult situation, as Irene attests:

Irene: Up to about six years before he died, he did the income tax, and oh, it was a hassle! And he'd have me sit beside him and he'd try to tell me how to do it. And *he* didn't know. This was miserable for two or three years.

The assumption of responsibility for dealing with finances, car repairs, lawn maintenance, etc., signifies the loss of the husband's role as protector and provider. The degree of trauma caused by these shifts in responsibility depends, at least in part, on the equilibrium of the prior relationship.

Before his illness, Angie's husband, a high-powered businessman, had not included her in financial decisions. Therefore, her assumption of those duties represented a particularly striking departure from the previous balance in their marriage. Her account is typical of what is often heard in the support group from women whose husbands had previously handled the couples' finances:

Angie: He's here, but he's gone. I've had the responsibility of taking over financially. We've been married almost thirty years. But, in those years, Hugo did everything. When it came to doing the income taxes, he did it. And it took me quite a while to find out what he had done. Because he wanted to be kind of closed about that. And it was all right with me. I took care of the house. I wasn't denied anything, and he took care of the books and provided me with what I needed.

So when this happened to him, it just . . . I just had to take over everything. And it was difficult. Because he was not the type of person that would talk to me about things, about what he was doing. He was pretty, you know, closed-mouthed about it. So I didn't understand a lot of things. I had to call the insurance man and have him explain things. I had to go to the accountant and have her explain things to me. In the last two or three years, I've learned quite a bit.

The development of competence in areas that were poorly understood before one's husband became ill is no consolation for the loss that necessitated that development. The assumption of new roles is an outward, tangible sign of a new phase in the marriage. Women learn what they need to learn and do what needs to be done, handling finite, manageable problems as well as they can.

What is not so amenable to management is the erosion of rewarding emotional interactions between the partners. In Bonnie's case, she and her husband had always worked together on business matters, so she was capable of taking over when the time came. However, she experienced the necessity of doing so as symbolic of the loss of Henry's partnership:

Bonnie: Taxes would come up. Preparing the taxes, paying the new taxes, thinking about decisions. It had been my habit so much to share, you know, you share everything. We have to make a decision on this, and knowing that any decision made, there was not going to be a coupling of it; there was just my own . . . If there was input from him, it wasn't anything that made any sense, and it wasn't anything that I liked, and I knew that I'd have to make the decision ultimately.

The assumption of new roles does not occur in an emotional vacuum, and it is not simply a matter of acquiring skills, as new widows are called upon to do all the time. If the reason for her husband's diminishing competence is poorly understood, the wife will be burdened with feelings of impatience, annoyance, and disbelief. The bond between the husband and wife is likely to be strained in the confusing period before the wife realizes that her husband's irritating behaviors are the result of a serious disease he has no control over.

Helen: In the beginning I used to get very cross. I'd say, "If you would listen to me once in a while you'd *know* where we're going," or, "If you would listen to me, Donald, you would know better than to ask that *dumb* question." I don't do that anymore.

Months or even years of exasperation draw heavily on the reservoir of love and good will in a relationship. By the time a diagnosis is reached, the fabric of the marriage may already have sustained damage. As Mabel describes it:

Mabel: I was not aware, too much aware at that time how bad Roy was. I didn't know what was wrong. I just started taking over more and more things. And screaming more and more. And of course, I yelled and I screamed, which we *all* do at the very beginning. I think that actually, I was angry at him. Because everything he said, and everything I said, there was conflict. Just constant. Constant.

The "constant conflict" that Mabel addresses is one of the most difficult aspects of the situation. People can start feeling very worn down when simple tasks and activities of ordinary living, like cooking dinner or going to the store, are all transformed into potential arenas of disagreement and stress.

However, it is not simply conflict itself that is upsetting, but the darker side of oneself exposed by that conflict. Several women told me that what was most distressing to them was seeing aspects of themselves that they had been unaware of or that they had managed to keep repressed in the past. As the limits of the wives' tolerance and compassion were approached, they were confronted with their own intolerance, anger, and even shrewishness. Outbursts of temper were almost always followed by feelings of deep regret and guilt. Such guilt feelings are indicative of another loss: the loss of an image of oneself as a gentle and loving wife.

> *Bonnie:* You know, I hated my position. I hated what was happening. I knew that I was sick, too. My persona, which had always been pretty positive, pretty happy, pretty able to adjust to things, was really going downhill as fast as Henry, and I could see it. I hated to be angry, and I hated to be this person who was yelling. I know I must have taken it out on him a lot. It's like a mother who regrets later, you know, that she said, "Oh, why don't you grow up!" So, the tongue can be very cruel. Everybody should know, if they're going to deal with this disease, that there's a part of you that comes out that is not very nice, and it can be very ugly and black.

Carrying on in the task of caring for a demented husband can mean having your own self-image redefined for you, as in Bonnie's case. The most basic understandings of what the marriage is based on and what it is all about are also subject to reappraisal. Like Bonnie, Mary alludes to the "mother" role in describing her new relationship with her husband:

> *Mary:* He had stopped looking at me as a wife. I had become a fairy godmother who was capable of making everything all right, but was being very ornery about refusing to do it. That's the way I began to realize he perceived me . . . I should somehow be able to make things all right. The way an infant looks at his mother and says, "But it hurts!" And holds it up to you.

Both Bonnie and Mary made it very clear that they did not regard their husbands as the equivalent of children, even though many people who deal with demented patients have an unfortunate tendency to do that. (The issue of whether or not dementia patients become "like children" will be discussed in more detail in Chapter Six.)

Identifying oneself as functioning in the "mother" role toward one's own husband could be considered an acknowledgment of the depth of the identity shifts that have occurred. Even with such acknowledgment, the new role is not a familiar one. If it feels something like motherhood, then it is a perverse, unfamiliar sort of motherhood.

The importance of the sexual relationship to the overall level of compatibility and satisfaction in a marriage is something that varies greatly from couple to couple, even in the absence of dementing illness. Regardless of the relative importance of the couple's prior sexual relationship, profound changes in that relationship, or the eventual complete absence of it, constitute a loss to the well spouse that can be devastating.

In the early years of a dementing illness, sex is not a problem area for some couples. Mabel and her husband Roy, for example, enjoyed a satisfying relationship up until Roy entered the nursing home. The sexual relationship between Aileen and Louie was also not adversely affected until nine years after Louie's Alzheimer's diagnosis. Then their sex life was suddenly disrupted, along with everything else in their lives, by his swift, catastrophic decline following the death of his mother:

Aileen: Most people argue about sex, money, and children. We never argued about sex. We never argued about money. We never argued about children. To us, it was not an issue. To other people, it might have been. He was just forgetful, up to that point. He had none of the other manifestations of Alzheimer's.

The emotional balance between a couple can undergo changes as a result of a dementing illness in one of the partners, and these changes generally do nothing to enhance the sexual relationship. A high level of tension between the partners, or on the part of one partner toward the other, is not conducive to the feelings of warmth, closeness, and mutuality that can lead to a gratifying sexual encounter. It is difficult, if not impossible, for most people to feel affectionate and romantic toward someone while simultaneously feeling irritated at him and harassed by him.

A patient's increased dependence on his wife can cause him to react differently to her, also:

Mary: I had to become his mother. That's what he wanted. And a mother and sexual activity don't go very well together. He stopped seeing me as a sexual partner. Why? Because he saw me as his mother. And it was a long time before I realized that. In the meantime, I'll admit, I was hurt. I mean, it was reasonably sudden, that our relationship changed completely. And when it changed, I became his mother. I was his caregiver, nurturer. But I was not his partner, in some respects.

Some women whose husbands are still able to have intercourse experience upsetting changes in their sexual relationships. One woman described how her husband suddenly got out of bed in the middle of lovemaking, with no apparent recollection of the activity he had just been engaged in. Others have spoken of feelings of being objectified and "used" in a mechanical way by their partners. The sense of being in bed with a stranger whose responses are unfamiliar has also been reported.

While it is impossible to generalize about this, a dementing illness can, unfortunately, have a negative effect on the patient's level of interest in sex, and on his ability to perform. Unsuccessful attempts to engage in intercourse are enormously frustrating for both partners, and can add one more stressor to the cumulative burden of the whole situation. A wife who wishes to be sensitive to her husband's feelings, and who would never deliberately do anything to contribute to his sense of inadequacy, must still deal with the disappointment she feels over her disrupted sexual life, and the angry feelings that disappointment can generate.

Bonnie, who never again had sex with her husband from the time of his diagnosis until his death, told me: "It made him totally out of it." As time went on, and Hank became incontinent, Bonnie's own attitude toward sex with her husband became stark indeed:

> *Bonnie:* As far as the body next to me in bed, my main concern was that he not wet it.

In some cases a dementia patient will become overly interested in sex, and act out his feelings in an inappropriate way. Obviously, a patient who is propositioning salesclerks, or fondling people, will attract more attention than someone who has simply lost all interest in sex, along with any inclination to seek it out. After many years with different support groups, however, both Mabel and Mary believe that such cases are the exception, rather than the rule.

A person exhibiting hypersexuality presents a management problem that cannot be ignored. Conversely, a complete lack of sexual expression on the part of the patient is just one more loss for his partner to accommodate:

> *Mabel:* I would say more of them just forget. But for the ones that it's still an issue with, it's quite an issue.

> *Mary:* Those cases are much more dramatic, but I think they are really a minimal part. They tend to be more the ones that stick in people's minds and get written up. Or maybe it's the ones that are brought out simply because they are something you have to do something about. With loss, you don't have to do anything about it except live with it. You're not comfortable, but you can live with it.

The loss of a rewarding sexual relationship is deeply symbolic of the bleak landscape a caregiver's life can become. Not only must she incorporate all kinds of new difficulties and frustrations into her life, but she must do so without the consolation of an enjoyable physical relationship with her husband.

> *Mary:* There's the void. The feeling that there's a huge chunk of your life that's just been plucked out, and has ceased to be a comfort and a joy. It becomes either something that's mechanical, or nonexistent, or an added frustration.

Aileen's simple definition of sexuality gives us a sense of both the nature of her marriage, and the enormity of her loss:

Aileen: To me, sexuality is the nurturing of one another, the look across the room. The way you look at each other and don't say a word. To me, it was a comfort. It's not about mad passion.

The loss of the husband's empathetic companionship creates a situation in which the wife is grieving for a person who is, physically, still there. Even as a woman assumes the role of caretaker and protector of her husband, he is less and less present to her as a person. Even as they are bound more tightly together by his increasing dependency and his overwhelming needs, she becomes more and more lonely. She must acknowledge to herself that her "personal supports" are, in fact, gone. She misses him.

Bonnie: His daily thing was a request, "Let's go. Let's go." Then we'd get in the car. He'd be okay for a while, and then he'd fall asleep. Those were the times when I began to feel that dreadful loneliness that was so devastating. Here's the body next to me, but we were alone. Here was this man that was so familiar. The body didn't change, the face didn't change, and I still expected him to be able to do things. And I knew, another part of me knew that that wasn't true. I still wanted him to talk to me, and the poor man couldn't. And I'd just plead, you know, "Please, Henry, talk to me." And I'd talk, and talk. And then I'd cry, because I wasn't getting any answers. I'd drive down the street, the tears going down my cheeks, and he's oblivious. Totally oblivious. The loss of the ability to have the companion was . . . That was really tough. My feeling about all those losses was . . . There was some anger with that, and there was so much sadness.

A wife's increasing isolation is felt in all of her relationships, not just the one with her husband. In addition to losing the husband as a social support, the woman's whole social world constricts. Mabel, for example, went through a phase that lasted several years, during which her friends couldn't, or wouldn't, grasp the fact that Roy was becoming seriously impaired. Their blindness, in turn, prevented them from offering her any support in her increasingly difficult situation:

Mabel: They absolutely could not see what was going on, no matter what I said. No one knew anything about Alzheimer's at that time.

Social isolation can also result when the woman fears being a burden to other family members and friends:

Angie: I have a daughter, but she's pretty busy with her own life, and I try not to ask too much of her. She's in her forties, and she'll have her time. Her time may come soon enough, and I figure, "Why bring it on her any sooner?" So I try to maintain as long as I can. I think I'm doing all right.

Sometimes, it is the behavior of the patient himself that serves to isolate his wife. Angry public misunderstandings, inappropriate responses or actions, and emotional outbursts at other people outside the family are sad and embarrassing for her. Understandably, she will try to avoid similar embarrassment in the future. Edith describes one such incident:

Edith: He was real friendly with the neighbors. They helped each other, and I'd asked the young men to come over and help me move a davenport. I asked them to come over some day he was up in the field, because I knew he would say, "Well, you don't need help with that, I'll do it." And I knew he couldn't do that himself, so I asked these two neighbor men to do it. And he saw them down there when he was up in the field working, and he came down before they were through, and wanted to know what they were doing. And he really lit in to both of them, told them to get off his place, "And don't come over here and do anything again!" He got so upset. And they'd been such good friends.

As the wife of a demented spouse tries to avoid anything that might upset him, a downward spiral of isolation is set in motion. Activities that were enjoyed in the past are dropped when they become more difficult and less rewarding:

Edith: He did start wandering after we moved here, so I just decided, no more trips with him, because it was miserable for all of us.

Even if the wife is motivated to seek out friends and companionship, she may have real or imagined practical reasons for not doing so. Bonnie, a naturally gregarious and approachable person, was worried that becoming friendly with the man next door, a man who had helped her to take an uncooperative Henry to the hospital on a previous occasion, might create new problems for her:

Bonnie: The neighbor was walking around, and I thought, maybe they should be friends instead of enemies, and I thought, nah, I'll leave it alone. I was gonna bring him in the house just to have a cup of coffee or something, but nah, I don't wanna do that. I just thought, Hank wouldn't understand it, and maybe he'd think again that I'm doing something crazy, because Hank never verbalized, like X's [a woman in the support group] husband. Hank never had any conversation, that he ever said to me, that there were other people in our house, or that I was doing anything that was sexually wrong, whereas X's husband was always accusing her of keeping people in the house, and a man in her bed, and stuff like that. Hank never did do that. But that's been things I've heard from others. Oh ho, that might have been something else!

Edith and Bonnie have described the sort of social isolation that can result from dementia patients' unpredictable behavior toward neighbors and friends. As if the loss of social contact with other people were not enough, it becomes extremely difficult for the wife even to take her husband on any kind of an outing without risking profound embarrassment.

Bonnie and Henry had enjoyed eating in restaurants before he became ill, and she continued to take him to one of their favorite places, where they were regular patrons. Bonnie did all of the ordering, having explained to the waiter that her husband had Alzheimer's disease:

Bonnie: This one visit, Hank got up and said he had to go to the bathroom. I didn't think anything of it. He was familiar with where to go. So he came back to the table, and then all these men were looking at us. And then there were mops, and buckets. There was a bunch of paper that had been stored in the corner, and Hank had just stood there and peed on the boxes, and paper towels, and paper bags. Well, I never did go back. I began to think, you know, I can't take him out too many more times.

Irene and Jim were dedicated churchgoers, and their church continued to be a source of comfort and pleasure to both of them even after Jim was very impaired. Like the incident Bonnie described, an excursion that had formerly been an opportunity to get out of the house and into surroundings that were relatively safe and familiar for the patient suddenly turned into a setting for the nightmarish mortification of his wife:

> *Irene:* I took him to church quite a bit, and we always sat in the same place, and he'd sing along. One time, he thought Saturday was Sunday, and he insisted I take him to church Saturday. Well, Saturday there's no church. But, to get him to leave me alone, when he had an idea he wanted something, you had to do it. So I took him to church. And I opened the door, and I saw this beautiful, beautiful bouquet. I saw that first. Then, of course, it dawned on me that there was a casket underneath it. I tried to pull him back, but he wouldn't let me. I had to go in. He wanted to sit up front, as usual. I tried to pull him to the back. No! He had to sit up front. So, we sat right behind the mourners. These little young kids. It was such a sad funeral, a young mother in her forties. Then, they had a soloist. And, lo and behold, he sang along with the soloist. He sang! He sang the whole song! I could have died. I could have gone through the floor, I was so embarrassed. And I couldn't shut him up. I couldn't get him out. I couldn't do a thing.

Being out in public with the patient carries with it the potential for incidents that the caregiver, at least initially, experiences as stigmatizing. Unfortunately, feelings of embarrassment become all too familiar. Wives are faced with the possibility of awkward scenes every time they leave their homes with their husbands, and they either learn to accept that possibility, or they become even more isolated and cut off from the rest of the world.

Sometimes family members and friends withdraw from the couple because they themselves are unable to face the situation, and sometimes the withdrawal is mutual. Angie describes the dynamics of how this happens:

> *Angie:* We were with a group that traveled, and we weren't able to do that, and what do you talk about? And then Hugo couldn't carry on a conversation. Hugo would sit there in the corner trying to figure out what was being said, and not conversing, and I'd

worry that maybe he's there alone, so it got easier for me to say, "We can't make it." I didn't say "Hugo's not feeling well." I'd just say, "No, we can't make it." So they quit asking after so many times. My friends are still there, but we just don't have friendships that we used to have, or do the things we used to do. So everything . . . I seem to have lost a lot.

I have heard women describe the pain that they feel when they run into friends who avoid asking them about their husbands, or who seem embarrassed and awkward. Yet, this is by no means a universal experience. Many people, like Bonnie, are fortunate to have supportive people in their lives:

Bonnie: Everybody was great, and nobody avoided us, or anything like that. And my friends in this area were always asking, "How's it going, Bonnie?" And "What can we do to help?" and all this. And I'm lucky to have two sisters in the area.

In most cases, friends and relatives vary in their ability to handle witnessing the decline of the dementia patient, and in the amount of support they offer his wife.

Aileen: I have a wonderful sister, brother, and sister-in-law. They come to see Louie, but my sister's husband couldn't handle Louie's situation. He came a few times and then went home to sit and cry, so I told her, I said, "Don't let him come anymore." I just knew him and I knew he couldn't handle it. We have another friend who periodically comes to see Louie, but when he goes home, his wife says he doesn't sleep all night. And I said, "Well, just don't come." And Louie has a cousin who came to see me, and he said, "I know I should go see Louie, but I don't think I could handle it." And I said, "Well, at least you're honest about it. You're not making excuses. If it's gonna bother you, I know your intent." I said, "That's okay." And he does call me periodically to see how everything is. But the rest of Louie's family has just, I don't know, just sort of forgotten he's there. But my family, I have a good family.

Irene's youngest son was still in high school and living at home during the years that her husband was most severely impaired. She emphasized the role that maintaining some semblance of family normalcy played for her, and how that saved her from total social isolation. She contrasted her experience with that of other people in the support group:

Irene: Having the boy here was a big plus, for the simple reason
. . . Just the fact that I had somebody here to talk to. And he
was gone a couple of times, three or four days he went out of
town. Then I realized what I needed him for. I needed somebody
to talk to. Living alone with the spouse, I can see where it would
send you up a tree. I had this kid. And he had his friends coming,
and all of that made commotion, and activity. It was different.

No, I didn't have the isolation that other people have. And you
know, so many of the people have real close family that just drop
them. Their sons, their daughters, their brothers, their sisters.
Just plain drop them, and don't want to have anything to do with
them. I can see where they must fall apart. See, I had all this
family support. And people understood, when they came to my
house. Although, people dropped me, too, I will have to say.

The theme of separation and isolation does not stop with
the loss of friends and social contacts. Women caring for
demented husbands find themselves cut off even from their
own emotions. Mary and Angie's descriptions of becoming
apathetic to their own reactions, and of putting their own
feelings in the background, sound very similar to each other:

Mary: I think we all do that. I think we have to do that. If you
concentrate constantly on one thing, it's just like they say about
pain: you can only feel a certain amount of pain at any one time.
In other words, one type of pain tends to cancel out another, to
a certain extent. I think the same thing happens emotionally, too.
If you're concentrating, whether it's a sick child or a sick husband, it's all . . . Your mind set is on that. You postpone your
own feelings. They're there, but you postpone your reaction.

Angie: I'm overlooking a lot. I'm learning to live with a lot more
than I thought I could. I'm living with more today than I thought
I could last year. And it's only because it gets a little worse every
day, but you overlook it. You overlook a little bit more, overlook
a little bit more. I think I'm coping really well. I don't know.
Some days I want to scream, some days I want to cry, but I just
figure I have to get going. I don't know how I feel differently
from before. It's just really hard to say. I've really lost a lot of
feeling.

CHAPTER FIVE

Turning Points

That thief went through all my files. He was in there, the marks are still on the wall, about forty-five minutes. And meanwhile Hugo is tied up in a chair, hadn't had lunch, and he was calling. Making noises. And very soon the thief walked out of my office, came down toward the closet I was in, and closed it. I had left the sliding door open about an inch. And as he walked by he closed that closet. And it scared me. I thought he discovered I was in there. And I thought, well, now he's going to get a knife and he'll really attack me. So I sat there for a split second and I thought: What will I do? He's going to harm Hugo. Hugo's helpless. He's going to harm me. And what will I do? So I thought, I'd better jump the gun on him. So I just threw that closet door open, and it really made a noise when I slammed it open. And he, at that time, was sitting in the chair next to Hugo. When I slammed the door, he jumped about two feet in the air, and over about two feet. And it startled . . . It scared him. And he said, "Oh my God, you scared me." And that's when I pulled the gun on him and said, "You just get back in that chair and sit there."

—Angie

Analyzing the stories of the eight women, I was struck by the fact that there often seems to be an identifiable incident, or moment, in which all of the accumulated frustrations, humiliations, and losses suffered and accommodated up to that point finally reach "critical mass."

The emotional state of the caregiver now undergoes an

abrupt shift, and the woman reacts strongly to the circumstances she is in with an assertive, even militant, response. These incidents could be viewed as either "the last straw," or as "the moment of truth," depending on your point of view. These turning points in the caregiving career mark the beginnings of new attitudes toward the situation and the wives' responses to it. A lifetime of "niceness," compliance, and deference to authority figures can suddenly be shed like an old coat if matters become sufficiently intolerable.

Mary, after encountering nothing but frustration in her attempts to get military medical personnel to diagnose her husband's problems, finally got results from the following conversation with an army-trained psychiatric social worker, after deciding that enough was more than enough:

Mary: I was very frustrated with the care he was getting. I was frustrated with the shrugging off of stuff, and I was frustrated with the fact that there had been no attempt to treat him when he was first found. I said, "I want him to see a psychiatrist." And the guy said, "No." And I said, "He *will* see a psychiatrist." And he said, "What're you gonna do about it?" Got real smart-aleck. I said, "I tell you what. If he doesn't see a psychiatrist, I will. Over at the clinic where they're sending him." And he said, "What do you mean by that?" And I said, "Well, I'll come over there, and I'll raise a fuss, and I'll probably raise enough of a fuss, and . . . Let me put it this way. I'll probably see the MP's, but I'll also see a psychiatrist." I couldn't take any more.

What I see in Mary's recounting of this incident is a dramatic turning point in her public demeanor. In other words, if she was previously constrained by conditioning that it was better to be "nice" in one's social interactions with people, events in her life finally overrode that conditioning. She realized that very assertive action was needed, and that no one would initiate it on her behalf. She had to do it herself. Not only did she have to be willing to do it, she had to be willing to state her case in extremely forceful terms.

When Aileen got on the telephone and told the person at her health maintenance organization, "I say you caused it, and I'm not paying it,'' after her husband had problems with his medications, she was setting new boundaries around her situation and defining for herself what she would, and would not, tolerate. As she said herself, ''That's when I thought, 'Hey, I'm in charge.' '' Having a husband in a nursing home was bad enough; she wasn't about to pay unfair charges, too. The genesis of clarity about what is or is not under the caregiver's control can come gradually or abruptly. Either way, a sense of reclaiming some control over whatever *can* be controlled emerges as an important coping strategy.

A major breakthrough in a caregiving relationship occurs when the woman realizes and accepts the fact that she has complete and total responsibility for her own situation. I have already described Irene taking her confused husband back down the church steps and directly to the hospital, unable to rationalize his deficits any longer. This act represents an assumption of her own responsibility that is much more open and frankly acknowledged than all of the gathering burdens that Irene had gradually been taking on for several years.

Sometimes this kind of personal empowerment comes about in previously undreamed-of ways. Angie's experience is, thankfully, very unusual. She discovered that some valuable pieces of her jewelry and coin collection had been stolen, and she did not know which of her three hired home helpers was the guilty party. She describes what happened when she turned to the police for help:

Angie: The woman who took the report said, ''Yes, I think the detective will help you.'' So that, when he said no, he wouldn't do it, I was really kind of shocked, because he said, ''Just fire everybody, and I'll start my investigation on Monday.'' And I said, ''I don't know if I can live with that.'' That was Thursday afternoon. I didn't want to involve anyone else. And here I am in this house, wondering who it was. If they went to that extreme to steal those things, then what would they try next? I didn't want to involve my family, for fear they'd get hurt, or whatever. I felt it was my problem now, and I had to do something about it.

The circumstances of Angie's situation took her from the accountant's office, where she had gone for information at the beginning of her husband's illness, to a chair in her hall closet where she sat with an unloaded gun, waiting to catch a thief red-handed. I asked Angie how she had felt after doing just that:

Angie: I was relieved. I could not have gone through the weekend without doing this. The police should have done it for me, or should have helped me. At that point, I had three suspects. And they were all going to be in my house that weekend. All three of them. So, how could I go the weekend with this man in my house? I *had* to find out. And there wasn't anything that was going to stop me from doing it.

It is hard to imagine doing something like Angie did, or how she must have felt sitting in her hall closet listening to the thief going through her drawers as her husband pulled against his restraints in his chair in the kitchen. The only thing I can think of that would be worse was the situation that led her to take such extreme measures. While what she did was a desperate act that could have turned out badly, it did solve her problem:

Angie: I felt very relieved that I found out who it was. I was shaken. I was mad. I was angry. To think that this person that I had trusted to take care of my husband had neglected my husband all these weeks. And went through my personal things. He knew everything about me at this point. He went through all my personal records. He went through my checkbook. I could hear papers, he was sifting through papers and everything. And then, to take everything that we had worked for, for sixty years. Just come in and take it away. Walk off with it. I was glad I caught him. I just had all kinds of things going through my head. I'm glad I did it. I wouldn't recommend that anybody do it.

(At first, the police were inclined to let the matter drop. However, thanks to Angie's persistence, the case eventually did go to court, and the thief served time in jail. Upon his release, he was ordered to make restitution, and was barred from ever taking employment as a home care aide again.)

Edith reached her own crisis point while her husband was still trying to run his apple orchard. A very mild-mannered, soft-spoken woman, Edith had been attempting for over a year to persuade Richard to move to a smaller place in town, or at least to hire someone to help with the apples:

Edith: He wouldn't have anybody on the place. I tried to get him to rent out the orchard to somebody and we'd live there. We'd move to town and get a family or somebody that could live there, try to get him to hire somebody to come and help. He wouldn't do anything. "Nobody is touching my apples. This is *my* place."

More frustration followed. Richard spent more and more of his time dismantling equipment, over Edith's protests that there was nothing wrong with it. One morning, she had finally had enough:

Edith: I had put the sprayer pump together four times, and he'd tear it apart, and I'd put it back together and say, "Well, go up and spray today." And maybe he'd go up and spray a little bit and quit or something. So then, the last day I put the pump together, he said, "That's not right. You don't know anything about pumps. We've gotta have the pump man look at that." The pump man said, "There's nothing wrong with that pump." So, we brought it home that night, and it was getting to be evening, and we put it back. I helped him put it back on the sprayer, and we filled it with water, and I said, "Now, in the morning, all you do is put the chemical in your sprayer."

Well, in the morning I woke up a little later than usual, and he was already up. And I heard metal . . . noises. And I knew what he was doing. So I grabbed my housecoat and went out there, and he had that pump, he was tearing it apart. And I could not tell him, or make him understand, that that pump was working. "Well, I've gotta spray and I've gotta fix that pump." And I just turned, and went into the house, and called three realtors.

If Edith, up to that point, was someone who had never contravened her husband's wishes, she found that she could do so now. The action that she took was not as important as the sudden, profound transfer of control within the marriage that it signified. Edith was confronted with the fact that appeasement was not working, and that it was up to her to take charge. We can also see in this case the giving up, or departure, from the self-imposed requirement of "honesty" with the husband.

Now honesty may be replaced by expediency. An attempt

at reasoning with the demented husband has not worked, and the wife's self-defensive blinders drop. Suddenly the situation is revealed for what it is, and the woman must ask herself which approaches work for her and which do not. Mary addresses this issue:

Mary: I generally used the quiet approach at first. You know, tried to do things according to the way they're supposed to be done. But, I'd become more and more aggressive as far as getting things done. The nice approach didn't work, so I used any approach I could. Quite frankly, for the first time in my life, I became somewhat dishonest. That, I had never been. I was painfully honest, even to the point that it was very much to my disadvantage. I was honest. Period. I'm very much afraid I learned not to be.

Mabel's husband Roy suffered a very rapid deterioration and entered the nursing home suddenly. She worked hard to find out all she could about Alzheimer's disease, only to encounter a lack of understanding of the problem even among doctors and nursing home staff. She describes dumping her "nice old lady" image in response to her frustration over this:

Mabel: In the skilled facility the nasty old lady came out in me. We walked around the facility every night after dinner. And one of the aides was sitting, doing some book work. This was down at the station different from where Roy was located. And the countertops were all marbleized looking. And we stopped at the counter and he took his fingers and traced all around this marbleized top, and the girl looked up and said, "Can I help you?" And I said, "No, no." And so, he went down a little further and he traced some more around, and so she looked at him and said, "What do you want?" And I said, "No, it's all right, go on with your work." And then he came back right over her head and traced some more of the marbleized figure on the countertop, and finally, she looked up, and she wasn't as sweet as before, and she said, *"What do you want?"* And I said, *"What do you know about Alzheimer's?"* And she said, "What?" And I said, "You sit there. You watch him. I'm getting a book for you." And I went down to the room, and I got a book on Alzheimer's, and I gave it to her. And I said, "Leave that paperwork alone and you read that booklet." Then the supervisor of nurses talked to me the next morning. And another lady and I went in and did a presentation on Alzheimer's to the staff. And we did that about every three or four months.

Mabel's example is also a good illustration of another change that successful caregivers undergo: they become less vulnerable to feelings of humiliation or embarrassment. Rather than slinking away from the counter, or trying to get Roy to stop his finger tracing, Mabel redefines the situation by insisting that the aide, and not Roy, make an adjustment.

A woman in the support group described what happened when she and her husband, a Parkinson's patient with heart problems and a very complicated schedule of medications, were stuck in a long bank line when it came time to change his nitroglycerin patch. Unsure of how to handle their predicament at first, she finally decided to put the new patch on her husband's back right there in the bank lobby. Shortly, one of the managers noticed the couple and ushered them into his office, where they could complete the procedure in privacy.

As this woman told the group about her experience, she said, "I wasn't embarrassed because it was a necessity. It wasn't obscene." The whole group then had a lively discussion about feeling emboldened to ask strangers to vacate a restroom for a few minutes so that patients could be given the personal help they needed. Several members described encountering people who had even offered to stand guard at the restroom door after getting such a request.

Aileen gives us a wonderful example of this "new attitude" with her comments about the way she handled the loud noises that her husband sometimes made:

Aileen: When Louie hollers, most families would say, "Shhh!" "Shhh," they tell the patient, but that's not going to shut them up. I say, "Give 'em hell, Louie!" I do! I do. I'm not going to shush him. It's not him, it's the disease. People laugh at me when I say, "Give 'em hell, Louie," because they're embarrassed. People are embarrassed because their loved one has a dementia. Well, I mean, they don't have a dementia because they *want* to have a dementia, the patient. It's a fact. To me, you know, if you can't lick 'em, you join 'em.

Mabel took it upon herself to educate the nursing home staff in a very direct way, by going over to the facility and giving presentations. However, every caregiver finds herself, even if only in subtle ways, in the role of public educator. This role is not one that most people would choose, but in the case of caring for a dementia patient, it is a role that caregivers find thrust upon them whether they like it or not.

Mary has spoken often of the need for greater public awareness of the problems facing families of dementia patients, and of the problems of disabled people in general. She was reminded of her own experiences recently after spending a long day in San Francisco with a couple she was assisting through the process of obtaining veteran's benefits:

Mary: You had some ugly reactions. Like Ira staggering, and you'd see people looking at him. And you knew darn well they thought he was drunk. I got mad Thursday. I'd taken Mr. and Mrs. Doe to Fort Miley, and we'd been gone all day. It was nine o'clock at night before we stopped in Petaluma to get some dinner on our way home, and we were exhausted and hungry. Mr. Doe had been pretty good during the day, but coming out of the restaurant he was staggering all over the place. He was tired. It was a long day. And we saw people . . . I felt like turning around and yelling, "He's not drunk! He's sick!" I mean, it made me angry to see the looks on their faces. I got a quick flash back to my old feelings, myself.

Ultimately, each caring wife must decide how she will balance the need to take her place, with her husband, in public, against her wish to shelter her husband from any unnecessary humiliation. Angie gives her thoughts on this issue:

Angie: He was diagnosed about seven years before he died, and for the first three or four or five years, something like that, I took him places. We went out to dinner. And there were times when we were at dinner, and the food was dribbling down the front of him, but I thought, "I'm not going to sit home and make him an invalid any quicker than I have to." So if he dribbled a little food, we'd put a napkin there, and take care of it. If he did do that, it would embarrass him a little, and he would look to me, as if to say, "Look what I've done," and I'd say, "It's okay, don't worry about it." There were many times when that happened. And he'd try to lift his food, and didn't get his mouth.

But we continued to go out until finally when we got to the point where he couldn't even use a fork or a spoon was when I decided that was the time we couldn't go out. For his dignity. I wasn't going to take him to a public place and sit him in a high-chair, so to speak, and spoon-feed him. But we did go out a lot in those first years, even though he was diagnosed with Parkinson's and a dementia. We did go out. And we had accidents. He would trip over the least little thing. And sometimes there was nothing, and he'd trip, and lose his balance very quickly. When we walked into a restaurant, we'd just walk arm in arm or hold hands or something like that, so we were kind of holding each other. You can tell when it gets to be a point of real embarrassment to them. And then I don't think it's right.

What I have tried to illustrate here is that the caregivers' accustomed responses to problems that they face must undergo some moderations if the caregivers are to see themselves as responsible and competent. Sometimes events make these changes take place in a sudden and brutal way, and sometimes the changes evolve gradually; but once they have happened, it is almost impossible to go back to the old ways.

Becoming a successful caregiver means becoming a person who fully accepts the responsibility not just for her own life, but for someone else's life as well; a person who has a firm sense of what she can control and what she cannot control, who speaks up when it is necessary, who has overcome the need to be sweet and friendly in all of her public interactions, who recognizes that sometimes what's needed is expediency rather than honesty, who is almost beyond embarrassment and beyond the need for the approval of others: someone who has enlarged and energized her personal resources in a way she may never have experienced before.

CHAPTER SIX

❧

Managing Day by Day

There's a sadness that's going to overcome every-body, the sadness that you say farewell in little bits and pieces. You say them as degrees happen. So you mourn and you grieve, and you grieve for the loss of each thing. *They* grieve. I saw Hank grieve for the ability to move about. I know he grieved for the change in me. I wasn't Bonnie. I was sick, too. Yes, I was different. And I think he must have grieved for that without knowing how to say it, or even say to me, "Damn you, you've changed." He would just get mad, but he couldn't verbalize that he was angry about . . . my new behavior. Which was: Jailer. Punisher. Verbal abuse.

—Bonnie

After a woman has fully accepted the caregiving role, and all of the varied responsibilities that entails, she is still left with the task of managing daily life with her impaired husband. After she has learned to be more effective with various service providers, and to speak up for her husband's needs, she must still live with the ongoing changes in the climate of her own emotional life. The strides that she makes in managing different social interactions do not constitute "magic bullets" that can change anything about basic, mundane situations like the one Helen describes:

Helen: I believe he is at a point now where he is hallucinating. I'm not sure that's the word I should use, but in the evening, when he is tired, he is more confused. Much more confused. It's almost every single night, now. It started maybe every third or fourth night. But almost without fail he'll look at me at the dinner table when we're just about finished with our meal and say, "Are we staying here tonight?" And I'll say, "Yes, of course, where else?" He accepts whatever I say. He accepts it, which I guess is pretty good. It would be bad if he didn't. But then he'll come in the living room, and sit in his chair, and say, "When are we going to the other house?"

Ironically, the sorts of behaviors and attitudes, such as forthrightness and assertiveness, that must be mastered to function and advocate effectively in the social world at large, are not the skills that must be learned in order to deal with an impaired person on an emotional level. Even after the patient loses many of his cognitive abilities, he may still have dramatic reactions to other people and to his surroundings, and a skillful caregiver becomes very sensitive and attuned to regulating the emotional climate around him. This is the key to avoiding catastrophic reactions from the patient, and to preserving access to whatever communication abilities may remain.

Each person in the caregiving role must learn, through trial and error, what works best in particular situations with her particular patient. However, there are general principles and guidelines that have helped many people learn to deal with dementia patients more effectively and with less strain and conflict. The key to creating harmonious living conditions lies not in learning a long list of inflexible "dos" and "don'ts," but in developing a sensitivity to the patient's fears and needs. As Scott Hale, the director of three Alzheimer's respite centers in Sonoma County, California, explains: "It's more of an attitude. It's how you act, rather than what you say. Your composure, your body language, who you are, how you come across in the caregiving position has so much more to do with what the relationship is going to be than any kind of technique you have."

The following discussion of general guidelines is presented with that ideal in mind.

1. Start with a safe, uncluttered environment.

This will involve removing throw rugs, or anything else the person could trip over. If you are someone who likes to rearrange the furniture often, now is the time to resist the temptation to do that.

Adequate lighting is important throughout the house. Night-lights in the person's bedroom and bathroom can help prevent confusion and falls if he wakes up during the night.

It is particularly important that the route to the bathroom be free of impediments. Some families find it helpful to put a picture of a toilet on the bathroom door, or even mark the way to the bathroom with colored tape. In the bathroom, grab bars can be installed over the bathtub, and rubber mats in the tub can help prevent slipping. If the hot water is hot enough to scald, the temperature in the water heater needs to be adjusted to 135 degrees or lower.

Check for toxic substances such as bleach and cleaning supplies in the kitchen and bathroom, as well as for sharp items and potentially dangerous electrical appliances about the house and garage, and find other, safer places to keep them. Evaluate the risks posed by any stairways, and decide whether or not you need to restrict access to them.

It can be helpful to have clocks with large, easy-to-read faces around the house, and labels on cabinets and drawers to help the person keep track of where things are kept. However, caregivers must realize that measures like these will only work for a limited time, becoming less effective as the person becomes more impaired.

Streamline the environment by removing seldom-worn clothes from the closet. Dresser drawers should contain only items the person uses or wears on a regular basis. The point is to eliminate some of the confusion that is caused when the person feels overwhelmed by too many options or choices.

2. Keep it simple.

This is good advice for life in general, but it is doubly important when you're taking care of a demented person. The aim is to keep frustration at a bare minimum. The concept of "simplicity" applies to many different aspects of care. Here are some guidelines:

• Stick to routine. Daily schedules and predictability are important for mentally impaired people. A comfortable, familiar structure to the day helps the person to know what to expect next. Strive for consistency.

• Never ask open-ended questions. The way we phrase questions and requests has a lot to do with whether or not the demented person will comprehend what we are asking. He can feel overwhelmed at needing to make a choice. Rather than asking, "What would you like to eat?" say, "How about a tuna sandwich?" This approach assumes, of course, that you are familiar with the person's tastes and preferences.

• Ask only one question at a time, and give only one direction at a time. A series of questions will make a demented person feel bombarded and defensive, and a long series of instructions will only confuse him further. The same principle applies when someone is engaged in a task: if the task is broken down into manageable parts, the person is more likely to feel successful as each part is completed.

• Use short words and simple phrases, and speak slowly and clearly, without shouting. As language skills erode, a simpler vocabulary becomes more appropriate. Any unnecessary verbiage only serves to muddy your message. Make your statement, and give it a moment to register. One pitfall to guard against is that the person may become angry if the overall tone of your words leaves him feeling patronized.

• Avoid long explanations. Some caregivers have trouble accepting the fact that explanations for things do not always sink in. It is much better just to help someone get ready to go out than to burden him with a complicated accounting of exactly where he is going, why he is going, and who will be there. Explanations, like any other messages given to patients, need to be given in small, manageable bits. For example, "Let's get your coat," will work better than "We're putting on your coat so we can go over to your sister's house with the Smiths for your brother-in-law's birthday party."

• Allow enough time. Hurrying and rushing are to be avoided at all costs. It is going to take longer to do things, such as getting ready for appointments, than it has in the past. Accept this, and take it into account when you're planning the day.

• Avoid abrupt transitions. The ideal is to have a smooth, relaxed flow from one activity to the next, and to ease into new activities so that the person has a chance to adjust to any changes. This applies whether it's time for him to go to the doctor or time for him to brush his teeth.

• Go places when they're not crowded, and try to use the least stressful means of transportation. If you must take someone shopping, try to do it when there will be fewer people and less noise in the store. The more commotion and noise there is, the more potential for confusion. It's also a good idea to minimize situations like having to stand in line with the patient. Consequently, you may want to avoid the mall on Saturday afternoons.

3. Use distraction, not contradiction.

Distraction can work for you when you are trying to get the patient's cooperation. For example, if you know he balks at the idea of going to the bathroom, it may work better if you forego announcing the purpose of the trip down the hall. Walk him gently through the motions, talking to him about something he enjoys, has pleasant memories of, or has always been interested in. This serves to keep the focus of his attention away from the immediate activity, whatever it may be.

One tool in working with a dementia patient is to refrain from saying the word "no" to him. By finding ways to phrase your messages so that you are not directly contradicting the person, you will be avoiding the sort of head-on confrontations that are usually no-win propositions for everybody. As far as catastrophic reactions are concerned, prevention is much better than cure.

If someone is headed out the door, or toward danger, the approach to take is to guide him gently over to something else and try to engage his attention there. Admittedly, this can be difficult at times, but it does get easier with practice.

4. Respond to the feelings, not the words.

It is difficult, initially, to fine-tune your own reactions so that they are in sync with those of a dementia patient. However, if you are able to discard the notion that every conversation you engage in must make logical sense, you will be making strides in that direction.

The key is to view the patient's actions, and interpret what he is saying, in terms of what it must be like to be in his situation at that moment. Unfortunately, two of the most common emotional states for demented people are anxiety and frustration. The value in understanding this is that your own reactions to the person will be different if you can see his actions as those of a frustrated, frightened person, and not as those of someone who is deliberately trying to make your life difficult.

If, for example, a patient repeats a question over and over, the caregiver must seek to understand the feelings behind the question. It does no good to tell someone who keeps asking where his wallet is that his wallet is in his pocket and that you have already told him that five times; the person is probably expressing a generalized insecurity about his sense of having lost control. On some level he knows, even if he doesn't say so directly, that he has not paid bills or balanced his checkbook or gone to the bank for some time, and this frightens him. The fear is made worse because he can't verbalize the vague unease that he feels, or understand why he feels it. The wallet, then, can be understood as a symbol. By speaking about this concrete item, he is also asking how these things are being taken care of, or if they are being taken care of at all. Rather than directly responding more than two or three times to the question of the wallet, a skilled caregiver will touch the person lovingly and say something like, "Everything is taken care of," and then attempt to engage his attention elsewhere.

Anything that helps the caregiver to develop empathy for

the patient will help her to keep him happier and more co-operative, as illustrated by Angie's understanding of her husband Hugo, who was very hard to deal with sometimes. She came to see his behavior in terms of what she felt he was expressing through it:

Angie: So I don't know what he knows, at this point. What he realizes is going on in there. But he's aware that there is something not right. And I think that's when he gets so frustrated and so combative, when he just wants to show that he's still in command of his life, and he doesn't want anybody to touch him. But he needs it because he can't stand up alone, he needs assistance to stand up. He can't do anything for himself. Nothing. He can't blow his nose for himself. He just has lost all coordination, and he can't even put on his shirt or *anything*. He's just lost it all.

5. Speak softly. Give lots of hugs, approval, and physical contact.

Since the dementia patient is operating on an emotional level rather than an intellectual level, a gentle human touch is a very effective way to reassure the person and get his cooperation. A hug will go further than any verbal explanation.

Irene had her husband at home for many years, and managed to accomplish the tasks of physical care by learning to work with him in a way that did not cause him to rebel against her ministrations. She describes what she considers the necessary attitude for caregiving:

Irene: You just love 'em a lot, and talk to them. You get more with honey than, you know, vinegar, so to speak. Just by being kind, you get more than by being pushy. By being good to them, and kind to them, and petting them, and loving them, you got them to do what you wanted them to do. More than pushing. If you tried to push him into the shower, he would get so rigid, and he would hang on to that frame. You couldn't do a thing with him. Forget it! You can't force them to do anything. Be kind, and talk softly and, you know, you might be calling them a bad word, but they respond to your voice and temperament more than what you're saying. You just have to push them around gently and sweetly, put your arm around them, and you can almost move them anyplace. They'll move. But don't try to push them. Don't try to force them, because, boy, they'll hang on to something and you won't get them off.

6. Keep your expectations realistic.

Dementia patients become frustrated when they are asked to do things that are beyond their capabilities, or when they are expected to function at an unrealistically high level. Caregivers invite stress for themselves and the patient when they are not realistic about what he is or isn't capable of, or when they fail to tailor their expectations to match the person's diminishing skills.

Sometimes the fact must be faced that the time for "reality orientation" has passed. It is always worthwhile to attempt to keep someone oriented in terms of time and place for as long as possible, provided you are able to recognize when the effort is creating more problems than it solves. As Scott Hale says, "If you're the caregiver, and your frustration level is increasing with telling the person what time it is, or where they are, or the day, or whatever, then that's probably a clue to you that this isn't working."

Caregivers must strike a delicate balance between encouraging the dementia patient to do all that he can, and not pushing him so hard that he feels ineffectual. Mary shared her thoughts on the necessity of keeping people as mentally engaged as possible, but doing it in a natural, unforced way:

Mary: I was visiting a friend on the neurological wing of a hospital recently. I was listening to a young woman talking to an elderly woman in the next bed, and she was asking her questions, obviously off some kind of a list of questions that, quite frankly, I would have had trouble answering, many of them. They were questions about obscure, unimportant things. Who cares? I think it probably increased the elderly woman's frustration and anxiety. I felt like telling this young woman to shut up. I felt she was being cruel.

And yes, I think we can play games, look at things, talk about things, try dredging up memories, encouraging the person to observe what they're seeing, and encouraging them to comment. But in a more or less natural way.

7. Respect and foster the person's dignity.

Even if someone is severely impaired mentally, it is crucial that he be treated with all the respect due to any adult. In the first place, he *is* an adult and, as such, deserves respect. In the second place, he may react with anger and noncooperation if he feels degraded or disrespected.

Respect toward the person is demonstrated by according him the same level of common courtesy that we would for anyone else. Everyone wants to feel that he or she is part of the group. It is unrealistic to expect *anyone* to sit quietly while a conversation he is not part of goes on around him, and a considerate caregiver will make every attempt to include the person she's caring for in social interactions. Ignoring someone in a social situation, even if that person is mentally impaired, is rude, and most people, including dementia patients, will become justifiably annoyed if they are treated rudely.

Another serious mistake that some caregivers make is talking to someone else about the dementia patient in the patient's presence, as if he were not there. No one wants to be discussed by others, particularly if what is being said is not especially flattering, and dementia patients are no exception. Respect for the patient and sensitivity to his feelings can go a long way toward preserving a harmonious atmosphere.

A tendency that caregivers must guard against, and one that has a direct bearing on the dignity of the patient, is to treat him as if he were a child, and not an adult. This inclination is strengthened when caregivers of newly diagnosed dementia patients are told that the demented person will eventually become "more childlike," or that he will lose skills in the reverse order that children attain them. The fact that both of those analogies are at least partially true compounds the problem. Also, caregivers eventually figure out that many of the management strategies that work well with children—for example, the principle of distraction rather than contradiction—also work well with demented adults. Nevertheless, successful caregivers are very concerned about preserving the patient's dignity, and most of the women I spoke with were wary of the "demented people are like children" comparison. They recognized that regarding someone as a child could be seen as a license to treat him like one, perhaps without even the minimal respect that children are, in fact, generally accorded in our society.

What all of this adds up to is a challenge for anyone living with a dementia patient. Do what works for you, but do it without losing sight of the fact that the person is still an adult, not a child. Angie and Bonnie speak on this issue:

Angie: We just tried to get him to do as much for himself as he could without making him look like he was a small child. He couldn't put his shirt on. Didn't know what arm went where. Well, we'd get him started on his shirt, get the other sleeve on, and leave him there and see if he could button it. Then if he couldn't, we'd just kind of go over and button a couple of buttons. Just so it wasn't lying open. But we tried not to make him feel like a child.

Bonnie: Well, I don't see where they're like children at all, in any phase from babyhood on. No. Dementia is not like that, in my view. Watching the destruction of someone's adult personality . . . each little thing that is lost, is certainly not going back to babyhood at all. I think it's an unfortunate thought to cling to, and I would hope that the medical community could find other ways to explain it, and not use that. I don't remember in our support group, anybody ever saying that their person, their spouse, was like a child. But I think there was some of that in the explanation to the well spouse, that your husband or wife will deteriorate to be childlike. Leading them around by the hand, that symbolic kind of thing. And being able to put them in the car and put the seat belt on and close the door, and that person sitting next to you accepts that, maybe in a childlike way, but that's the only thing I can think of for myself. Henry didn't ever turn out to be like a child. I think it's a misnomer if anybody's hanging on to that. They're strong, and adults, and they're still able to push their weight around.

8. Give the person as much independence and freedom as possible.

One of the basic problems that arises in caring for someone whose mental status keeps changing is the need to find the balance between protecting the person and letting him have whatever freedom of movement he is still capable of handling. It is important that the person, who is already severely constrained by his situation, not be made to feel more controlled and incarcerated than is absolutely necessary. Angie looks at this question in philosophical terms:

Angie: I had to get stronger. Because he was getting weaker. And sometimes I wonder. There's a fine line if you're taking too much control. Then that weakens the patient a little more quickly. So there's a fine line there, and when you have to do things, you're required to do more and more every day. And then you wonder, where is the line? When am I going to stop? Where is the stopping point for taking over his life? Where do I stop, and where does he come into the picture, you know? There is quite a big line there of when you back off, I think. And then let him see what he can do.

Bonnie, whose husband was more mobile than Angie's, saw the problem differently from day to day, according to her husband's behavior at any particular time. She also provides some insight into how hard it can be to live up to the principle of maximum freedom for the patient without becoming upset yourself:

Bonnie: On a peaceful day, when the medication worked, and things were calm, I knew he was okay and quiet watching TV. That was easy, and I could do other things. But if he got into things, I'd think, "Uh oh, it's quiet. What's he doing?" He'd be out in the garage fiddling with the automatic garage door opener. And then my skyrocket would go off. So if my husband, and I guess any other patient, stayed calm, that was a gift from God. The minute things happened that were causing concern for safety, destruction of property, loss of things because they were tucked away in little places that nobody ever found again, then for me, I would jump right in and be very verbal and vocal. And that upset him, because I would get strident and holler. So the autonomy of the person to have a calm day was really up to how he, in my case, spent the day.

Mary sees the issue of freedom for the patient in very practical terms, and acknowledges that the issue of appropriate limit-setting is something that always needs to be evaluated and reevaluated carefully:

Mary: I don't find it a controversy. I don't view it that way. Expect very little from them as far as help, or anything like that, but give them as much freedom of movement within a safe environment as you can. You have to set limits where they're safe. In other words, a person that's still capable of taking a walk, let him. But give them as much freedom of movement as is reasonable. I do feel, myself, that people oftentimes allow driving of a vehicle to go on well beyond the stage where they should be, but that's because it's not only the person driving that you have to consider. You have to consider the rest of the world. So I don't think you can separate the danger to self and the danger to others. Where that becomes an issue, you have to use good judgment. But if the person enjoys watering the lawn or the flower bed, I wouldn't worry too much whether they drown the plants. Just so they don't stick the hose into the window, or like one did, into the gas tank.

9. Get help and relief for yourself.

At first glance, this principle might not seem to have much to do with managing a demented person's reactions, but it is vitally important. The reason for this is simple: the patient, who is functioning on an increasingly emotional rather than intellectual level, is living with somebody who is under a great deal of strain! Since the moods of the patient are influenced by the moods of the caregiver, anything the caregiver can do to elevate her own spirits will improve the emotional atmosphere in the home. This issue will be discussed in more detail in Chapter Eleven: The Support Group.

10. Don't expect perfection.

As skillful as anyone becomes at dealing with dementia patients, there will always be times when the situation feels overwhelming. People sometimes lose their tempers, and that is understandable. Certain things are just extremely hard to deal with, and there is no way around it. The best you can do is to strive to eliminate as much upset from your life as

possible, and give yourself a lot of recognition for what you
are accomplishing every day.

> *Bonnie:* He got so he was paranoid about using a toilet. And
> getting started towards the bathroom he would use the closet, or
> he'd use the wastebasket, or the tub. The sink. Almost anything
> to avoid the toilet. And then the bowel movements, which I al-
> ways said, "I'll take care of him until he can't do that." And
> there would be these feces all over everywhere. And I would
> scream at him, "Wait! Let me put a towel down! Hold it! Don't
> move!" He'd be moving around and I'd say, "Don't move!
> Please!" But no, I never . . . never got control when it came to
> things like that. I don't know why the neighbors didn't hear me.
>
> He never did wet the bed, but he'd get up in the middle of the
> night, and the minute I heard rustling I'd be alert and right behind
> him and not saying anything and making sure he got to the bath-
> room. And there he'd be, peeing in the tub, in the wastebasket.
> And I settled for that. That was fine.

No matter how skillful she becomes at meeting the requirements of daily life, a caregiving wife must continue to
adjust and readjust to the decrements in her husband's condition. The caregiving experience is a very long process of
learning to accept the situation, and then learning to accept
a new situation all over again.

> *Mary:* It was strange. In the beginning, he did a little seesawing.
> He would, at times, kind of come up a little bit, and go along for
> a little while, and then he'd drop. And every time he'd drop, he'd
> drop to a lower step. He might come part way up, but when he
> dropped again it would be a lower step than the one when he
> started up. So it was a slow thing. After all, it was twenty-five
> years. In the meantime, of course, the children were grown,
> became independent, were off on their own. But Ira is getting
> more and more childlike. As the children were growing upwards,
> he was going downwards. But, he did hit a plateau there that
> lasted probably three or four years. One big plateau. And I kept
> on, because he would occasionally go up, and I'd hope. Hope
> does not die easily.

When Mary says that hope does not die easily, she is acknowledging the vast gap that can exist between the intellec-

tual understanding that the husband will never recover, and the emotional acceptance of that fact. When we consider that it is impossible to know what is actually going on inside the mind of a person who has lost the capacity for meaningful speech, the process of "acceptance" becomes even harder. How can a person "accept" something that there is no way of measuring, particularly when some emotional connection remains?

Helen: You can't live with somebody forty-eight years—or is it forty-nine?—forty-eight years and not have a very deep affection, and a very deep compassion, even though that person isn't the same person.

Angie: Once in a while I will understand something that he says. Just yesterday he said, "I want to go home. I'm leaving now. I'm going home." And I said, "Where's home?" Then he forgets. The mind doesn't register.

Aileen had no way of knowing whether or not Louie still understood her, but she was committed to trying to reach any level of understanding that might remain, even after he was totally uncommunicative and in the nursing home:

Aileen: Every year when it's Louie's birthday I have a party and all the family and a few friends come, and it seems on that day he's just sort of, I don't know, more content. But on my anniversary, I tell him, "Louie, I'm mad at you." I ask him for a kiss on my anniversary. He'll never give me a kiss. I do it with humor, though. I make a joke out of it, I tell him, "Louie, today's our anniversary, and you're not even going to kiss me." He just stares at me blankly. But then I tell him, you know, "I remodeled the bathroom and you'd really like it." I tell him everything. They laugh at me down there. I say, "Hey, he's understanding some of this." Maybe not, but I like to think . . .

The inability to be sure of her husband's thoughts and feelings is a source of anguish for a wife, who must still attempt to determine and respond to his needs after he can no longer communicate those needs to her.

Angie: He doesn't say if he has a pain. Sometimes I wonder, is he hurting somewhere? If he *is* hurting somewhere, does he know it? I don't know. I just . . . I can't understand it. I just don't understand it. I think at times, I don't know how this can go on. How much more can you take? Not only for me, but for him, too. It's hard on me, but what must be going through *his* head?

You wonder what people like that think, and you have to imagine yourself, that you can't find your car keys, for one thing. Where are my keys? Can't find my keys . . . and that freezes. That's it. Or you walk out to the parking lot. Have you ever walked out in the parking lot, and there's this sea of cars, and you think, God, was it this side? Was it the other? And let that freeze in your mind, while you're standing there, not knowing anything. And that kind of brought to my mind about some of the things he must be going through. I don't know. No one knows.

A woman taking care of her impaired husband must also deal in an ongoing way with the fact that her social status is ambiguous, at best. She is married, but she has lost her husband. She enters into a social limbo, a sort of twilight between marriage and widowhood, a state that has been called a "never-ending funeral." As long as the husband continues to live, the wife cannot truly proceed with her own life. Even after he is lost to her as a helpmate, she continues to have empathy and affection for him that make it difficult for her to move through the sort of mourning process that she would if he were gone physically as well as mentally.

Given the fact that their husbands eventually became incapable of providing the emotional and physical companionship that can make marriage rewarding, I wondered if any of the women had ever considered finding male companionship somewhere else. Angie found the whole idea appalling, and it was obvious to me that the question had never crossed her mind before I asked it of her:

Angie: I just think it's totally wrong. You're still married, you still have that responsibility, and you have to look at it, what if you were in his place, and in the reverse situation? How would you like that? I just don't think that would be right at all. I wouldn't even think about it. Never. I couldn't live with that. It's hard enough to live with the thought of Hugo having that illness, and then to turn around to satisfy *my*self. No, I wouldn't do that. It would just compound the whole thing. Then I would be sick, also. That would make *me* a sick person. I couldn't imagine anybody doing that. I don't care what the need is. I just don't think I could do that. I know I wouldn't do that. I couldn't do it.

Mabel told me that she did not feel judgmental toward other people who made different choices in the same situation, but that she herself would never have considered an involvement with another man:

Mabel: For myself, definitely not. Definitely, I couldn't.

Bonnie felt that marital fidelity was an important value in her life, but she had not categorically ruled out the possibility of a new relationship while her husband was still alive. She speaks very frankly about her feelings on this, and about the seriousness and care she brings to all of her relationships, even the theoretical ones:

Bonnie: I never met anybody that I felt would be worth the trouble to go hiding around and sneaking around. Just to get in bed and bang bodies around was not something I wanted to do. I would have to be attached to that person in all kinds of ways. I would have to think of that person as an alternative life partner. I never met anyone like that. If I had been sorely tempted, I don't think I would have let my marriage vows stop me. I said goodbye to Hank every month, every time something new was lost. I would have been able to adjust all that thinking and maybe I would lose some brownie points in heaven, but there wasn't any gut hunger, there wasn't anything going on going "feed me, feed me." Had that happened, I maybe could have lived a little differently, but I didn't have anything that was crying out.

When I asked Bonnie what her advice would be to anyone just starting in the caregiving role, she spoke about the difficulty of coming to terms with the situation, and of the importance of facing reality, insofar as that is possible:

Bonnie: I think the part that was most difficult for me to work with was to look at a familiar face, and not have the expectation that that person could do what they'd always been able to do. I used to say, "If Henry could wear a mask, I could be such a good nurse. I could do such a good job. But he's . . . there he is. It's the same old guy, dammit, and I want him to do what he could do." So I don't know how to answer that, except that, except for somebody to know that that person is going to be totally changed from what you know him or her to be.

When dementing illness strikes a family, the patient is not the only one who changes. No one could give care to someone else, day in and day out, sometimes for years, and not be deeply affected by the experience.

Angie spoke about the changes she saw in herself since the onset of Hugo's illness, and how she has made adaptations she would have thought impossible in the past. Her words speak for many in describing the evolution of a caregiver:

Angie: My sisters say to me, "How can you do what you're doing with Hugo? I couldn't do it." That's what they say. "I could not do it. And I *wouldn't* do it." And I can't . . . people can't say that. You can't say that. Because, until you're faced with the situation, you don't know how you're going to react. I would have said five years ago that I couldn't do what I'm doing with Hugo. I couldn't do that. And I wouldn't want to do it. But today, I'm doing it. Maybe I'd rather not, but I'm doing it. So it's . . . I think it's very difficult to say what you would do.

CHAPTER SEVEN

❦

Decisions about
Nursing Home Placement

I don't plan to ever put my husband in a nursing home.
I know I'm not the first one to say that.

—Helen

Placing a person in a nursing home is one of the most
difficult things that anyone is ever called upon to do in life,
and it is almost always the option of last resort. Not surprisingly, many of the people who eventually find themselves
needing to go through that painful process are those who
have vowed that it would never happen.

Aileen: Well, if anybody would have ever told me that I would
have ever put my husband in a nursing home, I would have been
really mad and called them a liar. Because I just . . . I was really
against it.

It is very common for people to continue giving care at
home long after they've reached the point of risking their
own physical and emotional health by doing so. This point
may be reached early or late in the course of a dementing
illness, depending on many variables, including the physical,
financial, and emotional resources available to the caregiver.
It is impossible to give a generic, across-the-board description of someone who "belongs" in a nursing home, just as
it is impossible to say whether a patient is "better off" in a
nursing home, or at home with a person who is having trouble caring for him. The important point to remember is that

93

the whole situation, and not just the condition of the patient, is what must be considered. Here are just a few of the variables that can make a big difference in terms of whether or not it is practical to keep someone at home:

• Can the primary caregiver physically handle the patient? Something as simple as the relative sizes of the people involved can be very important. A woman who weighs ninety pounds less than her husband will have a harder time helping him out of a chair than someone who is closer to him in size, and this consideration takes on more and more importance if the patient is losing mobility. If he suffers from rigidity, like Angie's husband Hugo did, the caregiver, no matter what her size, will eventually be physically unable to get him in and out of bed by herself, or help him on and off the toilet.

• What is the state of the caregiver's health? If the caregiver has arthritis, or any other disability, this will affect her ability to provide physical care. To use another example, a person with serious heart or lung problems would have a hard time keeping up with a restless, wandering patient. Physical considerations like these directly define the sort of help the caregiver will need if she chooses to keep the patient at home.

• Is bringing in any outside help an affordable option? Many families have been able to postpone a nursing home placement by hiring paid helpers to assist with housework, to aid in physically caring for the patient, or to provide supplementary companionship for him along with a respite for his caregiver. The amount and kind of help needed will vary from case to case, depending on things like the condition of the patient, the capabilities of the caregiver, the availability of free programs staffed by volunteers, and whether or not there are other family members and friends living nearby who are willing and able to pitch in.

In some cases, Medicare will pay for home health care. This care must be part of a doctor's prescribed home health care plan, and it must be arranged through a home health agency that participates in the Medicare program. Unfortunately, dementia patients are often denied these services when the type of care they need is judged to be primarily custodial rather than medical.

• What is the physical environment? A large house may present upkeep and maintenance problems, but be well suited to accommodate the comings and goings of home helpers. Also, having one's own bedroom can be a significant "quality of life" issue for the caregiver. A small apartment has the advantage of being easier to maintain, but it can feel very confining to live in one with a demented person who may sometimes be agitated.

Issues of maintenance, management, and privacy will be affected by the size and layout of the living space. Whether or not it is practical or even possible to change or adapt the physical environment can have important implications for nursing home placement.

Irene cared for her husband at home until his death. Since he was incontinent and required complete physical care for the last eight years, I asked Irene if there were any circumstances that would have prompted her to place her husband in a skilled nursing facility, or if there was anything she felt she would have been unable to handle. Given the immensity of what she had, in fact, handled already, her answer was surprisingly simple:

Irene: If I was sick, physically unable, you see. You never know. You can become sick, too.

Mary also had her husband at home until his death. Having health problems of her own, she recognized that there were limitations on her ability to care for him physically, and that nursing home placement probably would have been necessary if Ira had lived much longer:

Mary: The kids were very annoyed with me, knowing how exhausted I was, that I wouldn't do it. In fact, for a while, they weren't overly supportive. They were emotionally involved in the situation too. But he understood too much, and he would have felt so completely abandoned. I couldn't do it. Because, see, Ira was still able to communicate. My problem was going to be when he did become physically helpless. But with Ira, he was just on the edge of that, out to the point where I wasn't going to be able to take care of him anymore, when he had the final heart attack. I had him home up until two hours before he went.

The women who did not place their husbands in nursing homes, or had not done so as yet, acknowledged the possibility of not being able to give total care at home indefinitely. These women recognized the fragility of their situations, and that the delicate balance was vulnerable to being upset by their own future health problems or by a worsening of their husbands' conditions. Even so, the guiding principle for all of them was the goal of giving care at home until the last possible moment.

Helen: I hope I never have to do it. He would have to be physically abusing me, and I know that many of them do get to that point. It would have to be something that I could not handle. Physically or emotionally. I hope I never find myself in such a corner that I have no other way except to say, "Okay, he has to go to a nursing home." Or it would have to be that my health fails. I hope it won't. Or I just wasn't able. But it would have to be a very severe situation before I would agree to do it.

Irene: I said, "I'll keep him as long as I can." And I kept him, and there were times when I thought, "Oh, my God, how many more days can I do this, how many more months?" There were times when you just prayed that God would give you enough strength to keep on going, because if you didn't, you'd have to put him in a home, see.

Irene's words illustrate the horrible dilemma that these women find themselves in, which is: to continue giving over their own lives to the total care of a person who may or may not have any awareness of what is being done on his behalf, or to live with a terrible sense of guilt and failure at having consigned one's mate to "a home." It was difficult for me, personally, to see women who had given years of care feeling as if they had failed their husbands by placing them in nursing homes. Angie, who still had her husband at home at the time of our first interview, describes what trying to resolve this no-win situation feels like:

Angie: The condition with Hugo is such that, even though he is frail looking, he's still very strong, and I feel I'm getting a little weaker. I feel there's really not too much left. I could just be getting to the limit. But, I've tried to think about how . . . What would I do to make myself feel better? And I think, well, now, what can I do that will really solve some of my problems that I have? Number one, I could put Hugo in convalescent care. That would take care of that problem. But would it? I've tried to visualize it. I can visualize Hugo in a convalescent care home, and I'm here. Am I really going to be happy about that? I don't think so. I would be thinking, "Is he covered tonight? Are they taking good care of him? Did he eat his dinner?" All of these things would be tormenting me. I know myself. So I can say, I can put him in convalescent care, and I can just stay home and be happy. Or make a life for myself. But it won't work.

The necessity of finding balance between what is best for the patient and what is best for the caregiver is the critical issue in deciding when to place the patient in a nursing home, and solving this conflict involves complex and painful emotional issues. Since the caregiver herself almost always finds the idea of placing her husband in a nursing home extremely distressing, the question of what is really best for her becomes a complicated one.

Angie expanded on her feelings about not being ready to place her husband in a nursing home. Her report of going back and forth on the emotional seesaw between desperation about her situation, and faith in her continuing ability to deal with it, is descriptive of what many people experience. Her account is also typical of a process that many caregivers go through, in which they "try on" the idea of placement for a long time before they actually follow through with it, if they ever do.

She acknowledged how important her home helper, Manny, was in enabling her to keep Hugo at home, and how she would not be able to take care of Hugo by herself:

Angie: I've thought about it a lot. And that's as far as I get. I think about it. And there are some days . . . Yesterday, I thought, I'm going to call 911 and have him taken to . . . someplace. But I just can't do it. Last night was really bad. I had gotten dressed and I had a chain with a pendant hanging from it, and I reached over to help Manny give Hugo his medication, and Hugo grabbed me with this chain, and wouldn't let go, and he was turning it, and choking me. Well, it finally broke off, but I had a big scratch on the back of my neck and I just went out, very disturbed. But after a couple of hours it was okay. I got over it. So these are the kinds of things that, when it gets to that point, when he becomes really physical, that's when I think I can't take it. But it passes over and goes on to another day. Having Manny here . . . If I didn't have Manny, there is no way I could handle it. I wouldn't have a choice as to whether he would go. He would have to go.

Physicians played a role in placement decisions, even though the women often did not follow the doctors' suggestions to place their husbands the first time, or even the first few times, the suggestions were made:

Angie: Dr. M. said he will get a lot worse than he is right now. He said, "I have to warn you." And his suggestion is convalescent care. He has told me that for five years.

Most of these women had, over time, acquired a general unwillingness to follow their doctors' orders blithely, but once the decision to follow through on nursing home placement was made, a doctor's agreement with the correctness of the decision was seen as a source of comfort. This role of mitigator of guilt over a nursing home placement emerges as an appropriate and important function of a caring, supportive physician.

Edith's husband suffered a stroke after she had been caring for him for several years. The doctor had encouraged her to place Richard in a nursing home before the stroke, but Edith had chosen not to do so. Afterward, however, the doctor stated his case much more forcefully:

Edith: He was in the hospital a week. After a week the doctor called me and said, "He'll get out of the hospital today," and I said, "When shall I come and get him?" He said, "You're not getting him. I'm putting him into a rest home." We had talked rest home with the doctor before, and different ones that he said were pretty good, and so I was thinking there was going to have to be [a placement] because of the problems just handling him. The doctor'd been after me for a long time, too. He said, "You can't do that any longer." Of course, I'd done it a year or so after he told me that.

The decision to place someone in a nursing home may be arrived at gradually, or events may force the hand of the caregiver in an abrupt way. Mary and Irene never placed their husbands in nursing homes, and Edith placed her husband in one only after a stroke made his physical nursing needs too much to handle at home. Angie eventually placed Hugo, who was sometimes combative, in a nursing home for eight months, then brought him home for the last six weeks of his life. It is still too early to know whether Helen will ever have to make the decision. The remaining three, Aileen, Bonnie, and Mabel, all placed their husbands in nursing homes because of violent episodes, or the threat of a violent episode.

Even after the threat of violence enters the picture, the decision is still not an easy one, but once the wife perceives that the situation has become potentially dangerous, a turning point has been reached. It is also at this stage that other family members and medical advisers often become much more insistent that placement be considered.

As stated before, Aileen's husband Louie suffered a sharp worsening of his condition after his mother was attacked in her apartment and died of cancer shortly thereafter. Louie's agitation abruptly increased, and a long, peaceful holding pattern came to an end, overwhelming Aileen. As exhausted as she became, she was determined to keep Louie at home. Aileen describes how her sons worked to get her to carry out the recommendation of the doctor to place Louie in a nursing home, something she did not wish to do:

Aileen: I had to take him to the emergency room ten days after the funeral, when he just fell apart. And he was frightened. He didn't know what was going on inside him. So they put him on Mellaril. That didn't help, and then they put him on Haldol, which I hate. They put him on Haldol, and it made him more . . . paranoid, I guess. He'd think that people on the television . . . he'd want to know what they were doing in his house, he would just get very agitated. Not physically, with me, but verbally, which wasn't him at all, I mean, his personality. I blame it on the Haldol. I think, if he hadn't gone on the Haldol he would have been able to stay home longer.

It got so he never slept, day or night. It got so that I was up all the time, and finally it got to where I had my son put a lock on the hall door because he'd wake up and all the doors would be open. Louie had been outside, and I was so tired, I didn't even know that he'd been outside. Why I put him in a convalescent hospital was I was not only getting physically ill, but I was just exhausted. And my son noticed this, so he called my other son up north, and my son came down, and I said, "What are you doing home?" And he said, "You have to do what the doctor told you to do." He had told me to put him in a home about four months before this. I said, "I can't." So he stayed for two weeks, and then I waited him out another four days, and I said, "You'd better go back," and he said, "I'm not going back until you do it."

At that time Louie was very combative. In the middle of the night he would, if I would get up and say, "Louie, come back to bed," he would just grab my shoulders and he'd say, "What are you doing in my house?" He thought I was the intruder. You see, it all goes back to that. Oh, it was terrible. And my son thought maybe one night I wouldn't be able to get through to him who I was, and he might hurt me.

In Bonnie's case, by the time the doctor told her that he thought it was time to place Hank in a nursing facility, she had already started to consider that possibility, and had more or less reached the same conclusion:

Bonnie: One day . . . oh, it was early in the morning, and it wasn't a day-care day. He was dressed, but I was in my robe. I had turned my back to go into the kitchen, and I heard something, and I turned around, and he had the chair, about to crash it down on my head. When I turned to protect myself, he brought it down, and it crashed on my finger. So then I pushed him back, away from me, and he still had the chair. I picked up another chair, and we locked the legs together. I said to him, "Look what you're doing! We're like a couple of rutting deer! You big jerk. Put the chair down!" And he said, "No!" And I said, "You've got to, you can't hurt me! You *can't* hurt me." He said, "Well, I don't want to hurt you." I said, "Well, put your chair down."

So we put them down, and I said, "What was that all about? My God, why did you want to hit me?" He said, "You're such a jerk. You never say anything nice. Everything you say is nasty. You never give me any credit for anything." And on and on. He was sick to death of . . . and I *wasn't* nice a lot. I could be just real nasty, verbally nasty to him, and he'd had it.

But I was scared. When I went to the hospital to see if I had a broken finger, it wasn't broken, but it acted like a broken finger and was all swelled up, and I had to put it in a little splint. So essentially, I had a broken finger. And I lived with it, and looked at it. And felt it. And hated it, and felt victimized by it, and I was thinking, you know, my husband broke my finger. Really. And I referred to it a lot. It was sort of like a point that, hey, this has happened, and I don't want to ever have anything like this happen to me again.

When I went to the doctor for the finger, he said, "I think you'd better start looking for a place." I had started. I called around, and then I looked around. We really got on it.

In the case of Mabel's husband, Roy, the line between agitation and violence was also crossed. In Roy's case, the violent episode came suddenly, and almost without warning. Mabel and Roy had come home from a trip to New Zealand nine days earlier, and he had been restless since their return. He already had an appointment for yet another medical evaluation when the incident that landed him in the nursing home occurred:

Mabel: Every one of the nights that we were home, he had gotten up in the middle of the night, because there was somebody in the house. And he would turn on the lights. And then, eventually, he'd find out that there was no one there, and he'd turn off the lights and he'd come to bed. Well, this particular night, it was about one o'clock in the morning. He got up, and he took a shower, and he shaved, and he got all dressed up, and I looked, and said, "It's one o'clock." Well, he didn't care. Then he went out to the desk on the back porch to get the keys for the truck. He was going *out*. The doctor had given us some Valium. So I got up, and I went into the bathroom, and I drew a glass of water, and I said, "Come on, I've got this pill for you." And he just didn't pay any attention to me. I decided I would turn the bathroom light out and I'd walk out to the back porch with my glass and my Valium. I turned the light out.

Boy, the minute that light went out, he was in that bathroom, grabbed me by one wrist, and was twisting it the opposite way from where it should go. He finally found the "robber." [Mabel screamed for her neighbor across the driveway.] And so Denny, of course, came flying out. He came up and unlocked the door, and came and patted Roy on the back and said, "Roy, you're hurting Mabel. Roy, now, let go. You're hurting Mabel." And Roy didn't let his grip off a bit. I was black and blue on both arms from the wrists to the shoulder.

It took the neighbor, two paramedics, and one other man to subdue Roy enough to take him to the hospital. From the hospital, he was placed directly into a nursing home, where his violent episodes were an intermittent problem until his death a year and a half later. I asked Mabel how she felt about the way her husband's nursing home placement had come about:

Mabel: I didn't have to make the decision. I didn't have to. I didn't have any guilt. Because [the doctor, also an old family friend] put his arm around me and said, "Mabe, you know Roy can never come home."

Probably the most difficult aspect of placing a spouse in a nursing home is balancing one's own need for rest and safety with the reality that, due to the very nature of the situation, the person will not be receiving the kind of care he has received at home. There is a natural reluctance to see your own needs as legitimate when the price of getting those needs met is to place your husband in a nursing home. Angie had not yet reached that point, although she acknowledged that it was possible she might in the future:

Angie: Hugo is in such a bad state. He doesn't know what day it is. He is so vulnerable. Anybody . . . He could be mistreated so easily. And I would never know. I would *never* know. He wouldn't be able to tell me. And that's the thing that bothers me a lot. And that's why I have him home. Because I feel I have control. [Placement] won't work. It just won't work. I would feel real guilty and, on the other hand, Hugo might just like it there. He may find people that are like him that he can get along with. I don't know. Or, they may just medicate him so that he'll just lay there as a vegetable. That could happen, because of his combativeness. They're not going to put up with it. They can't. They don't have the time.

See, we can sit here, like yesterday. Manny had him in his chair yesterday, and Hugo didn't want to take a shower. He didn't want to be touched. He was very combative. Well, we can sit here and observe him, and let him cool off, and kowtow to him, and give him water, give him juice. "Hugo, when you're ready, you want a shower." And devote all of our . . . our whole day to him. We devoted the whole day to him. But he's not going to get that wherever he goes.

Bonnie also knew very well that the attention Hank was receiving from her would not be matched in a nursing home. She had no illusions about what nursing home care would be like, and described her expectations for it in very unvarnished terms:

Bonnie: Well, I went in with the attitude that it's not going to be great. And I knew it wasn't going to be great. I could stand almost anything other than abuse or total neglect. That the level of care there would be okay unless I saw something that was so bad that I could label it as abuse, or neglect.

When I told Bonnie that her assessment of the care she could expect sounded pretty minimal, I learned that she herself had worked at a convalescent hospital as a young girl:

Bonnie: Years and years ago, when I was in school, I took a job as a person working in a convalescent hospital, and it was sort of to see . . . a career move. I thought, well, I wouldn't dislike being a nurse. I might really like it. So I thought I would take a real shitty job, and see what it was like.

And I learned to love the patients, but I knew that you could work around one patient just all day, and never keep up with the need. So, I did go into nursing, but it was during the war, and I didn't finish. Anyway, I had nursing experience, and I had office nurse experience, so I knew that you could have overstaff, which nobody has these days, and you still would not keep up with the need. Knowing that everything is understaffed, if he's kept reasonably clean, if his food was given to him, if he was able to handle stuff, if he was moved about and he was given the opportunity, at least, to walk when he could walk, then I'd be happy with that.

Bonnie visited most of the nursing homes in two counties, and was not very impressed with what she saw, so she initially tried placing Henry in a board-and-care home. Such places, also known as "rest homes," or "residential care facilities," provide care that is basically custodial and non-medical in nature. People who live there may need help with getting dressed and caring for their personal needs, but they do not require the sorts of medical services that are provided in a "skilled nursing facility," as nursing homes are also called.

Board-and-care homes may be large places with many residents, or they may house only two or three people who live in the private home of the owner/manager. Such facilities cost less than nursing homes and are an appropriate placement for people who are mildly confused, but who don't require daily nursing attention; who can transfer in and out of bed and chairs by themselves, who are continent, and who are not violent.

Bonnie tried a small home for Hank, hoping that he would do better in a different environment with another man around. The placement did not work out, and she was forced to place him in a nursing home very quickly:

Bonnie: I heard about a board and care, and I took him up there to show the owner all about Hank, giving all the gory details, what he'd be dealing with. And J. thought he could handle it. He had all these ladies, and I think he was kind of thinking, well, this will be nice to have a man instead of all these little ladies.

And so I packed a bag and came back the next day with Henry, so he's looking around this really nice bedroom with a beautiful view, and I said, "Well, Hank, you're going to have a little vacation here in this wonderful spot. And J. and his son are going to keep you busy, and this lady cooks the meals."

I didn't know that they left her alone at night with all the patients. She slept in a room next to him. Well, when he got up disoriented, and didn't know where he was, she got up to show him how to get to the bathroom, and he grabbed her by the neck, which just totally frightened her. Somehow, she got some help.

But I got a phone call about seven in the morning, "Come get him." It was very short-lived. Then I tried to get him into the HMO hospital just for overnight until I could figure out what to do with him, and they wouldn't accept him. So I called one of the places I had looked at before, and said, "It's an emergency.

We tried a board and care and it didn't work, and the HMO won't help. Can I bring him in?''

The experiences of Mabel and Bonnie provide good illustrations of why it is very important for caregivers to take the time to familiarize themselves with local nursing homes. Nursing home placement is traumatic under the best of circumstances. When it must be done under hurried, crisis conditions, it is less likely that the best possible choice will be made.

Even if the situation at home still feels manageable, and it appears that placement is far in the future, looking over the available facilities is still a good idea. One reason for this is that the most desirable places sometimes have long waiting lists. Also, filling out lengthy preadmission forms prior to need is one small way to ease the complexities of placement, particularly if that placement comes about suddenly.

Quality of care in nursing homes runs the gamut from excellent to awful, and choosing the right one may not be easy. People who are called upon to make that choice find themselves needing to weigh competing considerations. Often, the ultimate decision, just like the decision to place someone at all, is a subjective one. Suppose a family must decide between two hypothetical nursing homes: the first one is cheerful and clean, and staffed by warm, caring aides, but it is two hours away. The second nursing home is right in town; it doesn't have any glaring flaws and seems generally adequate, but the administrator is not warm or likable and the residents look listless. Obviously, the solution in a case like this will take careful thought.

The following suggestions are intended as general guidelines in the search for the best nursing home situation.

• Determine how the care will be paid for. If the person will enter the facility as a Medicaid patient, or if he will need to go on Medicaid in the future, the home he enters must be certified to accept Medicaid patients. (See Appendix A, Financial and Legal Considerations.) Unless you can pay two to four thousand dollars a month from the family funds for an indefinite period of time, this question will apply to you.

• Identify any needs or special requirements pertinent to your family member. Physical therapy is an example of something that is offered in some nursing homes, but not in others. If rehabilitation services are important, the search can be narrowed by eliminating facilities that don't offer them. If the person is on a special diet, find out if the nursing home can provide it. If he or she is a member of a religious group or fraternal organization, you may wish to look first at nursing homes that are run by that group.

• Be sure that the facility and the administrator are both licensed by the state. Do not even consider a place without such licensing. Each facility must also post, in plain view, a copy of any deficiency notices and citations they may have received. Check for these.

• Examine the contract of admission. This document should be very specific about which services are covered in the basic daily rate, and which are extra. Items that may or may not be included in the basic charge are things like laundry services, the use of a wheelchair or walker, and frequent bed changes. If the contract doesn't itemize these charges, ask for an itemized list.

• Take someone else with you when you visit the nursing home. This way, you can check out your impressions with the other person after you leave. He or she may notice something that you have missed.

• Note the overall impression you get when you walk in. Is the place well lighted? Is the temperature kept in a comfortable range? In terms of cleanliness, the ideal is for the place to be clean without feeling sterile. If residents are receiving personal care in a timely way, the odors in the facility should not be overpowering. This goes for the smell of disinfectants as well as the smell of urine and feces. A strong disinfectant smell can be masking other smells.

• What is the physical layout of the nursing home? The dining room should be pleasant, with small tables rather than long ones such as those in a school cafeteria. Is there a nice room with comfortable chairs where residents may go to visit or watch television? Are the hallways wide enough for two wheelchairs, or two people using walkers, to pass through with ease? Is there a safe, enclosed place for residents to sit outside? Are fire exits clearly marked?

• Most places will offer prospective families a tour. Make sure that you see the whole facility, including the kitchen. If there are entire wings or floors of the facility that are not included in the tour, or if you are discouraged from looking around on your own, consider that a bad sign.

• Look at the individual rooms. Residents should be able to have some homey touches, such as family photographs, in their rooms. Each room should have a working call bell and a reading lamp. Check for the presence of fresh drinking water within each person's reach. Bathrooms should be clean and have safety bars next to the toilet and over the bathtub.

• Go at different times, including a mealtime. Look at the trays going back to the kitchen to see if the food has been eaten. This will give you some indication of whether or not the food is any good and whether or not people who need help eating are receiving it.

• Look at the overall condition of the residents. Accept the fact that some of them will be in a sad state, which is part of the reason why they are in a nursing home. However, no matter what is wrong with the people in the facility, what you are attempting to determine is whether or not they are clean and well cared for. Are the majority of them dressed and out of bed? Are residents being walked by aides? Large numbers of people sitting restrained in geri-chairs are an indication of inadequate staffing.

• Notice the attitude of the staff. Do they seem reasonably cheerful? Do they speak to the residents respectfully? One indication of the sensitivity of the staff toward the residents is the degree of privacy that is accorded. Intimate personal care should always be given behind a closed curtain, and it is important to be alert to whether or not this is the case.

• Nursing homes are required by law to provide varied

activity programs for the residents. Ask the administrator or
activities coordinator about them. Find out if community
volunteers regularly visit the nursing home, and what they
do there. The degree of interest and enthusiasm expressed
by the administrative staff toward these issues can be an important indicator of the level of concern they have for the
residents' psychological as well as physical well-being.

Even though Bonnie had to place her husband in a nursing
home very suddenly, she had already made herself familiar
with the places available to her. Bonnie talked about the place
she chose for Hank, and why she chose it:

Bonnie: I liked it because it was small, and there weren't
hundreds of people all milling around crashing into each other
with wheelchairs. At least they know the name of the patient.
I went in to some facilities where they had to put the picture,
and the name, so they'd know who's supposed to be in that
bed. That's too big. I felt that that part was the best. And the
fact that I tasted the food, and it was fine. One of the things
I noticed was they had some male attendants. And I thought,
if he gets out of hand, they can handle him. They had all the
activities they could offer. They had, even, a little tiny group
of volunteers, and I'd say, to people who asked for a recommendation, "I can't really recommend it in the sense that it's
wonderful, but they have room, they do take Alzheimer's, and
somewhere, you're going to be turned down. So it might look
to you like it did to me: a haven."

Mabel's logic in choosing a nursing home for her husband
was somewhat different from Bonnie's, and illustrates the
fact that the choice itself is often subject to intangible, personal considerations:

Mabel: He had to be out of the hospital by noon that day. There
were two beds open. One at Hacienda, and one at Beverly Manor.
Now, at Hacienda, next door is the donut shop. He had donuts
and coffee there at six in the morning for *years*. So, I thought he
may recognize that place, that neighborhood. We'll put him in
Beverly Manor. It was just a matter that he might recognize
where he was. And if he knew he was in a convalescent hospital,
he'd have had it burned down in ten minutes.

We have seen that a person's development into a successful caregiver involves the process of becoming much less concerned with, and burdened by, the judgments of other people. This can be particularly true when the time has come for nursing home placement. No matter how much trauma a caregiver has gone through, and no matter how long she has been going through it, there always seems to be at least one relative, acquaintance, or neighbor who tells her that they themselves would never, ever, put someone in a nursing home. The only thing she can do in the face of such remarks is to remind herself that people who say such things have probably never experienced the situation themselves. If the caregiver is truly compassionate herself, she will hope for their sake that they never do.

In order to do what is truly best for her husband and for herself, a dementia patient's wife must develop the ability to rely on her own determination of what is correct. Perhaps what makes placing a spouse in a nursing home the hardest decision of all is that she must learn not only to rise above the judgments of others, but above her judgments of herself, as well. She must grant her own needs as much legitimacy as those of her husband, and this is something that it is virtually impossible to do in any rational, systematic way.

The determining variable might even be the quality of the emotional relationship between the two people involved. Mary, who never placed her husband in a nursing home, speaks with understanding on behalf of the people who ultimately have to do just that:

Mary: I can't help but think, sometimes in the nursing home situation, that it might seem to some of us that the person isn't that hard to handle, that if they were *my* spouse, I would keep them at home. But when I see that there's a great deal of irritation and resentment going on, and a person really has very negative feelings, sometimes I think maybe, in that case, they would be better off to put them in the nursing home early. Because of their mixed feelings. There are some people that put them in there because there is no other way to handle it at this time, because the patient has deteriorated to the point that they *have* to be in, for their own protection. Sometimes both the caregiver and the person being cared for are better off if they're separated. It isn't necessarily bad. Sometimes it's the best solution. It wasn't for me, because I was able to cope with what I had. It would have been the only solution for me if my husband had become more completely physically helpless. Then I would have, because I don't have the physical strength to handle it. You see, in other words, there's too many variables to say.

CHAPTER EIGHT

❁

In the Nursing Home

It's about, oh, fourteen months ago, when the hospital just started deteriorating. The floors were filthy, they just were really neglecting the patients, and I thought, hey, I'm paying seventy-eight dollars a day for this. For skilled nursing care. Louie isn't getting skilled nursing care. He isn't even getting care, so I wrote a letter to the owner, and I explained to him in detail how bad things were, and that I felt that he may be going according to what is required by state law, but he wasn't giving skilled nursing care. And he called me, and we had a twenty-minute conversation on the phone. And he told me he wasn't aware of this, and he would check into it, and that he would personally go every day to check Louie, and to see how he was being taken care of. And I said, "I'm not complaining because I want my husband taken care of before anybody else, or better than anybody else. I want them *all* taken care of. And I feel that if you're neglecting my husband, and I come every day, what is happening to the people that have no one?"

—Aileen

The first days and weeks after a dementia patient is placed in a nursing home are tremendously trying for his caregiver. Even after all of the problems and stresses have finally culminated in a demented husband being moved to a nursing home, his wife may go through a period of intense questioning of her own judgment, asking herself if the placement was really necessary. Once a woman has had some much-needed rest and a chance to regroup, she may begin second-guessing her decision, sometimes even entertaining the idea of bringing her husband home again.

At this time, more than any other, a caregiver needs emotional support; affirmation from her family and friends that she has done all that she can do for her husband at home, and reassurance that she is doing the right thing now. Aileen's two sons, who were instrumental in getting her to place their father in a nursing home, continued to offer her support when she wavered about keeping him there:

Aileen: You know, it was their intervention that really made me realize that I had to do it. But I didn't want to do it, and I didn't like doing it. In fact, I'd go in and say, "He's pretty good today, I can take him home." And my son here in town said, "Mom, you really want to take Dad home, we'll take him home. But you have to realize, he just had a good day today. You're just postponing the inevitable."

No matter how terrible the situation may have become at home, there is almost always an equally terrible sadness that follows nursing home placement. Placing a relative creates tremendous feelings of guilt for family members. They are often tormented by the question of whether or not they have really and truly done enough for the person, and the years of devoted care that they have already given do very little to insulate and protect them from such feelings.

Mixed with any feelings of relief is a sense of a void, or vacuum, in the rhythms of daily life. The constant work, vigilance, and expenditure of energy that a caregiver may have been required to give in caring for the demented person over the years can't be turned off like a faucet once he has been placed in a nursing home. She may not have realized until now how thoroughly she has become accustomed to a heightened intensity of stress, concern, and attention. Hence, it is unrealistic to think that she will suddenly be able to relax, unwind, and immediately start living on her own spontaneous schedule.

One of the women in the support group spent the first week that her husband was in a nursing home (that is, when she was not visiting him) filling her time with bustling activity.

She cleaned her house meticulously from top to bottom, dusting behind the furniture and inside the closets. She did a particularly thorough job in her husband's bedroom, she said, "in case he can come home sometime." As she related this to the group, she was overcome with emotion. She acknowledged that she really did know that her husband was never coming home, but said that she was having a terrible struggle within herself accepting that.

Adjusting to the fact that the patient is no longer living with her is only part of the new picture a caregiver must now face. Recognizing the deeper, rarely spoken meaning of nursing home placement requires an altogether different level of acceptance. The woman who cleaned her house so thoroughly in anticipation of a possible homecoming was only just beginning to absorb the reality that her husband would, in fact, die in the nursing home.

Aside from any considerations of what nursing homes are like, or whether the care in any particular facility is excellent or terrible, the brutal truth is that nursing homes are places where dementia patients go to wait for death. On some level, caregivers know that, and that knowledge causes the unbearable, though mostly unexpressed, feeling that they are somehow responsible for consigning the person to that fate.

Nursing home placement, then, can be understood as something that produces a very real grief reaction in caregivers. Unfortunately, this grief, like the grief they have already been living with for a long time, is still not the kind that allows a clear, straightforward process of mourning and reconciliation.

It is heartbreaking to see a formerly strong and healthy person reduced to the status of someone receiving nursing home care. One of the saddest aspects of placement in a facility is that it represents such a stark and definitive break from the life the patient lived in the past. His very personhood, already violently assaulted by the disease process itself, is perceived by people who care about him as even more diminished.

Mabel chose to discourage friends from visiting her husband Roy in the institution, and that decision was based on her wish to have her husband's friends remember him as he had been before he got sick. Her remarks point up one of the dilemmas that arises when a wife wishes to be emotionally faithful to the husband as he used to be, even as she is confronted with what has happened to him:

Mabel: People went to see him in the nursing home occasionally. But they weren't doing him any good because he didn't know who they were. Roy, of course, was in business here in town for forty-nine years in the same place. So everybody knew Roy, and everybody loved him. And he had visitors by the dozen.

But, when I met people downtown, and they asked me, "Can I go over and see Roy?" I would say, "Please don't." My feeling was that it just confused him more, and he would have been furious if he knew that people were seeing him in that shape. I have a lot of different views than most other people. He was a very proud person. And he was always fussy about how he was dressed. Lord, he had his hair cut once a week whether it needed it or not, and it never needed it. And I felt that I was doing him a favor by not letting people see him as he was.

The process of adjusting and readjusting that is enacted over the years of caregiving does not stop with nursing home placement. The burdens of hard, physical care and constant vigilance may have been lifted, but a tremendous emotional burden remains. Aileen, whose husband Louie was still alive and in a nursing home at the time of our first interview, describes what it was like for her right after Louie entered the facility:

Aileen: I was just tired. I was overworked and I was tired. So I feel, him being in a nursing home, the time I'm with him is quality time. I mean, I don't enjoy going to the nursing home. In fact, when he first went in, I'd get to that front door, and, to be honest with you, I didn't want to go in. Because I didn't know what I'd find. Not only in him, the care he was getting . . . If I felt he was being neglected or something.

If he had a good day, I had a good day. If he had a bad day, I had a bad day. When I got out to the car, out of the nursing home, I'd sit there and bawl my eyes out. And I'd have to sit there, because I couldn't drive. And how, all those days of going back and forth, how I never ran into somebody, I'll never know. Really and truly. Because I was so preoccupied.

Even though Aileen's description is very bleak, she reminds us of the potentially positive aspects of placement when she says that "the time I'm with him is quality time." That sentiment has been echoed by many people in the support group, who often report welcome feelings of renewed compassion and affection for the patient once they have been relieved of aspects of care that had become exhausting, odious, or completely impossible.

Being freed from the relentless demands of physical care enables some people to experience emotional warmth for the patient once again. Simply stated, the caregiver now has more to give, and she may feel more love for her husband than she has in quite some time. As one woman put it, "He will get more loving care from me if he's not in my home." Mabel speaks on this issue:

Mabel: I'm honest about everything. I really felt, when Roy went into the hospital, it was a relief. And there's another thing that I will tell people that are feeling so guilty. I think Roy was ten times happier after he went to the convalescent hospital than he was at home, on a one-to-one basis where we *both* did everything wrong. Screaming at each other. No idea what was wrong. Doing the weirdest things.

Unfortunately, it is sometimes very hard to see anything positive about a spouse's nursing home placement.

Angie: It gave me a chance to unwind and get away from it, and what I didn't see didn't hurt me, I guess. When I got home, I could maybe put it out of my mind for a while. That was the only positive thing about it.

Once a person is in a nursing home, it is up to the caregiving spouse to decide how much time she chooses to spend there with him, and how involved she chooses to be in his care. Most of the women from the support group visit the nursing home daily for the first several months that their husbands are there.

Not knowing what is going on in the patient's mind, always a problem in caring for a dementia patient, is very hard on the caregiver in terms of her inability to assess how the patient himself may be feeling about being in the nursing home. Angie's inability to be certain that Hugo was unaware of his surroundings caused mental anguish for her:

Angie: There were times when things would happen or he would say something that would make me feel . . . how aware was he of the whole thing? In the hospital I think there was a man in his room that was having some sort of a problem and was calling for a nurse. And Hugo heard him, and Hugo yelled out, "Somebody! Front and center!" So he was aware that somebody was calling for someone.

Many days I would think, if he could just give me some idea of what he is thinking, what is going on in that mind . . . What is he trying to say? To give me an idea of what is going on with him in there. It's hard to know. It's very hard. I would almost dig to get something to come out of him. I was looking for answers. Sometimes I'd ask him questions to try to pull out an answer that would make some sense. He couldn't talk very well. It was just a few outbursts, but to carry on a conversation, he couldn't do that.

It is very common for family members to become upset when a newly placed nursing home resident keeps telling them that he wants to go home. There is very little that can be done to make hearing that request any easier, since it's hard to say whether the person is expressing his generally confused state of mind or a genuinely bad reaction to the facility. However, Mabel reminds people that it is worth remembering that sometimes an assertion that someone wants to go home predates his placement in the nursing home:

Mabel: Roy would say, "Let's go home." And I'd say, "Yes, over there, by the stairs." And by the time we got to the stairs we were on a cruise ship somewhere.

Sometimes it becomes easier to reevaluate the amount of visiting, and cut down on the number of visits, once there is doubt about whether the person even recognizes his wife or other family members anymore. When this happens, caregivers begin to question how much benefit is derived from the visits. However, it can be very hard to know if her husband does, in fact, recognize her or not.

Edith: I don't think he knew where he was. He would recognize me. When I'd first go in, his face would light up, and he'd say, "Hello," the first few times. And after he'd been in there awhile, he wouldn't even say anything, but his face would light up. His sister and brother-in-law came up to visit him a few times, and the first few times he said, "Hello, Jack. I haven't seen you for a long while." But, in just a few months he didn't even know Jack was around, and things like that. And me, he would know who I was when I came in. But I'd sit there awhile, and he didn't recognize me.

Many people in the support group have talked about how hard it is to wean themselves away from daily nursing home visits and really begin to try and rebuild their lives. Advice from well-meaning family and friends that the caregiver shouldn't go to the nursing home so often is rarely welcome and often actively resented. Each person must come to this balance in her own life in her own good time, and the process cannot be rushed.

Aileen: My main focus while he was in there was, I would go to the nursing home, and if I was asked to do something or go somewhere it was okay if it worked out around Louie. But, if it didn't work around Louie, I said "No," because he was my main focus.

Angie lived near her husband's nursing home, and she went there several times a day for the eight months he was there. Her main reason for doing so was that she felt it was important for her to monitor the care Hugo was receiving:

Angie: I felt like I had to be there a lot to see that he was being taken care of the way I wanted him taken care of. I had to be sure that he wasn't in bed and in his urine. I had to be sure that he was up when he should be up, and not just in bed all day long. I found that I was running down there a lot. I felt I had to be there.

Aileen's husband was in the nursing home for four years, and she visited him almost daily for that entire time. Her reason for doing this was partly so that she herself could feel that she had truly done all that she could for him. She also had a practical reason for visiting every day, which was that she felt Louie received better care from the staff if she did:

Aileen: You can't do anything for them after they're gone. And the doctor says, "Why do you go see your husband every day? It's not good for you." And I said, "I have to do what I feel in my heart I want to do, because when he's gone I can't do it." I know I'm going to go through another mourning, but this way I won't have any guilts or any regrets. Because if I was there, he would. It would be the same, it really would. And I go because I want to go, and I do miss it occasionally. But I also think that when you go, and *you* care, the hospital cares. I think your action of going shows them that this person has to be cared for, I really do. I know my mother, she was four months in a convalescent hospital, and I went every day for her, too. If you care, they care. It's a psychological thing.

Aileen intuitively recognized the importance of having her husband perceived as valued and loved by his family. While not everyone, or even most people, would choose to visit their institutionalized relatives as often as Aileen and Angie did, visits are important. Even if the patient is largely unaware of the visits, or forgets a visit as soon as it is over, a clearly established family presence lets the staff of the facility know, in a nonconfrontational way, that this resident's relatives are liable to show up at any time.

It is beneficial to be a little unpredictable in the timing of visits. Since the quality of care can vary a lot depending on the work shift, it makes good sense to go to the facility at different times of the day. In this way, family members will be able to see the sort of care that is being provided on the different shifts, and address any problems as they come up.

Angie and Aileen's accounts underscore the fact that being the wife of a nursing home resident means being an advocate for the person's care, and this is a job that is learned as you go along.

Aileen: When things were right, it was okay. The first four months were just horrible. Then, gradually, it was a day here and a day there. But up until the end, if things weren't right . . . Of course, I had learned to handle myself, speaking out. I became very assertive.

Bonnie describes Hank's first day in the facility, and how that experience gave her a taste of what would be required of her in her new role:

Bonnie: The day we took him to the hospital, my daughter and I, he was in a really good mood. The young women that met us at the door and took him to his room were cute. Cute young ladies. And, of course, he always responded to a good-looking woman, so he's standing there singing, "Wellll . . . I'll tell ya now, we're gonna be in a new hospital ahh cha di da!" And the girls were all looking. "It's a live one here." And I said, "Yea, you watch him now. You watch him." I said, "I came here twice to look at the facility, because he walked out of my house many times. I don't think your security is too good." They had a little alarm at the door, and a little alarm at this door, and a little alarm at that door, but not very much. And they weren't locked, because I think through the day you're not even allowed to lock them, for safety reasons. So, the one taking his count for his clothes said, "Now, don't worry about it."

What I was naive enough not to understand was that, although he came in with the Haldol, the physician that was going to take care of him changed his medication within twenty-four hours to Thorazine. Within twenty-four hours after he gave them a hard time that night, he was zonked out so much that . . . Well, they walked him around, but as far as finding the door on his own . . . Thorazine was something I objected to, and I kept telling the doctor I thought the Thorazine zonked him out too much.

Bonnie's struggles over the drugs Hank was given were similar to those that Aileen, whose husband had to receive physical therapy to combat the cumulative effects of drugs, experienced. Mabel also found it necessary to work with the doctor on the drug issue:

Mabel: And there were times that I'd go over, and he'd been overmedicated. And naturally, within an hour, I was telling the doctor to back off.

The experience of these women points up the fact that in spite of adverse publicity, overmedication of nursing home residents is a continuing problem that families need to be vigilant about. Drugs have a role to play in patient care, and can be a boon for a fearful, anxious person as well as for the people taking care of him. However, they are subject to abuse as long as they are used as a substitute for adequate supervision.

Drugs are not the only problem that families encounter in nursing homes. Occasionally a family will feel that a resident is being treated insensitively, or too roughly, by a particular staff person. Even if most of the staff members are caring and conscientious, this is a problem that must be dealt with.

Angie: I think the majority of the staff were very concerned and very caring. There were a few that were a little on the rude side, the way they handled the patients. I just resented some of the ways they handled him. When they'd pick him up and kind of throw him in the bed. And when they did that, it would startle him, and his eyes would just . . . Two women just take him and throw him on the bed. And I thought, here is a man that had control of his life. He's a man. He's a person. He's a very educated man. A smart man. And here these two women were tossing him around like a bag.

Inadequacy of staff training, particularly as it relates to dementia patient care, can also be a serious problem. Aileen encountered this difficulty, and did her best to teach the aides how to work with Louie, using the sorts of techniques that Irene described in an earlier chapter:

Aileen: If they'd start pulling the blankets off the bed, Louie would pull the blankets up. They'd go to take his pants down, and he'd put his hand there, and by golly, he was strong. They had to work to get his pants down. When I used to go in, they'd say, "Oh, you can sure tell when you come in. Louie is just a different person." And they'd say, "Why doesn't he grab your hand like he does mine?"

And I would explain to them, "When he grabs your hand, relax it, and he will relax his." "Oh." You know? And I did a lot of that for other patients. And the aides would say, "Oh, I couldn't even dress him." I'd say, "When you dress him, tell him, 'Louie, we're going to stand up. Louie, we're going to sit down.' Don't just take him and grab him and shove him here and shove him there.''

And you know, they talk about how they need men to care for these patients. My husband did better with the little women in there. They'd say, "Louie's no problem." He cooperated with them. They weren't shoving him around. They'd say, "Come on, Louie, honey, we're gonna do this," or, "We're gonna do that," or, "Let's take a walk," and he would do it. But, you get a man in there that would grab him here and shove him there, and then, sure, I mean, then he would become defensive.

I still feel that these people who have Alzheimer's are so frightened, if you really watch them. When people would come in to care for Louie, they'd just take him and they'd put him here, put him there, and he'd just tighten up. He wouldn't sit down or anything, and I'd say, "Talk to him. Tell him what you're going to do. Don't just pounce on him." And then they would listen and say, "Oh, that works better, doesn't it?"

Learning to function effectively in the role of "wife of a nursing home resident" means learning how to work out problems as they come up. Aileen became very good at determining whom to talk to in specific situations, and whom to target for her complaints when things were not going well. For example, if Louie's laundry was missing, she went directly to the laundry room. Her actions were influenced by a practical, result-oriented attitude, and by her respect for people—both her husband and those who took care of him.

Aileen maintained good relationships with the staff of the nursing home, and had sincere respect for them as people, but that never stopped her from stating, in a very direct way, what she felt her husband's needs were. She was completely uncompromising about speaking up when she felt Louie's needs were not being met:

Aileen: I don't just complain. When things are wrong, I go in, and I talk to them again. But when things are nice, I go in and say, "I'm really pleased." I do it with the help. I say, "Gee, Louie looks good today, he looks so well groomed, and I really appreciate it." And when they have an extra-special nice dinner, I go in and tell the help. I do! Because people like to hear the good things they do. And there's a lot of good help in that hospital. I don't know what they say behind my back, but a lot of the young people come up and say, "Oh, here's Mrs. B.," and they give me a hug. They call me Aileen. I get a lot of hugs from the help out there. They're overworked and they're underpaid, but they're kind. I have to say that they're good to Louie.

And if you do explain your position . . . I go in, he's not shaven, I'm not going to complain about that. I have an extra razor, I shave him. That doesn't bother me. But if he's soiled, or if I feel he's been neglected, I do state how I feel.

I went in one night, and Louie was in bed at five o'clock. And I went down to the nurse, and I said, "Why is Louie in bed?" And she said, "We're short of help." And I said, "That's your problem, not mine. I want Louie up now." So she went to the aide and said, "You have to get Louie up." Now when I go in, if he's not up, they meet me in the hall, and say, "I have to explain why Louie isn't outta bed." And so then periodically now, I go in at different times. I went in the day before yesterday and they hadn't made the bed up yet, they were just going to make it up, and I sat down on it and it was damp, so I stripped the bed and put the sheets in the laundry. Nobody said anything. I figured if they say something, I'll just say, "I don't want Louie in a wet bed." I don't make a big fuss about it. I just do it.

After having a husband in a nursing home for four years, Aileen learned to choose her battles carefully. Part of knowing which matters are worth pursuing lies in having a realistic assessment of what can reasonably be expected, and a good understanding of how to address issues effectively. Bonnie was able to deal forthrightly with important care issues as they came up, but she did it without being constantly upset whenever things weren't exactly the way she wanted them to be:

Bonnie: I think because I had some nurse's training, I could go into the kind of nurse mode, and deal with some frustrations that had to do with the hospital situation, knowing that you could never, ever have enough people to do the things that are needed around the clock. A couple of times I was an observer of a frustrated family standing there with just the nastiest look they could have on their face and just tapping their feet, and arms akimbo, saying, "Well! I think this should be straightened out!" And feeling, "Yea. I'd like it all straightened out, too."

Angie, a tireless advocate for her husband, also was not naive in terms of what she felt she could expect from the nursing home staff:

Angie: I talked to a couple of women, and their complaints were the same as mine. The food wasn't as good as it should be. The cleanliness wasn't as good. One of the patients would go into the bathroom, have an accident, and there's nobody there to clean it up until tomorrow, or whatever. The way the aides handled some of the patients could have been a little better, but I can understand they are overworked. They've got so many patients to take care of. They couldn't feel about Hugo the way I do.

Hugo was my patient, my person that I wanted taken care of just the way I wanted it done. Well, I couldn't expect them to feel the same way that I do about him. And there were how many others? Fifty other people in that place. And if they tried to take that personal interest in each and every patient, those aides just physically couldn't do that. It's just another job for them, and another person. I'm sure they had a certain amount of interest in caring, but not like you would personally have about your own. I just don't know how it will ever be resolved. The only way that can help, the nursing homes are going to have to get more people, to get more personal care.

No matter how carefully a family has chosen a particular nursing home, the fact is that staff turnover is a very common problem in many facilities. What this means in practical terms is that even if you are very happy with the care your relative is getting now, the overall quality of care can plummet if key personnel leave.

If a good cook is replaced by a bad one, or a conscientious and able director of nursing is replaced by a less competent person, the residents' quality of life can be swiftly, dramatically, and adversely affected. Somewhere along the line, most families of institutionalized people will get the opportunity to polish their assertiveness skills, even if they have spared no effort in choosing the best possible nursing home available to them.

If difficulties do arise, a clear, frank statement of what the problem is, phrased in a noncontentious way, if possible, will often be sufficient to resolve a troublesome issue. If it is not enough, and you continue to experience frustration about the care your family member is receiving, begin keeping a record of the conversations you have had with staff members about those problems.

Nursing homes are extraordinarily hierarchical institutions, and complaints about care are best dealt with by going up through the ascending staff levels, if you continue to be unsatisfied with the responses you are getting to your stated concerns. These levels are:

- Charge nurse, or head nurse of a particular unit
- Director of nursing
- Nursing home administrator
- Family and resident council. Check to see if your facility has one of these. If not, you may wish to consider starting one.
- Long-term care ombudsman. Mandated by the Older Americans Act, the ombudsman's office investigates complaints in nursing homes, and works to resolve those complaints. The ombudsman will not reveal the identity of the complaining person without the permission of that person. Your state's department of aging, or state agency on aging, can put you in touch with your local ombudsman.
- State licensing office

Angie was very assertive about her husband's care. She describes going up the chain of command in the nursing home when she felt her concerns were not being addressed adequately:

Angie: I think I was an annoyance to the administrator because I would look at the menu and, by law, they have to post the menu, and [the meal] was never what the menu said. I can't say never, but many times. So I called that to their attention. Their excuse was, "The cook that was supposed to be cooking is not here, and she's the one that made up the menu, and so we'll have to fix that." But they can just post the menu, and if no one looks at it . . . The patients aren't going to look at it. So it has to be some member of the family that would go in there and make sure that what was being served was what was on that menu most of the time. I can see that at times maybe it might change a little, but it shouldn't have changed as much as it did.

I reported them to the ombudsman, and they kept a close watch. I reported the menu thing, and they approached the owners about it. There was no secret about it, I even told the owners about it myself. And the ombudsman came in on a regular basis and checked on them. I complained to the owners before I complained to the ombudsman.

The food wasn't very good. A lot of it was sandwiches. A lot of cheese sandwiches. Dry. Little thin slices of cheese. A lot of bread. Tuna sandwiches with just a very fine spread of tuna, no lettuce, no nothing. And then, when you make a sandwich, if you don't cover it, you know what happens to the bread. So finally the ombudsman told them they were going to have to cover those sandwiches.

Actively confronting a problem like bad food can have positive benefits for all of the patients in the nursing home, and this is something to consider if you are trying to decide whether it is worth the effort and aggravation of pursuing a solution to a particular complaint. Although Aileen's primary concern was for her own husband, she did care deeply about the other residents of the facility, and often acted on their behalf:

Aileen: One day I was going through the lobby there, and I saw this woman in a wheelchair, and she was sort of crying, "I can't breathe, I can't breathe." And I went down and told the nurse and she says, "Oh, she always does that." And I said, "Well, go check her. Now." And she looked at me very resentfully, but she did go check her.

Aileen's attitude regarding what constituted good service and compassionate attention encompassed more than just the needs of her husband and the other residents, but those of other caregivers as well, and her ability to get things done was a skill that she tried to impart to people she met visiting their family members in the nursing home. She describes her efforts toward the wife of Louie's roommate:

Aileen: You go down the hall, and there's a person in bed, and they don't have the rail up. The person falls and breaks their hip. If I go down the hall and the rail's not up, I go tell the nurse, and

I don't think they like that. Like the man in the bed next to Louie, he's supposed to have a soft restraint. He's a stroke victim. He tries to stand up and he'll fall. Well, a lot of times I've gotten in there before his wife, and I find him trying to stand up, and I'll go down and ask the nurse. And so I even made a sign, because his wife is very meek. She doesn't speak out. I'm making her better. I used to do it for her, and now I say, "B., you go down to the desk and you tell them." And she says, "But, they make me feel like I'm complaining." I said, "You're not complaining. You are your husband's advocate. If you don't see that he's well cared for, who's going to do it?" And so then she'll go down.

The interchange between Aileen and the other woman illuminates one of the differences between successful caregivers and women who are victimized by the situation to a much greater degree. "B." is still subject to the tyranny of the "nice lady" role model. The last thing that she would want to be is a "complainer." Other people are still capable of "making" her feel a certain way. While it is, unfortunately, true that speaking to people in a forthright manner is unaccustomed behavior for many women, particularly older women, and that Aileen is better at it than most of us will ever be, we see over and over again that this is exactly what any caregiver must learn to do when she is in the role of spokesperson for someone who cannot speak for himself. And nowhere is this more true than in the nursing home.

Aileen: I don't think I was ever unreasonable. I just wanted them to do what they were supposed to do. I always tried not to intimidate them. I hate people who intimidate other people. But I didn't want them to intimidate me, either. When Louie first went in, I was meek. I had to learn to speak up. After Louie died, I ran into the pharmacist from over there, and he told me, "They respected you. You didn't ask for anything that Louie didn't deserve."

Nursing home placement can break the last fragile bonds between a dementia patient and his wife, but it does not always do that. Securing the best possible care for an institutionalized husband may be the last remaining way that a wife can express her love for him. She is now faced with the reality that the time will eventually come when her husband will not be needing her care. Before that time comes, each woman must continue to determine for herself the balance that she will strike between her own life and that of her husband. Each person with a spouse in an institution must decide what she will accept and what she will attempt to change, just as she has done all along.

Bonnie: They took him in, and they've done the best they could. And when you go in and you look up and down the corridors for somebody to help you do something, and they don't exist—they're somewhere, you know—and you hear the bells going off, and nobody answers the bell, you think, "My God." But eventually somebody comes. And eventually somebody answers your question. Eventually, you either accept it or you move. And if you're going to move, where are you going to go? Will it be any better? It probably won't. But the most important thing, in these long-term, terrible things, is, don't be . . . What is the word? A martyr? And hang on forever doing something that's beyond what you're capable of doing. Then you get sick, too.

CHAPTER NINE

Death, Bereavement, and Widowhood

> I knew something was going wrong the last couple of months, and I said that, if Roy was . . . if Roy was in pain, that I would move heaven and earth that he is not in pain, and whatever is going to go wrong . . . Just let it go.
>
> —Mabel

A woman who cares for her husband through the course of a dementing illness has a long time to adjust to the idea of his death. In many important ways, her husband has been lost to her for months or years before his physical body actually expires. Physical death lingers in the wings as a sort of formality, a final detail that will make the state of widowhood official, even though that widowhood has already been well established in terms of the number and magnitude of the losses she has already sustained.

Even so, the fact that a wife may have long since reached the point where she is ready and willing to accept the death of her impaired husband does not mean that she isn't still vitally concerned with his comfort and well-being. As long as he lives, she must continue to monitor the quality of his care and speak up as his advocate when his needs are not being met.

The inability of demented people to communicate effectively about their thoughts and feelings, a major problem all along, remains so until the very end. Mabel gives her view on this as it relates specifically to the death of the patient:

Mabel: As far as I'm concerned, I can't feel sad when an Alzheimer's patient dies. I think, ''Thank goodness, they're at rest.'' Because I think, right up until the last breath, they are suffering. Not physically, but mentally. I really do. Some of the things that they say and do, I'm just sure that there's a little bit there. Unless they're overmedicated, and, goodness knows, you don't want that. If they're going to get progressively worse, I think you're doing the patient a favor when you let go.

There is great variation in the ways that people approach the very idea of death. While death is seen by many as a welcome end to suffering, and as a long-awaited release for both the patient and his family, that sentiment is not, by any means, shared by everybody. Some of the women who have come to the support group seem to be burdened with the feeling that somehow it is not proper to have a welcoming attitude toward the death of someone else. Even if they do, privately, welcome that death, they are extremely reticent about verbalizing it. It is almost as if they feel that they are supposed to wish actively for the patient's continued existence, no matter what condition he is in, and no matter what that continued existence is costing the caregivers themselves in personal terms. A small number of people genuinely dread the patient's death, and have an enormously hard time accepting the fact that it will happen.

I asked Aileen what her interpretation of the term ''death with dignity'' would be. She reiterated Mabel's concern about unnecessary suffering, and emphasized the fact that dementia patients cannot make choices for themselves in terms of the treatments that will be given or withheld:

Aileen: I believe in quality of life. I believe in freedom from pain, as in my husband's case, and that should be the main consideration. Prolonging their life with extraordinary measures is not in their best interest. I think each case is individual. I think if they . . . how can I put this? If they are mentally impaired, then the spouse, or the ones closest, should make the decision not to prolong their life, or use extraordinary measures.

Decisions about whether or not to provide aggressive treatments for people with no hope of full recovery are extremely difficult, and are by no means always clear-cut. Caregivers also have different feelings about what constitutes heroic treatment, and their decisions, to the extent that they are allowed to make them, are made on the basis of those feelings. Aileen's husband Louie died of cancer in the nursing home. She had made the decision not to move him to an acute-care hospital:

Aileen: I chose, if he had a heart attack, not to send him to the hospital. Which he didn't. But I also chose that when he needed an antibiotic, he did get an antibiotic. Because I felt that wasn't really life-threatening, and because of his lungs and everything. But I just asked that they don't take any steps to prolong his life, because he wouldn't have wanted it. Knowing him, he wouldn't. You know, why keep him . . .

It would have been another week or ten days he would have stayed alive. This is what I'm talking about. It wasn't a matter of months. They gave him three or four days, and he lasted twenty-two, because he was strong. He was younger, and he was strong. He stayed at the nursing home, because sending him to another hospital would have been very disturbing, and he would have been so disoriented and frightened.

After a consultation with his doctor I consented to put him on oxygen around the clock and morphine as needed to ease his suffering. Three days before his death he was looking at me and I leaned over and hugged him and told him that he had my permission to let go and be at peace.

Families must communicate their wishes about terminal medical care for the patient to the professionals involved in his case, and hope that those wishes are carried out. Irene, who had her husband at home with her until his death, had conveyed her concerns about this to the doctor long before Jim's final hospitalization:

Irene: The doctor and I had talked, and he knew what I wanted. He asked me first, "Now, if ever you call me and want me to treat him, what do you want me to do?" I said, "Well, what *can* you do for a person in his condition? Keep him comfortable. I guess pain pills, or something on that order. But there is no sense keeping him going on life supports.'' He realized that, and I realized that. We had agreed to that ahead of time, that they wouldn't keep him on. Because he had nothing to keep.

In accord with Irene's wishes, when the time came, Jim was not maintained by artificial means, and his death, from food aspiration, was rapid:

Irene: He aspirated food into his lungs. And this is also common. This happens to a lot of them. He kept on eating, and it went into his lungs. They pumped out a handful of food when I took him up to the hospital. And the doctor told me, ''Well, after aspirating food, these people usually don't make it. It goes into pneumonia.'' Well, the second day he was so happy, and just ready to jump out of bed. They couldn't keep him in bed. The doctor said, ''Well, I think he's going to make it. If he keeps on, he can come home in a couple of days.'' Well, the third day he went down, and was gone. Just three days he lasted. So, he had just one day of feeling better. Of course, they were giving him oxygen. They fed him intravenously or something. But then they pulled all the plugs, and then he went right down.

Angie actually decided to bring Hugo home from the nursing home when it appeared that his life was very likely drawing to a close, and part of her reason for doing so was to retain some control over the treatment he received. She was prepared for a long haul, but as it happened, Hugo was to live for only six more weeks. She was able to manage by hiring a part-time helper and a couple to live in. (It should be pointed out that, for financial reasons, this option would not be available to all, or even most, caregivers.)

Angie: I knew I was going to be faced with round-the-clock help here if I brought him home, and people in and out. It was not going to be peaceful, and there were going to be a lot of problems, but I weighed it and I thought, ''Do I really want him to die in that hospital?'' I figured it all out. Financially, it was going to cost me a little bit more than the hospital, but I felt that if Hugo had the means, he was going to spend what he's entitled to. If this is a better way, and a more comfortable way for him and for me, and if I had the finances, and if I was going to have to stretch it a little bit, I was going to do it. Just for the comfort of it, and the security, the feeling better about it. Rather than in the hospital. I wasn't happy with the hospital. I'd walk in there and there were flies all over the place, and that drove me crazy. It wasn't clean like I wanted it to be.

I was prepared to go quite a while. Within six weeks it changed. The doctor warned me that this was probably what would happen, his muscles just . . . He couldn't swallow anymore, and if he did try to swallow, he would choke. And so he stopped taking food. And then it went into pneumonia, and when that happened it was pretty fast. The only thing that would have saved him would have been tube feeding. I wasn't going to let that happen.

Sometimes the involvement of more than one doctor in a case can complicate matters, and that is what happened with Bonnie and Hank. Understandably, in life-and-death situations, the doctors themselves may feel a need to verify and affirm that they understand the family's wishes:

Bonnie: When I'd talk to Doctor #2 I said, "We have durable power of attorney for health care in his chart, and Doctor #1 told me that she would honor the fact that we didn't want any code, or code blue, or whatever, and any life-support systems, or any stomach feeding. I hope your opinion is that you would honor that, too." And he said, "As long as we've got it in the chart, it helps. I'll honor your durable power as much as I can." And I said, "Well, thank you for that." And then time went on, and I didn't hear from him again.

I heard from Doctor #3. He introduced himself. He had gotten a call from the nursing home, about how Hank had been running a fever, which they had told me. So he said he'd gotten a call from the nursing home about possibly changing his antibiotic for the fever. He said, "What is your opinion of that?" And I said, "I don't know what to tell you. If you're asking me to change it, fine. If you're asking me to discontinue it, fine."

I said, "I don't want to prolong any of these horrible days, these horrible times. This man is a living skeleton. I don't want it prolonged. I've tried to make it very clear to his primary physician that that is my wish." He said, "Fine, that's all I needed to know." And he hung up. Whether he discontinued it, I don't know. Whether he changed it, I don't know.

When the patient has become completely debilitated and helpless, a loving family may move beyond simple accep-

.nce of his approaching death, and begin actively wishing
.r it, both for his sake and their own.

Bonnie: I think he did what I've heard happens. He just forgot
how to swallow. I know that he had over his bed, "force fluids,"
and I'd bring him what I thought he wasn't getting there. Things
like V-8, which he loved. And I'd bring him root beer and things
like that. It was hard to get it down him. He would push out a
straw. And you couldn't use a straw. Hold his head, open his
lips. It would mostly dribble down, so it was sort of like he . . .
My daughter said, "Whenever I go visit him, I just say, 'Dad, I
love you so much. Dad, let go. Just let go. Just see if your life
could be better somewhere else, Dad. Let go.' " And maybe he
heard, and maybe he had it in his ability to do that. I don't know.

In speaking of the actual deaths of their husbands, Aileen
nd Bonnie emphasized their appreciation for the nursing
ome personnel who took care of Louie and Hank in their
nal days. As we have seen, Aileen was a very assertive
dvocate for Louie's care while he was in the nursing home,
nd was not shy about seeing that he got what he needed.
Iowever, she had a deep appreciation for all that was done
or him, and acknowledged the sensitive treatment she and
.ouie received at the time of his death:

Aileen: They were very good about it. Very sensitive, very caring. I can't really quarrel with them there. Other things in the
past I have, but at this point, they did everything they could for
him, and for me. They were in the room every day, hugging us
and checking in on us. So I have no quarrel with them.

Bonnie's husband died right at Christmastime, and she
ave presents to the aides who had cared for him:

Bonnie: He died on Wednesday, and I picked up his belongings
on Thursday and talked to all the girls. It was getting close to
Christmas, and I made arrangements that everybody get a little
Christmas present from Henry. It wasn't a good time to think
about it. Well, maybe it was, in a way. It was something that I
might not have even thought about, to say, "Thank you," but at
Christmastime you think of gifts. I might have missed, totally,
giving a thank you, because I told the director of the nursing
home, "You know, these nice women have done what I couldn't
do. And have done it for eight months. I want gifts to go to the

workers that are down on the bottom of the list. I'm going to gi
the administrators some cookies, but the gifts go to those girls.

This kind of appreciation for the contributions of others
the very time when one could be forgiven for exhibiting
more self-absorbed outlook on life is one hallmark of th
successful caregiver. These are women who have becom
very strong and forthright, but they have not done so at th
cost of losing respect and appreciation for the people aroun
them.

No matter how predictable a death may be, it can still b
an unexpected shock precisely because a patient has been i
an unhealthy condition for a long time, or may have alread
survived several serious health crises. Once a patient ha
approached and then veered away from death a number c
times, family members strive to accept the possibility that h
may be around for quite a while. A caregiver who has bee
through near-misses with the patient learns to monitor he
own feelings, since she must guard against letting go of af
fectional bonds to him while he is still alive and still in nee
of her care, love, and advocacy.

Angie was told by the doctor that Hugo would not liv
much longer, and her reaction to that news provides a goo
illustration of why it can be difficult for a caregiver to believ
that death will come soon:

Angie: I wasn't sure that Hugo was dying at this time, becaus
Hugo had been almost at the same stage twice before, with pneu
monia, and I thought that he'd pull out of it. He had pulled ou
of it twice before, and he'd looked just like that. But the Saturda
that he died, I thought he didn't look very good, and I staye
with him all day. But I still did not think that he was dying. I
just did not occur to me that he was going to die.

The announcement of the death of a person who has bee
demented and deteriorating for a long time is often greetec
with reactions of openly expressed relief by family anc
friends. The primary caregiver herself is also likely to feel a
great sense of relief, at least initially:

Bonnie: Well, everybody, all my friends, and everybody that I shared with, "Henry died," said, "Oh, what a blessing," and that sort of thing. And I felt that it was, too. I said, "He gave me the only Christmas present he could give me, and that was just to release himself and go." He just got out of that terrible little body, and whatever is happening for him has to be so much better.

Aileen used the occasion of Louie's death to make a public statement about Alzheimer's disease, in accordance with her belief that families should be more open about it:

Aileen: I think people think it's a stigma. Because a lot of people in the group, I see when their spouse dies there's nothing about Alzheimer's in the obituary. And I feel people are just afraid to say it. Alzheimer's didn't kill Louie. Cancer killed Louie. And I didn't have anything about cancer in the obituary. I had about Alzheimer's.

Several of the women I spoke with, and other people in the support group, have described feelings of numbness and unreality in the time right around the death of the patient. Angie used the word "blurry" to describe how she felt immediately following Hugo's death.

Unpleasant, though necessary, administrative chores must be attended to after someone dies, and these tasks can serve nicely as a temporary distraction from feelings of sadness. Many people spend a great deal of time and energy cleaning out their garages and closets, and attending to legal housekeeping chores.

Aileen: A lot of it was taking care of a lot of things that have to take place after a person passes away, like getting paper work done.

It is not always easy to rebuild a life for oneself after spending years looking out for someone else's welfare and tending to that person's needs. Caregivers have different experiences in terms of the ease with which they can get back into their social lives. Some people have little difficulty in this area:

Aileen: I've become more social. My friends insisted, right away, that I have a good social life.

Other people find rebuilding a social life intimidating. Mabel describes her first attempt at hostessing a little dinner party after Roy's death. The guests were two other couples she and Roy had socialized with for years. Mabel was fine until she set the table. At that point, she became very emotional at the realization of Roy's empty place at the table. She called her friends and canceled the dinner:

Mabel: I was not going to be able to sit at that dinner table with those two couples.

Mabel's experience illustrates the way that some people avoid social encounters. Widows who don't get back into the social stream easily do, nevertheless, often realize that they must force themselves to take the plunge. Angie describes her feelings about this in a conversation that took place four months after Hugo's death:

Angie: I've lost the last seven years. I've devoted every bit of energy, and I've given up friendships. I've given up a lot of things I could have done on my own. I could have done some things, but I chose not to do them, because I felt I had a number-one priority, and I had to do that. That was my number-one priority. Five years ago I was living day by day. I'm still doing that today. Five years ago I could see that Hugo's health was getting worse every day, but you never know what will happen. You just can't make too many future plans, because you just have to kind of play it as the day goes.

It's just been a few months. It's still here. It's hard for me to just all of a sudden say, "I'm free. I'm going to do this, and I'm going to do that." I'm still right here where I was six months ago. And I have to pull myself back up a little bit. I thought, okay, now I should start thinking about doing a little volunteer work. Getting involved, out with people more. See, other than my family, I didn't do too much. I didn't see many of my friends. And at times I have to tell myself I have to get out, and do some of these things.

I was invited yesterday to play bridge with a group of ladies, and it's very easy for me to say, "I can't make it because I don't have time." And I was tempted to do that, but I thought, "You've got to quit doing that." So I went out and played. I can't say that I enjoyed it that much, but I think I have to. I'm starting all over again. I have to start. Going out and playing bridge yesterday was a start.

A woman who is attempting to rebuild her life may find that her values and priorities have changed as a result of everything she has been through. Adjusting to widowhood does not necessarily mean reestablishing connections with old friends. The life that a former caregiver fashions for herself may bear scant resemblance to the one she had before her husband got sick.

Mary: I guess through the years with a reclusive husband, I've lost much of my ability at purely social interaction. I've been too serious for too many years. I don't really know a great deal of chitchat. I don't find that I get any particular pleasure out of it. So, what do I do? I find things that *do* give me pleasure. Through my work in peer counseling, and the Alzheimer's group, and what have you, I meet many delightful people.

Aileen: I do volunteer at the church. I help with the mailing. I do the Italian Cultural Club, and I've become active in that. I just try to keep my yard up. And the Alzheimer's work is needed. It's needed. People still don't understand.

None of these women would pretend that assuming leadership roles and working for good causes can fill all of their personal needs. A large loneliness remains, and Mabel speaks for many other women when she says:

Mabel: When I'm out, it all looks fine, and everybody's always saying, "Oh, you're effervescent, you're full of pep." There are other days besides that, believe me. I can't say I'm not depressed a lot of the time. If I'm out, and I'm talking to others about Alzheimer's disease, and pointing out something that happened, and maybe they can use some of my suggestions, I'm coming home feeling good. But, if I go two or three days without going to some of the meetings, I can get very depressed.

Every woman who has lost her spouse after his long dementing illness will experience grief in her own way. Even if the husband's death has come as a welcome relief, grieving can still be a long and painful process characterized by feelings of conflict. It can be difficult to truly grieve, at first, for a person who was very sick for a long time, and who died with no hope of ever returning to an enjoyable, productive life.

Aileen: Well, it took me a long time, because when he died I didn't cry. The doctor told me he had from one to three days to live. I don't know, I just got a real cold, numb spot in my heart, and it just stayed there. I think I just must have blocked everything out. I kept thinking: well, you didn't cry because you cried so much when he was in the hospital. But I didn't feel right about it. It really bothered me. And then I kept saying to myself, "Well, you went through so much, so you cried all you're going to cry." But I still didn't feel right about it. I didn't feel guilty. I just didn't feel right. The cycle wasn't completed. Maybe that was it, the fact that it wasn't completed.

No matter how much sadness a bereaved caregiver has already felt over the course of her husband's illness, and no matter how well she may have accommodated to his decline over the years, she is still confronted, after his death, with the loss of their shared life and future together. That loss comes into sharper focus as times goes on, and it must be reckoned with.

Angie: I think I probably grieved more before he died. It's still hard for me now. It's hard in the respect that I remember the plans that he had, and what he would like to have done with his retirement, which he couldn't do and never did. That makes me feel sad. So, when I think about it, I grieve for that part. It was very difficult to watch him go downhill so bad, too.

The deceased husband's birthday, the couple's wedding anniversary, and the anniversary of the husband's death are all days that can be painful for a widow to observe alone. Sensitive family members can help the grieving wife in small but very significant ways, as Aileen's story illustrates:

Aileen: They told me about the baby on my anniversary. They called me specifically to give me something happy to think about. My daughter-in-law said, "I just came from the doctor, and we have some happy news." So I have two things to think about on my anniversary. I'll always think of my anniversary as a special day for me and Louie, but also the day I learned about the baby.

As it turned out, it was the birth of Aileen and Louie's new granddaughter a year after Louie's death that finally provided Aileen with the opportunity to move beyond her numbness and to start really acknowledging her grief for everything that she and her husband had lost:

Aileen: I think I was numb before, but it's been thirteen months. I feel differently than I did before. And I was fine when I went up to my son's to help with the new baby, but I was there about ten days, and I'd hold the baby, and I'd think, "Gee, Louie was so short-changed, getting sick so young." It bothered me that he missed out on this beautiful little girl, my son's first child. He didn't even know this daughter-in-law.

When I was up there I walked a lot. It's a forest, and I walked the road twice a day, and I'd think about Louie and how he should be walking by me and all this, and that's when I really . . . I started to cry. I went through a really bad two-day period. And then once I cried I felt better. Really a lot better. I discussed my feelings with my son, that when I was walking I just cried, because I was thinking about his father, and about the baby, and that I felt sad that Louie wasn't enjoying this time with me. Because he just loved his granddaughters so much, the other two. And I felt sad that this one would never know.

Speaking over a year after her husband Hank's death, Bonnie gives us a summation of her feelings of grief both before and after he died:

Bonnie: My grieving was very much before he died, and in steps. Depressing kinds of steps. The realization, and anger. I was so mad. The "golden years," quote unquote, were so bad, and I was going to be cheated out of them. When we probably would have had some nice times together, where we would be good buddies, and not adversaries over funny little issues, the little things that always get people, the unimportant little things. I just felt we probably could have handled that really well. We were starting to.

And I felt so bad that Hank's business which he had been so proud of had been ripped away from him, and that all these other things were being pulled out from under him and destroyed. My sense was not so much that things were happening to me, but what a horrible thing's happening to him. As I was not being able to talk to him and have him talk back to me, that set up immediate recognition of how lonely and how sad all of this was going to be.

And as I live my days now I still have that sense of loss. I don't have a companion to share things with. I have, thank God, wonderful friends, and I can pick up a phone and get together with anybody in a minute. I am handling my oneness okay. I still sort of feel kind of like the color went out of life for me.

The grief after he died was just relief for him and relief for me. Now I wasn't going to have to worry about all of it. Now I knew that he wasn't going to be that poor old guy hunched over in the chair. I couldn't imagine what the back of his neck felt like, after those months and months of his head down on his chest. The skinny little body that you knew was never going to fill out again. This poor little guy.

No, the grief was before, certainly not too much after. Things will pop up and I'll have a little quick cry, and every once in a while I'll say, "Henry, did you hear that?" Or when somebody else has gone I'll say, "I hope you found him. I hope you're together, the two of you. I hope you're up there." So I think it was the loss of each step that I grieved. Some of it was grief, totally, for his loss, and the other part was my grief for the loss of us both. And also, I was so glad not to be sick all over again. Not to have that illness. Not to be a bitch, bitch, bitch.

The task of healing from a painful experience, facing one's losses, and accepting life on changed terms is an exercise in discovering meaning both in all that has gone before and in what is to come. This is not easy, yet it is possible to have faith in the significance of one's experiences, even if that significance seems elusive in the present moment.

Bonnie: I certainly wouldn't want to say that it was meaningless, because it was so heavy. But I guess I haven't reached out to anybody with this experience to be helpful. I think I'm staying closed in or something about it. Maybe there's somebody that someday I can be super helpful to. I'm not there yet. That person isn't there yet. I'd like to say that the Lord and I have come together, bang, like that, but I don't say that.

Part of the search for meaning in a terrible experience embraces the creation of a coherent picture of how everything that has happened fits into the story of one's life as a whole. All of the events of that life, and not just the ones connected to a husband's dementing illness, are subject to review. What stands out over time, and what fades into the background? What is lasting, and what is only temporary? The nature of the love between two people provides at least a partial answer to those questions.

Angie: I think with experience throughout your whole life you become stronger. Whatever happens to you in your life, you learn a little bit more, and you get a little stronger to go on. For me there've been some wonderful things that have happened in my life, but there's also some things that were very difficult and hard to take. And it hasn't been easy. When I look back over my whole life, the grief sticks out more than the good times.

The wonderful times went by so quickly, when I should have taken more time when my daughter was little to enjoy her more, to enjoy my life when I was younger more. But you're busy, you're too involved, and you're doing too many things, and it just flew by. So now I look back, and the grief stands out. Seven years of grief with this illness. It's got to take a toll, and it's not like it's going to go away real fast.

So I have to remind myself, "Where were the good spots? Where is that nice, wonderful thing that happened?" I can do that. I have to search back. I think in my case God put me to the test. I think that could be almost true. I think God took Hugo at the right time. I watched Hugo die a little bit every day for seven years. That's really hard to do. I think God decided that Hugo had gone through enough, and He decided that I had gone through enough.

I was hoping that Hugo could spend, maybe, the summer, enjoying a little bit here. We could have walked around here and maybe gotten a little more enjoyment. I had planned to take him over to the coast, just for a drive or something. I kind of wish that He had given him just a little more time.

CHAPTER TEN

🐾

An Overview: The Basis of Coping

> I couldn't control that he had Alzheimer's. I couldn't control that, at fifty-two, he got Alzheimer's, or that we wouldn't have our "golden years" together. I couldn't control that. But I could control to the point that my husband was well cared for, and that I would just do the best I could, and I look back, and I think, at the time, I did the best I could.
>
> —Aileen

Each stage of caregiving makes its own set of demands; from the early days before a diagnosis of dementing illness has been made, to making decisions about nursing home placement, and, eventually, to bereavement. We've been looking at a very select group of people: people who have met those demands in an exemplary way.

What is it about these people as individuals, aside from the specific facts of their particular situations, that has enabled them to survive the experience so well? How do they help to illuminate the psychological basis, or foundation, of coping? What is it about them that the rest of us can learn from?

Responding effectively to the diverse requirements of caring for a dementia patient while maintaining some sense of personal equilibrium and well-being is a very delicate balancing act indeed, and it requires a variety of different coping skills. These skills can be innate to a particular individual, or they can be "grown into" over time as circumstances call for creative solutions.

142

One of the obvious points that emerges from an examination of these women's lives is that there is no one correct way to respond to someone else's dementing illness. For example, what works to calm one agitated, wandering person may not work to soothe another, and the needs of a wanderer are different from those of someone who sits quietly in a chair all day long. The caregiver's basic temperament, the emotional support available to her, her personal system of beliefs and values, the degree of affection and empathy she felt for her husband before his illness, and her perception of her own situation all come together in a complex interplay that crystallizes uniquely in each case.

As different as the women we've been following throughout this book are from one another, they share several important traits that serve as the basic foundation, or structure, of their psychological survival. These traits are: the ability to assess difficult situations realistically, thereby keeping their expectations realistic; the ability to adapt to changing conditions; and a well-developed sense of which things in their lives are subject to their personal control, and which are not.

In an effort to provide some insight into how the personal resources each woman brought to her own situation helped to shape this basic framework of coping, I will enumerate some of the attributes that these women appear to share to varying degrees.

Personal Attributes

Experience of prior hardship
Having a husband with a dementing illness was not the first major life crisis the caregivers had faced. As far as I was able to ascertain it, the experience of varying degrees of prior hardship was a feature in the lives of most of the women:

Edith: Well, my first husband went to work one morning and had a cerebral hemorrhage. He was forty-eight. So I had the five kids. My oldest one was in the first year of college. My baby was thirteen. So I had to go to work to feed them and keep a roof over their heads. But, I've always been like that. If something came up, I took care of it. It might not have been the right way, but I did something about it.

Helen: When our daughter was a year old, we learned that she was profoundly retarded, and would never walk or talk.

Irene: I came from North Dakota, and I was used to severe weather, and severe this, and severe that. I had a hard childhood. I started to support myself when I was in high school. See, so I was a hardy person. I think that's part of it.

Mabel: It was nineteen years that I was married the first time. I was thirty-six when I was widowed. I was alone for seven years, but I worked, and I went to college.

Bonnie: I met a marine, and married him. When he came out of the service, he was an alcoholic. That's why I say I knew lots of different alcoholic habits. That marriage was four years.

Aileen: My mom had a stroke at fifty-seven, and I took care of her for a year. I would go down there every day, pack little Jon off to school and go down there because my dad was having a bad time. I've always been taking care of somebody. Then my father-in-law had a heart attack and my mother-in-law just fell apart. Then my mother-in-law was sick and I took care of her. So I guess that was just my lot in life.

Mary: I was an army wife. I had kind of a rough upbringing to begin with, and so it was tough. I had a lot of survival ability, and the ability to look at things and say, "Okay, this is the way it is. Now what are you going to do about it?"

When the crisis of dementing illness struck these women's husbands, the women already had some experience in dealing with unstable conditions, and with solving their problems on their own.

Forthrightness
The caregiver's ability to speak out honestly and without timidity is essential for getting both her own needs and those

of the patient met. Some people, like Aileen, are forthright by nature:

Aileen: Well, I've always spoken my piece. I've always said what I felt. That, I've always done, it's just me. I figure, if I don't tell people what I feel, they don't know what I'm thinking. I was a teacher's aide. I worked for two sixth-grade teachers, and the first thing I told them was, "I haven't done this before, and if I make a mistake I want you to tell me, because if you don't tell me, I don't know." And I had a beautiful relationship with those two teachers.

Even with my children, when I raised my children, I never didn't tell them anything because there might be a confrontation. I would say, hey, this is the way I feel. That doesn't mean I'm right, but I feel this way, and I'm your mother and I have a right to tell you. What you do with it is your own prerogative, but I have a right to tell you. And I expect you to listen.

The necessities of caregiving help some people to discover that they can be assertive and firm if they need to be:

Angie: I was surprised, to a certain degree, at the extent of what I could do. I just didn't take "no" for an answer. From anyone.

If a person has not been open, self-confident, and straight-forward all along, the escalating demands of the husband's condition can bring her to the point where she is able to speak for herself and for her husband as effectively and forcefully as she needs to. Mary does not put a fine point on this when she says:

Mary: I'd say first off to accept the fact that your name is going to be . . . not very nice. That you're going to be considered a bitch. And just accept the fact, and don't take it personally.

Optimistic role models

Several of the women spoke of people in their lives who had been models of stalwart good humor. Someone who is caring for a dementia patient walks a very fine line between her need for emotional support from the other people in her life, and the realization that those same people may become less accessible to her if she projects nothing but unremitting gloom to them. Someone in an ongoing unhappy situation may find that being absolutely honest and genuine with her feelings at all times is not necessarily the most adaptive way to behave. Role models of optimism, good humor, and cheerfulness can serve as a source of encouragement.

The attempt at maintaining some semblance of cheerfulness around people may actually help the caregiver to carry on in a positive way. Interactions with others who reflect back to her that she is handling things well, and that her strength is admired, can go far toward bolstering her feelings of competence.

Bonnie describes the example set for her by her father, whom she considers to have been an important role model in her life:

Bonnie: There are the negative people and there are the upbeat, positive people. I'm like my dad. I had a very positive dad who'd say, ''It's a beautiful day! Look at your beautiful mountains!'' I'm glad he did. I might not have noticed what a beautiful mountain it was, but he saw it.

It must be stressed that a brittle, forced cheerfulness that is assumed as a stiff mask that never allows any expression of negative feelings, or that serves only to keep other people at arm's length, is not the same thing as a genuine attempt to maintain an optimistic demeanor, and it is definitely not a positive survival strategy. Helen, like Bonnie, admired her own father's optimism. She addresses the ambivalence she sometimes feels:

Helen: I'm tired. I don't know about anybody else, but I feel like I'm two different people. I'm the person that you see, and everybody else sees. On the outside. And another person on the inside. Sometimes I don't know whether I'm deceitful, or whether I'm a sham, or what I am, but I put on an outside Helen that I want people to see, because I don't want them to know that I'm sad. So I sort of hide that.

And I *am* happy a lot of the time. My father was a very happy person. He had a good sense of humor, and everybody wanted to be with him. He was always the head of everything he ever belonged to. He was the kind of person that people wanted to be around. I have a lot of that in me.

Honesty about their own feelings

A striking thing about all of these women was the fact that they never pretended to be happy all the time, or that things were always going fine. They acknowledged the full range of their own feelings, and honored those feelings that were unflattering, or that are culturally labeled as "negative."

Bonnie: I get told a lot, "Well, you're such a wonderful person, and you're so nice, and you're so bright. Your attitude is bright, it's not dark." And I think it was important for me to let people know that I'm not that all the time, you know. I have always been glad that I could look at life, and almost always see the bright stuff. And want to see the bright stuff. I'd lie to myself, even, that it would be bright, but could recognize, too, when this other part of me was very present, and a little bit dangerous. A little scary.

To accept the full range of one's feelings in a situation that is demanding, frustrating, and terribly sad, is to accept the reality of the situation. The concept of acceptance is important, for only in accepting what cannot be changed is it possible to move ahead with the clarity that flourishes when no illusions remain.

Aileen: I've handled a lot of my unhappiness with humor, and I feel it helps other people around me, too. Because nobody wants to be around a weeping, you know . . . And I say, "Okay, I've had my pity party." I give myself a pity party. I allow myself to have pity. And then, I had the pity party. Now I go on. I've never been one to suppress. You have to have a release, and my humor and my pity parties really are my release.

Like I'll say, to my granddaughter one day I said, "Oh, Maria. Poor Noni, she just is really unhappy today." And she got these big eyes, and she patted me on the shoulder and she said, "Noni, life is tough!" So whenever I start feeling like that, I think of Maria with her big eyes looking at me saying, "Life is tough." And I know my son must have told her that when she was complaining. And I really thought, she was looking at me just so sympathetically, so it was kind of funny. "Life is tough." I thought I was really going to get some real wisdom. And I did. It helped. [laughs] Life is tough.

A wish to be strong for others

The concept of "positive role models" can work in both directions. Aileen, for example, derived comfort and strength from her own desire to serve as a worthy exemplar for her family:

Aileen: I've hurt. I've hurt. But I just felt that my strength would be a positive thing for my children and grandchildren. I didn't want them to see me fall apart completely, you know. But they've seen me cry. They've seen my sadness.

Since Mary's children were very young when their father's problems began, she felt that it was essential for her to serve as a positive role model for them, and she sought the help she needed to continue functioning in that role:

Mary: I know that I talked to every psychiatrist they ever had down there at the VA, simply because Ira was off and on under treatment all those years. And periodically I would talk to them and say, "Hey, I need to talk to somebody myself. I have to have somebody I can talk this out with. I don't want to talk to my kids too much, simply because they're growing up. They need some feeling that *somebody* is okay. I don't like upsetting them by telling them just how bad off I am right now. It's not fair to kids to put that kind of strain on them. They have no security."

A supportive family

Strong family ties were a great asset to several of the caregivers, and they recognized the contributions of the other people in their lives:

Irene: Jim was more of a person, more personable, you might say, because of the family. They came in and they hugged him, and they loved him. You see, we had togetherness. The family came home all the vacations. My daughter from L.A. came home every vacation she had. I think more for me than for him. But it helped. It helped all around, you know, it helped . . . Not like some people have, complete isolation.

Aileen: Like I say, I'm a survivor because of the people around me, and a lot of people don't have that.

Family support could be expressed in the absence of close emotional ties. Edith, who had been married for only two

years when her husband became forgetful, found this to be
the case:

> *Edith:* His sister understood, but, of course, we weren't close.
> His other sister in Oklahoma has had a stroke and can't talk. So
> I really didn't have any support except his sister. We hadn't been
> married very long. I hadn't been in the family very long when
> he got sick, and when we found out there was something wrong,
> they told me, "Anything you do is all right with us. We're with
> you. We're behind you 100 percent, regardless of what you do."
> They came up on a Sunday and said, "Don't cook anything for
> dinner today. We're going out to eat." They came up quite often
> and visited. Even after he was in the convalescent home, they'd
> come up.

A sense of humor

Early in the interviewing process, I noticed that the women
each had a good sense of humor. It is hard to imagine being
able to find humor in situations that are fundamentally un-
funny, and yet I saw it happen many times.

> *Irene:* If you put his food in front of him, he fed himself. When
> dinner wasn't ready, like at Christmastime and holidays . . . the
> kids, the older ones, the girls, they would take and put grapes on
> his plate, and then they gave him a fork. In other words, they
> wanted to keep him entertained until the food was cooked.

> *Aileen:* I've told the nurses, "I used to be a real nice person
> before Louie came in here." I've told the director of nursing that
> I've told my children never to put me in this hospital. She says,
> "Well, why?" and I said, "It's not that you wouldn't take care
> of me, but that you're going to get even with me." And then she
> started laughing. I do find that a sense of humor carries me
> through an awful lot.

> *Bonnie:* I hope Henry's in a great body somewhere, having great
> sex.

Ability to "distance" from the patient

The ability to disengage from the patient emotionally
emerged as a coping skill. Irene, who gave total personal
care to her husband for many years, explained how distanc-

ing herself from the emotional aspects of the situation and focusing on the practical ones enhanced her psychological survival:

Irene: You deal with it down to earth. You get to the point that you are dealing with something that is apart from you. Even though they are your spouse, they are some sort of a little something you take care of. You separate yourself from them.

Mary applied the idea of "distancing" in her pursuit of outside activities that were meaningful to her, and that had nothing to do with caregiving. The issue of letting herself enjoy life without her husband along took awhile to reconcile. At one time, she took courses at the local university:

Mary: When I needed to be away, I just skipped a class. I was a good enough student. I could do it, could get by. It gave me an outside interest. I remember the professor asking me, "What are you trying to do here? Why are you going to school?" I said, "Well, to tell you the truth, the most important thing to me right now is the fact that I can come in to school, get a problem, and solve it, and it stays solved."

I sought my own ways of coping with my problems, and one of them was, I had to keep myself functioning mentally in order to keep myself functioning physically in the situation, and I had to get enough distance from the situation to feel like I was having some kind of a life.

I didn't have too much guilt for the simple reason that I didn't do that until it was so far down the line, and had become such a desperate need. I had to force myself to have fun without my husband. And by the time I forced myself to do it, the need for guilt, I already realized, wasn't there. It had become absolutely necessary to stay alive.

Perceptions of the Situation

The way a person perceives any situation will have a great deal to do with the way that she responds to it. If she makes no attempt to improve things she is able to change, she will simply be ineffectual. But if she tries to exert control over things she really has no control over, she will be frustrated. A critical step in the caregiving process, and one that is vital to the development of the all-important ability to be realistic in expectations, is acceptance of the limitations of other people and of oneself.

Disappointment and anger will be the inevitable result of unrealistic expectations, and this is true across the course of a dementing illness. From the very beginning, a caregiver subjects herself to endless trouble, aggravation, and grief as long as she persists in dealing with her demented husband as though he were not, in fact, demented. Until the fact of the dementia itself is acknowledged, some people persist in their attempts to reach the patient through logic and reason. This leads to nothing but frustration.

The acceptance of the unpleasant reality of dementing illness, as difficult as that may be, is the first recognition that must take place before the caregiver can move on to a determination of what she can control, and what she cannot control.

Irene: They start wetting the bed. One of the first times, he came to me, and this was about ten or twelve years before the end. He came and he said, "My bed is wet, and I don't know how it got wet!" That's an idea of how their brain is working. That bed was wet, but he did not wet it. He did not make the connection. He did not wet the bed. I didn't argue. I *knew* he wasn't all there.

When Aileen told Louie to "give 'em hell," rather than trying to quiet him, she was acknowledging that his noises were beyond anyone's control. She felt no shame or guilt, because she knew that there was nothing she could do about it. Nothing, that is, except to make sure that he wasn't overmedicated as a result of his noise.

A caregiver must make the distinction between the unavoidable realities of the situation, and the practical steps that she can take to help alleviate them. For example, she can accept her own need for some time to herself, and also recognize that her reserves of patience with her husband, and compassion for him, are replenished when she has some time away from him. Acknowledging this, she can enroll her husband in an adult day care program. However, she has no control over his reaction to being taken there, or whether or not he enjoys being there.

Unrealistic expectations might stand in the way of a care-giver receiving gratifying responses from the patient, the doctor, or the staff of the nursing home. When Aileen stripped Louie's wet bed in the nursing home, her aim was to have her husband in a dry bed, as opposed to ''getting somebody to change the bed.'' She was willing to take a practical step to alleviate the problem of the wet bed. This approach worked well up to a certain point, but on those occasions when the level of Louie's care fell below what Aileen accepted as minimal standards, she knew which person to target for action. When his clothes were missing, she went directly to the laundress. When the nursing home was understaffed, she went to the director, rather than criticizing the aides, whom she recognized as being ''overworked and underpaid.'' In this way, she spared herself and other people from useless, wasteful aggravation.

This sense of knowing the right person to approach for solutions to problems is important both from the standpoint of getting better results, and because it helps to preserve good relations with hands-on service providers. Mary, who has dealt extensively with the byzantine bureaucracy of the Veterans Administration, knows this:

> *Mary:* So far, I've received pretty good treatment. I can't com-plain. I say things about them, but the individual doctors often-times are very nice. Their bureaucracy is horrendous. But as individuals, oftentimes the doctors are very nice.

The perception of what can be controlled and what cannot bears a relationship to one of the important personal attrib-utes of successful caregivers, which is a forgiving attitude. This attitude can be applied both to oneself and to others. Aileen understood that some of Louie's friends and relatives were unable to deal with seeing him in the nursing home. Although she was disappointed, she did not hate them for it.

Someone with a forgiving attitude does not become bogged down in useless resentments and recriminations. As hard as

Aileen had to work to see that Louie got good care in the nursing home, she knew that the people who worked there had problems of their own:

Aileen: At first, when things happened, I was more aggressive. Then I became more assertive, and picked the right person to talk to, and got the situation cleared up. And they knew what I expected, and I have to say, as I look back . . . I guess they did the best they could.

The same flexibility that allows a person to have a forgiving attitude allows for adaptive, rather than rigid, responses to problems. Sometimes caregivers must make adjustments in their outlook on life and in their accustomed ways of doing things.

Helen: I always wanted everything yesterday. Was very impatient, had to do everything at top speed, had a whole bunch of things I had to do. I couldn't wait to get them done, and now I think, well, if we don't do it today . . . But it took a lot of work for me to get to that.

A person who insists that everything must be done in a certain way will have a harder time dealing with a dementia patient than someone who is willing to be flexible and overlook unimportant things. If the dementia patient is sitting quietly in a chair looking at a book that is upside-down, the flexible caregiver will forgo acting on her own response. She will not risk a bad reaction by going over and turning the book right side up. The more she is able to overlook, the more contented everyone will be. Finding new ways of doing things, and working with the patient, rather than against him, facilitates daily management.

Irene: I think he could breathe better sitting up. See, I would put him to bed, I'd get him in his bedclothes. I'd put him to bed, he'd get right up. So I just adjusted to his system. I never put him in bedclothes anymore. I just let him keep his everyday clothes on. I just made sure that his pants were loose. He'd sleep sitting up in the chair.

At this point, it should be apparent that several of the critical coping skills required for successful caregiving are intertwined. A flexible attitude toward problem-solving is more likely to be found in people who do not adhere to rigid ways of doing things; people who do not adhere to rigid ways of doing things are more likely to have faith in their own judgment; people with faith in their own judgment have more freedom from the opinions of others; and people who are free from the opinions of others are better able to state their requirements in a frank and forthright way.

It is important for a caregiver to face and accept her own limitations. Until that happens, she is not likely to seek or ask for the kind of help that will be of real value to her and, by extension, to the person she's caring for. Asking for help is very difficult for many people to do, but until they do it, they risk being overwhelmed by the situation. Mary describes her feelings, in the early days of Ira's illness, about seeking counseling through the VA:

Mary: I had no qualms about asking for help at a time when it was unacceptable. I was able to ask. Let me put it this way: my family needed me. I had to somehow hang on to my own sanity through this. I had four kids. They had nobody else.

The caregiver must learn to recognize and give weight to her own needs, doing what she needs to do to get those needs met. Some people find this difficult and guilt-producing at first, but it is still extremely important. A caregiver who tries to do everything alone, or who attempts to ignore her own needs, is not responding to the situation in a way that will be effective over the long haul.

Angie: Several times I did take one or two days and I went over to the Sonoma Mission Inn, but that was more of an R and R. I went over there, and took some of the treatments that they have. It was just to clear out my mind so I could have the energy to come back and devote my energy to him. It never satisfies you completely, but it does kind of clear up some things. You think, okay, now I've had a couple days, and now I can do these things for him that need to be done with a little more energy than I could have before.

Values and Belief Systems

The idea of *meaning*, by its very nature, is subjective. People derive personal significance from their experiences from within the framework of their own values and belief systems. Some of the women seem successful, at least in part, because they have willingly assumed roles as mentors for others who are new to the situation that they themselves have faced. For them, the ability to help others gives added meaning to all that they have been through.

Aileen: Being a peer counselor, I get so much satisfaction out of it. I really do. Because I think I'm preventing somebody else from going through a lot of what I went through. With support. And imagine the poor people out there that don't have support. I feel for them.

These women have faith in their ability to make a difference, and they believe that their contributions are valuable. Mabel has been very active in supporting medical research into dementing illnesses. She has been instrumental in arranging, and in some cases funding, autopsies for dementia patients. The death of her husband assumes a different meaning for her in terms of the work she has done:

Mabel: Roy was the first tissue sent from Sonoma County. And, at the end of one year, we had sent twenty-eight tissues. In one year's time, we had twenty-eight tissues sent down there. [To Dr. George Glenner's research lab at the University of California, San Diego.]

The awareness of eventual life beyond caregiving puts the immediate situation into the framework of a larger picture; a picture that includes the woman's basic values and standards for herself. Actions taken in the present are analyzed in terms of how the caregiver will feel about them in the future.

Throughout the caregiving career, successful caregivers know that they will have to live with the actions they take, and this realization informs their decision-making. Aileen was aware that one day she would no longer be caring for Louie, and she did what she could to ensure that she would have no regrets when that time came:

Aileen: I just felt, with Louie, that at this point in my life, this was what I was supposed to be doing.

An ability to grasp the fact that life will go on in spite of the demands of the current situation is a strength that these women share.

Mary: Life is a continuum. This incident right now is just an incident. Life started way back there, and it's going way over there, and you're going to have to live it.

Paradoxically, a person in the midst of the situation must also be able to deal emotionally with the reality that things may get even more unpleasant in the future than they already are. Helen addresses this issue:

Helen: It isn't easy some days. I do get depressed because I feel I'm up against the wall, you know. You can't get ahead of it. You can't look ahead to see the brighter side of it, because there isn't any. But, a lot of the things you worry about never happen. I know it could be worse. I know it could. It may be. But in the meantime, I'll just keep it as good as I can.

One needs to take each day as it comes without worrying too much about what the future may bring, and to do this while maintaining a sense that life, as a whole, has meaning and that, when all is said and done, it will have been worth living. Obviously, this is a very tall order, and none of these women would say that they have always been able to maintain that balance perfectly at all times.

As difficult as their lives have sometimes been, the women seem to share a sense that those lives, taken as a whole, have been rewarding. They perceive themselves as having blessings to count, and that in spite of everything, they are still more fortunate than some other people.

Aileen: I've always been a realistic person. I've always felt that certain things happen, and you just handle them the best way you could, because nobody's life is peaches and cream. But I always looked on the good side. I guess I'm sort of a Pollyanna. I live on a budget now. I feel that I'm better off than most, even at that. I have my house. A lot of people don't have a house. I do things that I want to do. I have to choose, but I'm better off than most.

Mary: In spite of the bad things, there have been many good things, and I can take an overview of my life and say that, on the whole, I would not be willing to give up the good to erase the bad. I mean, you can't pick and choose. If I could pick and choose out of my life, sure, eliminate that thing. It would have been better. But still, do I have a basic satisfaction with life? Yes.

Mabel: What coming to the support group does for me is I see how much better I had it than some of these people in the group now.

Some of the women felt comforted by the bond that had existed between them and their husbands before the onset of the dementing illness, and their actions in caring for their husbands were influenced by the deep affection they felt.

Part of the benefit of a long and gratifying marriage may be that it nourishes what I will call "faith in reciprocity," or the belief that the husband would be giving loving care to the woman if she herself were the ill spouse:

Angie: If Hugo had been an abusive husband, or a scoundrel of any kind, maybe my feelings might have been different. But he was so sweet to me, and so good to me, that how can I not take care of him? How can I not do the best for him? He did the best for me, when he could. Now why can't I do what I think is the best for him?

Helen: I said to my friend, "You know, I'm never going to put Donald in a nursing home, because he wouldn't do it to me."

Aileen: Well, I always focused on him. I really did. I always felt that if I was there, he would have been doing it for me. He was very protective. And I put myself in his place and I felt, not consciously, but you just know how, if the situation was reversed, what would Louie have been doing?

Although a long-standing devotion to her husband gives a caregiver a distinct advantage in terms of her ability to withstand the strains she will be subjected to by his illness, this is by no means a prerequisite for effective coping. A generally responsible and steadfast character can be a source of strength and support, also.

Edith, who had been married only briefly when her husband got sick, never wavered in her assumption of responsibility for his care:

Edith: I imagine it was easier, probably. I don't know. If you were married to somebody for a long time or something like that, you would probably feel worse than I did. But I've always been one to do what had to be done, regardless of what it was. To the best of my ability. I was married to him, and I should take care of him, as much as I could.

Mary also had a firm sense that taking care of her husband was the morally responsible thing to do, although she lacked the faith in reciprocity that provided comfort to Angie, Helen, and Aileen. Mary's own analysis of her marriage is practical and unsentimental; the care that she gave flowed from her own values and self-image, thereby providing meaning for her, even though it was meaning of a different sort than that experienced by some of the others. Mary describes what she felt was positive about her marriage, and contrasts her experience with Aileen's:

Mary: Well, I didn't have the same assurance as Aileen, and I used to envy her that feeling. I can remember being very, very resentful of some of the things that Ira would ask of me, and thinking, at the same time, "Hey, big boy, you would never do this for *me*." And feeling that resentment. And, I mean, it was there. It was real. I don't know what he would have been like if we could have grown old gracefully together, but at the same time, the psychiatrist he was seeing advised me to leave him. And off and on through the years, other doctors have made the same comment, and, you know, I won't say there wasn't many a time I really contemplated it.

Well, one thing, I happen to believe in marriage vows. And the other was that I just knew, in my own heart, that the man was not responsible for a lot of his actions. And, in spite of that, those were the bad times. You have to remember that every life has bad times in it. But there were a lot of good times, too. So, by this time, of course, it wasn't a very passionate marriage, simply because of the circumstances and the conditions, but there was still a lot of companionship, and that may be a better basis for marriage anyway.

The original character of the caregivers' various marriages was, overall, an unreliable predictor of the degree of seriousness with which they approached their caregiving responsibilities. They all took their husbands' care very seriously, and continued to do so long after the men had become incapable of providing them with any emotional support.

A strong belief in the inherent dignity of human beings can be a source of emotional sustenance. This sense of human dignity is what made Mabel discourage her husband's friends from visiting him in the nursing home; she considered the visits an affront to the person he was before he got sick. The same instincts made Mary want to yell ''He's not drunk!'' at people who stared. This recognition of human dignity extends to everyone, not just the womens' own husbands. Aileen addresses the feelings that she has now, when she sees a person who is disabled in some way:

Aileen: You get so mad. You think, how can people be judging this person? They don't even know him. That used to be one of my feelings, you know. I've always been more or less that way, though, too. When you see someone, you smile at them. If they do something strange, you smile at them. I mean a nice smile. Like you are a friend. Just a friend.

The Role of Religion

Irene has been a faithful churchgoer all of her life; Aileen rediscovered deep religious feelings within herself right after Louie went into the nursing home. Aileen's ability to stop worrying about things she had no control over was enhanced by her belief that God had a controlling role in her life:

Aileen: When he first went in, I'd just walk around this house, bawling my eyes out. The day he went in the hospital, I remember coming home, then I went back at five o'clock, and I came home and it was about eight o'clock and I went in my bedroom, and I locked the door of my bedroom. It was a fear. It was. I think everything was so uncertain, I didn't know where to go. And that's when I really went back to my religion.

I've always prayed and had religious feelings, but I was not active going to church. I went, but not on a weekly basis. And that's another thing that has helped me. I'm at the point where, like I said at the meeting the other day, I do what I can do, but I can only do so much. I can't do any more. And I say, "Hey, I've done everything I can do. The rest is up to You." And I really feel that it's going to be taken care of, and I relax. Until I did that, though, I wanted to be in charge. And you're not in charge.

Angie also found renewed comfort in her religion:

Angie: I found that I'm a little closer to God, and I find myself driving down to the Saint Rose Catholic Church. I find myself going into the little chapel there. I feel that, really, God has helped me through many things. With Hugo. My daughter had some throat surgery and now she's faced with some more. He helped me through that. But I feel a little closer to God, and I find myself, although I don't go to church every Sunday, I do drive down to the church and I do go in to the little chapel. A lot.

Helen found herself getting back in touch with the same religious faith that had helped her to deal with caring for her retarded daughter:

Helen: I have a lot of faith. And when I say that, I mean that I just know that somewhere, somehow, the Lord will give me strength. Because He always has. The reason I didn't lose my sanity is because I knew we had done everything humanly possible. We'd been everywhere. We saw every person who could help her . . . change her. You say, "Am I religious?" I said to the Lord, "I have done everything I can do. Please show me what I am to do. I don't know what more I can do."

Edith, Bonnie, and Mary, though they are not regular churchgoers, are individuals with deeply-felt values, and they derive meaning from their attempts to lead worthwhile, up-standing lives:

Edith: I never went to church, or anything like that. Well, I went, but I don't go like some people, every Sunday. But I do live, or try to, by the Golden Rule. I'm honest, and I try to do what's right, and take care of what I have to take care of. And I do say a little prayer every day, to God, thanking him for giving me the day, and taking care of me. I think I'm religious in a way. I'm

not one that goes to church and thinks that that covers everything.
I mean . . . takes care of everything.

Bonnie: Once we moved I didn't go to church anymore, and I
still haven't. I got involved with the chaplaincy at the hospital.
What I saw for the chaplain was that his church was in the hospital. We could be doing as much good in the hospital, by the
side of a bed holding a hand. We didn't have to be in a building.

Mary: Well, I get a certain amount of satisfaction out of being able
to help others, and I have a feeling that we do owe the world something. You don't take everything off the plate and put nothing back.
And others have helped me through times of stress and strain. I
find meaning to my own life, and to the world, in being active and
contributing something to the world. That's my meaning.

The womens' ideas of "meaning," their own personal
feelings about what it means to be a good, decent person,
and about what it means to be a survivor, were all different.
Yet, the belief systems of all of them were important to their
individual survival. Just as there is no one right response to
the demands of caregiving, there is no one right attitude or
philosophy about it. There is no one right philosophy of life
in general.

I thought it would be interesting to ask these women who
have been through so much to respond to the statement,
"God doesn't give us any more than we can handle." It's a
statement we hear often, and I have just as often wondered
if people who say it have really thought about what it means
before offering it to someone who is enduring a hardship of
some kind.

Each woman responded to that statement in the way that
was true for her. Each woman has been highly effective at
meeting the demands of her own particular situation, and yet
their collected answers reveal that the philosophical bases of
their belief systems are highly individual.

Mabel had a very practical reaction, which was not
couched in spiritual terms:

Mabel: That's true. I don't know why, but that's the way it is.
Because there's a lot of us that would have been snowed under

long ago. You think you can't take one more day, but you wake up the next morning and you do. Sometimes you keep wondering why. It's just what you've been handed to deal with. That's the way it's always been. We meet people in the support group where you think, "They can't make another day." But two weeks later, they're back. And two weeks have gone by, and they've gotten through it.

Aileen and Mary, who have great respect for each other, and who are good friends, reveal that divergent views of reality can serve to give order and meaning to the world:

Aileen: Well, I think it's true. I really wasn't that religious before Louie became so ill. I felt abandoned at first, I really did. I felt abandoned. And I didn't go to my regular church because I'd see everybody I know, and they'd ask me how old Lou was, you know. What's Lou doing? And I'd cry. I was able to get through that after about eight months.

But I feel that when things just got too hard for me I'd just look up and say, "I've done everything I could. Just give me the strength to know what to do." And it isn't that I'm religious, but I do have faith. I just feel it's going to be taken care of. I used to worry about everything and finally I'd say, "I'm just one person." It goes back to "Thy will be done." And I truly believe it. I really do. That's been my salvation. That's what helped me, was this saying. Before, I always thought I was in charge. It was very humbling to find out that I wasn't.

Mary: I don't agree with that saying. In the first place, I'm not sure I believe in the kind of a God that would test people in that way. I mean, depending on how you define God. And yes, people do get more than they can handle, at times. I see that all the time with what I'm doing, is some people cannot cope with what they have to do. Look at the poor Alzheimer's victims. They didn't do anything to deserve that. I don't think that God inflicted it on them. I think it just happened.

And if you take that statement literally, the person who's caring for the Alzheimer's patient, do they have more than they can handle? Maybe they do. We've had some of them die from cancer. I think of Geri, she took care of her husband. She wouldn't go in and have the cancer surgery because she'd have to leave John. Well, she left John. She died from cancer before he did from his Alzheimer's. Yes, she had more than she could handle.

She obviously couldn't handle it. She died. Did John ask for Alzheimer's? He was a sweet person. He was a lot of fun. That's the reason Geri devoted her life to him, and this was a mid-life marriage, too. What did he do, ever, to deserve something like Alzheimer's?

Yes, they had more than they could handle. That's my response to that. I've never agreed with that statement. I can remember being told that, and feeling very tempted to say, "Okay, *you* handle it for a while. I'd like to give you my burden for a while."

Angie and Bonnie's replies raise questions about what it really means to cope with life. They know that it doesn't mean being happy all of the time, and it doesn't mean having the answers for everything:

Angie: I think what happened to me, is that having someone to care for like that just made me stronger. Somebody had to take control, and go on with his life and my life and take control of it. And luckily I had the strength to do it. There's an inner strength that you have to develop. And maybe I am a little stronger type, although I wouldn't have considered myself to be. I look at some women and I think, "God, if something like that happened to their husband they probably couldn't handle it." But, you know, I think they could.

Bonnie: Oh! Well. I never railed at God for Henry being sick, or for my burden. I never saw it as He was doing anything terrible to either of us. It was just one of those things that happened. If I were told that, "God doesn't give us any more than we can handle," in the middle of a crying spell, and was angry and upset, and feeling terrible, I'd say, "Shut up! What do you know?" And "Damn!" I'd say, "That's very inappropriate and I'd like you to leave!"

But now, this day, where I am today . . . In retrospect, whoever decided that was a very good statement probably was right. I don't see anybody falling down after all they've had to do. I see tears, and I see wringing of hands, and all that, but I don't see anybody crashing to the floor in an absolute inability to handle it, so I guess we all can. I've never seen a case of anybody . . . that happening to them.

We all have our inner strength that can be called upon. Maybe nobody will ever, ever find out how much.

CHAPTER ELEVEN

❧

The Support Group

It's unbelievable. Alzheimer's brings people very close.
The people in the group are closer than your own relatives.

—Mabel

There are, as yet, no medical remedies for dementing illnesses. In light of that fact, treatment for the patient consists
of doing whatever can be done to improve and strengthen the
management and coping skills of *the person caring for him*.
This will, ideally, create a positive emotional climate for
both the patient and the caregiver.

Mary: It's true that it's not treatable, but if you treat the surrounding problems created by it, you make life easier. Not just for the
patients, but for the family.

Some people have had to learn on their own, through long
and arduous personal experience, the techniques and attitudes that make it possible to care for a dementia patient
effectively. Fortunately, every person who is new to that situation does not have to reinvent good coping strategies all
by herself. Newcomers can reap the benefit of other people's
experiences, learn new survival skills, and get some of their
own emotional and social needs addressed in a support
group.

Support groups come in many different forms. A group
can meet for a specified period of time, or be open-ended.
It may be a small, loosely-structured gathering of people who

meet in each other's homes, or it may be a large, organized group sponsored by a church, charitable organization, or local government. Some groups employ facilitators, and some do not. Any group will have its own tone and character, and even within the same group, continual changes take place as new people come in and other people leave.

The group that my observations are based on is ongoing and meets twice a month under the dual sponsorship of the Redwood Caregiver Resource Center and the Older Adults Program of the Sonoma County, California, Mental Health Department. Attendance at the meetings usually ranges from ten to twenty people, and the group is facilitated by leaders with training in social work or counseling.

The dementia patients that members of this group are caring for are at all different levels of disability. Some people in the group are caring for their parents, or parents-in-law, and some are caring for their spouses. Some of the patients are in nursing homes, and some are not. Some of the caregivers feel deep love and affection for the people they're caring for, and some do not.

The people in the support group represent a mix of personalities, temperaments, age groups, religious backgrounds, and financial conditions. However, the situation that they all have in common easily overshadows those differences. In some ways, the support group members have more in common with each other than they've ever had with anyone else, and it is the very diversity of the group that serves to spotlight the universal quality of their shared experiences.

Irene: By going to the support group, you hear all the different people saying the same things. And you cry a little, and then you laugh. You know what it's like.

Caregivers are comforted in the realization that their demented relatives are not the only ones exhibiting exasperating behaviors. Hearing other people describe similar frustrations and annoyances can do a lot to reassure new group members that their own feelings are normal and shared by others, and that the patients they're taking care of are not, for the most part, deliberately trying to make life difficult.

There is one small catch: a person must attend a support group before she can derive any practical or emotional benefit from it. Unfortunately, there are many people who, at least initially, strongly resist the idea of attending. They find it difficult to admit to themselves, much less to others, what a hard time they are really having.

Some individuals are burdened with the feeling that walking into a support group meeting constitutes an admission that things are becoming too much to handle alone, and that this is the same as an admission of personal weakness, or of a deficiency in their own character.

Adhering to an ideal of being an emotionally self-sufficient and independent woman may have served a person well throughout her lifetime. However, independence, as an ideal model for behavior, only works so long as the circumstances of life cooperate by never requiring her to ask for help from anyone for any reason.

Many people have, in fact, reached an advanced age without ever having to turn to others for help. They have little practice in seeking advice or assistance, because their "rugged individualism" has not let them down until now. As these people eventually find out, caring for someone with a dementing illness means that relying solely on oneself will probably not remain a viable option indefinitely.

It must be pointed out that not everyone who avoids a support group does so because she is denying the level and intensity of her difficulties. Feeling that one has done well on her own can, in itself, be a genuine source of comfort and gratification. An attitude of "independence at all costs" only becomes a problem if it prevents the person from seeking help when the time comes that she really needs it.

Helen: One of the workers at the hospital, who works in my daughter's wing, asked my friend Lucy, "Has Helen ever thought about having some counseling? I don't know how she carries what she carries." And Lucy said, "You don't remember, because you're too young, but Helen and I grew up in a generation where you fought your battle no matter what it was. Period.'' And I said, ''That's absolutely right. That is how it was.''

Now, I don't mean to say that I don't need help. Maybe I do. And maybe I'm going to seek it. I mean, I don't want to say no, I won't ever do that, because who knows? But I know myself pretty well, and I just know that I have to be strong. I can be strong. If I decide I will be, I will be. But that doesn't mean it's easy. You do what you have to do.

People who avoid support groups may attach a strong identity value to being someone who doesn't complain. Older people appear to be particularly tyrannized by the cultural expectation of noncomplaining, as if an honest statement of one's own problems and struggles is the same as an indulgence in tawdry gossip. It is almost as if there is only one acceptable way to be: upbeat and cheerful.

People who avoid support groups sometimes feel that it is wrong to ''air the dirty laundry'' in public, or that they are being disloyal to the patient if they tell a roomful of people how difficult it is to take care of him. An open admission of conflicts within the family feels very threatening, because it means the end of the pretense that those conflicts do not exist.

For spouses, particularly, coming to the group can symbolize a painful disruption in the prior relationship. Going somewhere without the spouse represents a disturbing new mode of behavior that is upsetting for some people. One woman's feelings of disloyalty were focused on the discomfort she felt when she was untruthful with her husband in response to his questions about where she was going on the days of the support group meetings. This woman experienced her own untruthfulness as a very harsh break with the way she had always communicated with her husband, so much so that her continued participation in the group was at risk.

Apprehension about what the future may hold is another factor keeping some people away from the support group. This is especially true for those whose demented relatives' symptoms are still mild compared to those of patients other group members are taking care of. Support group leaders are careful to point out that not everything one hears about in the group will happen to any particular patient in the future. Even so, it can still be very upsetting for a new support group member to listen to stories about some of the unpleasant things other members have had to deal with, knowing that she herself may eventually have to deal with them, too.

Helen: You go to those meetings, and you hear all those stories, and you know you're in this thing, and how it could be, how it could progress, and what would be ahead and everything. It's very depressing for me, and I think it's because I'd really rather be on a happier note. But life is not that, and I know that it isn't, but I think I'm always striving for the happier things because there's been so much that's really sad.

On the other hand, a caregiver who does not come to the support group until very late in her husband's disease process may perceive that she has little in common with the other people there.

Angie: Well, I've only been there about three times, and to find out about the [new drug] was a big help to me. Other than that, I don't know. Most of them are at a point about where I was two or three years ago. And, as they were talking I thought about that. I thought, they're talking about something that went on in my life three years ago. And these poor women are still having to face all that.

As a result of this reluctance on the part of some caregivers to participate, there is an element of self selection in the makeup of any particular group. Sometimes, people who have been initially resistant to attending a group may come to feel differently as time goes by.

It should not be surprising that caregivers are often in very fragile emotional shape by the time they finally do come to the group, and it is common for people to cry at their first meeting. As the Kleenex box makes its way around the circle, a newcomer begins to reawaken to something that has probably been missing from her life for quite some time; namely, emotional support. The familiar phrase "break down and cry" takes on an important new meaning in this context. To cry within a group of unfamiliar people represents the breakdown of resistance to getting help for oneself, and it represents the beginning of a new phase in which the caregiver starts to honor her own needs.

The loss of friends and social support structures that caregivers can sustain has been addressed already, and the group serves as a replacement for some of those lost supports. In the group, newcomers find new peers; people who can understand their feelings and who do not judge them harshly for having them, because they have had many of the same feelings themselves. I have heard more than one person say something like, "You people are my real friends now."

Even people who have close family and friends may eventually choose to share the bulk of their feelings of exasperation, fear, and sadness with the group, thereby preventing their important personal relationships from becoming centered solely around discussions of their caregiving. This substitution can help to keep those other valued relationships as unaffected as possible. A sense of normalcy is important because without it, the caregiver may come to feel that her whole life has been taken over by someone else's disease, and that she has nothing left.

Aileen: My daughter-in-law, bless her heart, she said, "Are you going to go to the support group?" And I said, "Yes, I think I'll go," and she said, "Well, I'll come the first day with you." So she did come the first day with me, and I've been involved ever since. And I felt that people there knew what you were talking about, and I felt very comforted, and I did have family support and everything. But still, this was another dimension. This was a person my age in my same generation that was supporting me. And I really have good friends and good family, it's not that. But it's another dimension.

In the support group, negative, angry feelings are not brushed aside or criticized. Fear and apprehension about the future are not belittled.

Mabel: And so I talked to her [a woman in the group], and I ended up my conversation by saying, "The reason you come to this group is to let off your tension. You can laugh. You can cry. You can scream if you want to.'' She said, ''I think I'll scream.'' And she started to scream. And we had the darndest time getting her stopped.

No one is required to speak in a meeting if she doesn't want to. Benefits can be gained by sitting back and absorbing what other people have to say. This is particularly true for newcomers, or for people who have trouble expressing their feelings.

Mary: I really feel that some of the very embarrassing, uncomfortable things that happen in the family when you're caring for an Alzheimer's person, or any other dementia, need to be brought out. Some people can, some people cannot talk about it. But in the group, those who cannot talk can still listen, and they can still react. They don't have to open their mouths. They can sit back there and listen to somebody else bring it up. You can still participate in a group without saying a word.

The basis of the support that people receive in the group is the concept that caregivers have the right to address their own needs as well as those of the patient. Sometimes people have lost sight of that, and need to be reminded. It can be difficult to see oneself as deserving of help when the sick person has lost everything. There can be an element of survivor's guilt.

A person's sense that she is entitled to take care of herself is often in need of strengthening. Women in particular have been raised to provide care for others, even if that means endless self-sacrifice. A lifetime of conditioning does not fall away quickly. The support group enables participants to gain some perspective on how skewed the balance in their relationships with the patients they care for may have become.

In order to encourage someone to respect her own needs, it may be necessary to appeal to the very altruism and dedication that make it hard for her to do that. She must be supported in including her own well-being in considerations of what is best for the patient, even if she initially finds that uncomfortably ''selfish.''

The question caregivers are asked is, ''If *you* break down, who will care for the patient? Isn't it important for you to take good care of yourself, so that you can continue assisting this person?'' These are by no means idle questions: several of the caregivers in the support group have predeceased their husbands, and we are left to wonder whether the strain that they were subjected to was a contributing factor in their deaths.

Almost always, when someone is struggling with a particular management problem, others have something from their own experience to offer. One woman told the group that her husband fussed about going to the respite center two mornings a week, and that he protested loudly in the car for the last few blocks before they arrived there. The suggestion was made that she vary her path to the center, even if that meant driving there via a circuitous route. Support group members emphasized to this woman that it was important for her to get some relief, and that she must not waver in her resolve to take her husband to the center, even if the logistics of getting him there were unpleasant.

Group members are reminded to tell themselves, ''It's not him, it's the disease,'' when they are faced with maddening behaviors. Once a caregiver is able to view obnoxious, difficult behaviors as manifestations of a disease process, it is easier to stop holding the patient accountable for his actions, and to begin accepting his functional losses. This is an important perceptual shift, because as long as someone persists in holding a dementia patient accountable for his behavior, she is at risk of subjecting herself to the immense frustration that results from attempts at getting him to ''change.'' If caregivers persist in treating patients as though they are rational when, in fact, they are not, they will be making their own lives harder than they need to be.

The outcome of the debate over whether or not every single aspect of a given patient's unpleasant behavior is, in fact, a direct result of the disease process is not as important as the attitude that his caregiver takes toward that behavior. If she is able to view it as something the patient is not doing deliberately, she will be better able to maintain her own sense of personal equilibrium, and that, after all, is what is most important.

Aileen: When my mother was ill and came to live with us, she had Parkinson's. Louie was still working then, and I'd get upset with her, and he'd pat me on the shoulder and say, "That's okay, babe, everything's okay." He'd make her laugh, and she was always on her good behavior around him, which made it a little bit easier. But with me she wasn't. It took me about two years after she died to get it straight in my head that it wasn't her, it was the Parkinson's.

Once the insistence on logic and rationality is abandoned, management becomes much easier. However, people can be understood for having trouble letting go of "reasoning" with a demented person. To treat the person as if he is demented is to accept, once and for all, that the dementia is a fact of life. Acceptance represents a new phase in the caregiving career, and some people need more time than others to arrive at that point.

It is only when the caregiver fully recognizes that the patient's ability to express himself logically is irreparably impaired that she can begin learning how to communicate with him in a new way. Once she learns to respond to what his words convey about his emotional state, rather than to the literal content of his utterances, it will be easier for her to begin to let go of the "reasoning" habit.

Expediency is promoted as a coping strategy. For example, it feels strange at first to pick up someone's foot and put it into a shoe. Yet, if one persists in standing over the dementia patient and repeatedly asking him to put on his shoes, she risks provoking a negative reaction, and he still will not have his shoes on. As the group leader once said, "It feels as though you are insulting the person's dignity by doing things like that, but sometimes that is what you have to do."

One woman told the group about the terrible time she was having getting her husband to stay in their bed at night. He kept taking his pillow and a blanket, and sleeping on the floor. She was becoming exhausted, waking up several times during the night to get him back to bed. There was an awkward silence. Finally someone asked her if there was really any reason why he shouldn't sleep on the floor, since he seemed to like it there. She thought for a moment and then said, no, she really could not come up with a good reason why not.

This example is virtually identical to the situation of Irene, whose husband slept sitting in a chair in the living room. While Irene was able to arrive at the "noninterference" solution on her own, the woman in this case derived the benefit of other people's experiences. Practical coping strategies are just as effective whether a caregiver arrives at them through brutal, tedious experience, or has been taught them by others.

Great truths are sometimes imparted in support group meetings, such as: "Nothing really bad will happen if your husband's socks don't match."

> *Mabel:* There's lots of ways I can help. Such as, if the patient is having trouble handling a belt, use suspenders! And if they put the suspenders on the underwear, just get another pair of suspenders! It is much harder on a person who says, "It's going to be done my way."

The recurring theme of "What can I control? What do I have no control over?" is important. A woman whose husband was in the "shadowing" phase of his illness, marked by his wish for her constant presence, had tried to hire people to come in and stay with him so that she could go shopping or just get out of the house for a while, but four successive sitters had not worked out. When other group members asked her why not, she replied that her husband was "just not happy when I'm away," and that it "wasn't much fun" for the sitters.

It took quite a bit of energetic campaigning to convince this woman that even though her husband was, indeed, unhappy when she was away, there was nothing she could do about that. It was not within her power to keep him happy all the time. And wasn't she herself very, very unhappy at home with him constantly? In addition, she was paying the sitters to stay with her husband. They had accepted the terms, and had not taken the assignment because it would be fun. Slowly, this caregiver came to the recognition that she had to get away once in a while or risk a breakdown. Very simply, this meant that she had to leave her husband with other people. It did not mean that he had to like it.

In addition to replacing lost social supports, the group is an important educational resource. Caregivers have numerous practical matters to address, such as getting the patient's name onto waiting lists for adult day care centers and nursing homes in a timely way. While group facilitators do not offer legal advice, they stress the importance of obtaining it. Financial planning for eventual long-term care must be dealt with, and group members are advised that such details are better handled sooner than later.

The group always encourages participants to arm themselves with information. The practical advice dispensed at a group meeting can range over a wide variety of subjects. Certain topics, such as effective ways of communicating with health care professionals, and solving problems in nursing homes, are common. Members steer each other away from insensitive professionals, and toward those with whom they have had good experiences, comparing notes on people who are particularly understanding about dementing illnesses.

People in the group offer each other approval and permission for following their own instincts. At one meeting, two women who would both soon be faced with making funeral arrangements told the group that they felt awkward because they had formed close relationships with clergymen from outside the churches they themselves belonged to. Both women wondered if it would be proper to include these new clergymen in the funeral services. The consensus was that the important thing was for the women to do whatever gave them the most comfort in the situation.

Just as there is a progression in the way a caregiver responds to her own circumstances, so there is a progression in her participation in a support group. In the support group, there are people who are taking care of patients at all different phases of dementing illnesses, and who have been doing so for varying lengths of time. As people continue their involvement with the group, newcomers gradually become veterans, and their feelings of competence and mastery grow as they themselves have the opportunity to offer help and support to others.

It is important for all of the members to respect each other, and take into account the fact that not everyone is operating with the same level of experience. Some caregiving relationships, particularly in the early days, are marked by a reluctance on the part of the new caregiver to frankly assume burdensome new responsibilities. An important function of the support group is to assist people in recognizing that their demented family members are no longer capable of taking full care of themselves, or of making responsible choices, and that the assumption of the new role, as odious as that may be, is necessary.

The group can serve as the voice of "community conscience" in convincing people that they must take distressing but necessary steps such as separating an unsafe driver from his car, or making new living arrangements for someone who can no longer safely stay alone. Encouraging and supporting the caregiver in doing what she probably already knows she needs to do is an important function of the group.

I asked Mary and Aileen how they handled their roles as veteran support group leaders in situations where they felt concerned about the way other people were handling things:

Mary: Well, oftentimes, I keep my mouth shut. And other times, I don't. I'll disagree, at times, but I also recognize the right of everybody to make their own decisions. Their own individual situation might be similar, but it's still unique. What's right for me is right for me. And maybe I'm wrong. But I have no right to make that decision for other people, unless what I feel they're contemplating doing is harmful to somebody else.

Then I will speak up, and I'll speak up quite clearly, and express my opinion. Sometimes, when I've heard them say things that I felt uncomfortable with, I've just said, "Always remember, before you take any action, that some of these situations cannot be reversed completely. I mean, you might do what you can to change it, but you're going to have to live for the rest of your life with the knowledge of what you have done, or haven't done. Make sure it's something that you can be comfortable with, because you live with yourself for the rest of your life."

Aileen: I agree with Mary. That's my feeling, too. I speak up. As you know. [laughs] That's a given. And I still, at the same time, feel that the other members of the group are entitled to their decisions and feelings, and I honor that. I don't feel that mine is the right one. It's just that sometimes, in situations, people are so confused, they don't know which way to turn. Because in Mary's and my situation, we've been through it, and we're looking back. When you're right in it, like when I started out, it's just terrible.

Teaching caregivers how to deal more appropriately with dementia patients not only makes life a little easier, it can help them to achieve the goal of keeping the patient at home for as long as possible. With good management skills, some time away from the patient, and social support, people can care for dementia patients for a long time. The support group facilitates all of these things.

Yet, the same group that assists a caregiver in keeping a patient at home for as long as she can may ultimately be the source she turns to for support when she can no longer care for him. Nursing home placement is sad and traumatic, as we have seen, and caregivers who are in the process of placing someone, or who have just done so, are in tremendous need of understanding and reinforcement. They may face overt or implied criticism from friends, relatives, and neighbors who don't really understand what they have been through.

There are people in the support group who know what it feels like to put someone they love in a nursing home, and they also know that all of the coping skills in the world will not ease the pain of doing it. Sometimes support is silent.

Some people remain with the group for a long time after the person they've cared for has died, and some do not. Bonnie, who had been very active in the group, stopped coming to meetings very soon after her husband Henry's death. She describes her ambivalent feelings about sharing with newcomers the gruesome details of some of the troubles she had faced, such as her husband's violence and fecal incontinence:

Bonnie: I knew they hurt. And I knew it helped them to hear about the frustrations and the anger. We could express them and say, "This is what we did. And the reason I put him in the hospital was that he was shitting all over, and doing these things." And so I think, you know, they heard that, and thought, "Oh my God, my husband's going to start messing in his pants. What am I going to do?" Without pointing the finger and saying, "You're going to have to deal with that," you just do it through your sharing. But it's a message that does say that. It says it, and if they want to hear it, fine. I think they do, and they put it way, way back.

A message that was given to me in one of my first meetings was from a man who had a wife that was scary and wielded knives and scared him like that. And he was a big, burly guy who handled horses and everything. He had to really protect himself from a knife in bed. And I heard that. He said to me one day, "Well, you'd better start thinking of a place for him, because a man can always overcome a woman, and he just might overcome you." I heard that, and I didn't push that way back. I kept that up front.

Why do veteran caregivers stay with the group? Each woman has her own motivations, yet the wish of each one to derive meaning from her experience is always important.

Mary: That's one thing that kind of slays you after they're gone, or after they get in a nursing home, or something like that, when you start to feel your own feelings. They're overwhelming. I continued to defer a lot of it. That's one of the reasons I stayed with the group afterwards. It's been a healing process for me, because I'm out of it now, and yet I certainly empathize with everybody there.

I had felt that staying with the group, working with them . . . It not only helps them some, but it also increases my own understanding of some of my own emotional problems at the time. I didn't think it was a good idea to continue to push them in the background. I needed to bring my own feelings out in the open, and deal with them.

Aileen: When we started there wasn't anything out there, and so, if we could just help a little bit, help someone a little bit, by just a few words . . . I mean, that's what it's all about, is helping the other person.

CHAPTER TWELVE

❧

Talking with Two Support Group Leaders

I thought that God and I just had an open, running
disagreement about how much I could handle.
— Sharon Lieberman

In connection with their jobs as counselors at the Sonoma
County Mental Health Department, Sharon Lieberman and
Jeanne Goff have served as facilitators of the support group
profiled in this book. Both of them have fulfilled that role
with understanding and sensitivity, and their ability to do so
has been enhanced by their personal experiences.

Sharon, one of the current leaders, began her association
with it as a regular member during the time that she was
caring for her mother, who had Alzheimer's disease.

When Jeanne was in her thirties, her husband died of cancer, leaving her with three young children. The need to assume complete responsibility for a family and to do that
without the emotional support of a mate is something that
she is very familiar with. Jeanne is now retired.

I've been curious to talk with both of you about your roles as leaders of the support group. To begin with, what are some classic signs that should alert people that they're dealing with more than ordinary forgetfulness?

SHARON: Well, there's an old joke I like, and it's a bit outrageous. If you misplace your glasses, don't worry about it. If you forget that you wear glasses, there's a problem.

JEANNE: It's not "I've lost my keys"; it's "What do keys do?" And I think you see all different levels of that, because we all get kind of scared when we forget things. We may wonder what's happening. But it's the impact of the forgetfulness that's important.

Do you think that there are any basic personality traits that help a caregiver to cope better with caring for a memory-impaired relative? For example, a flexible attitude comes to mind. Can you think of any others?

J: It's hard, but I think a sense of humor helps. In spite of all the tragedy, there's humor, if you can keep it in perspective. Another thing is learning not to take it all personally. I think that's terribly important, because people do get caught up in what the patient is "doing to me," when they're not doing it to you at all. I don't even know what that is, but the ability to distance yourself from the person you're caring for. I think that would be extremely helpful to people.

S: Well, I think it really helps if a person has a lot of inner strength, and I think it helps if a person is independent. Oftentimes what we see with people who come to support groups is that they're from an older generation, and because of their cultural training, and since most of them are women, they've really not been encouraged or allowed to be independent, and all of a sudden they have to be, so it's very difficult.

What I find is that a lot of those people have that spark of independence, but they don't know it. And so we try to identify that for them and help to bring that out, along with their inner strength and an optimism about life.

I think people do better if they tend to be less negative and more optimistic about life. And I think part of the whole thing is to help people to become aware of the strength that they have that's in them. We call it empowerment, which is not about gaining power over someone else, but about trying to catch their own personal power and using that. It's a wonderful thing to see when that happens, as people start to grow, like Aileen.

Yes. And we see that in the support group.
s: And we see that all the time. Yes.

It's been very rewarding to see that happening with different people.
s: Well, I remember when I first came to the support group, Mary and Mabel and other people would tell me that I was a basket case. I remember being a basket case, but I don't remember much about it! And I know that the group helped me to evolve.

It just has a way of doing that by supporting you, and encouraging you, and giving you permission to try, and to fail, and also to get better, and do better in the process. So I think those characteristics are really important to people's succeeding.

To a certain extent, people can be helped to develop those things.
s: That's right. It's not the people in the group, or the facilitators, who "fix" people. I think it's imperative that the person in the group knows that people who come there have within themselves the skills and knowledge to problem-solve, but they just need encouragement, and some guidance.

By the time you come to a support group, it either looks like there's no road at all, or it looks like there are so many choices you're not sure which one to take. Both can be pretty frustrating, so I think that's really the role of the group: to encourage and allow for individuality, growth, and decision making. And the right to fail. To succeed or to fail.

As you mentioned before, many of the people who are currently finding themselves in the situation are members of the older generation, and it seems as though people in that age group suffer more from the sense of stigma about "mental illness" than younger people do.

In your opinion, to what extent does the sense of stigma about mental illness feed into denial of the presence of dementing illness, or keep people from acknowledging memory-impairing diseases in their relatives? What other factors would lead somebody to deny her relative's problem?

J: I agree that there is a tremendous stigma. I know that from personal experience in my own family. There used to be a lot of denial about cancer. Certainly there's all kinds of denial about alcoholism. People don't want to face the reality of what this terrible burden is, this terrible situation that they might be in.

But I think that the stigma of mental illness, with people of my age group, and that's the age of a lot of the people we deal with, is just starting to get a little bit of a breakthrough.

I can remember as a kid, sitting in my window looking out at night, and the neighbors would let this man out at night. He was an older man who had a mental deficiency. And he was never allowed out during the day. It was as though they thought, "If we keep it quiet and locked away, it isn't happening."

And I think there's still a lot of that with people. I can't tell you the number of people who have said, "I *never* thought I'd walk through the doors of a mental health building." Like this would be the absolute end. The only other thing as bad as that would be going on the dole, or something.

S: You have a lot of questions in there, cloaked in one. I think the stigma is still there, and I don't think it's just for older generations. I think it's in my generation. I think in the generation of my kids, there's a little bit less of that, but I think it's still pretty strong.

I think that it's been kind of interesting, because we fought for so long, myself and others, to really educate people about the fact that Alzheimer's is a neurological disorder. And when that was finally recognized, that it was a neurological disorder with psychiatric symptoms, it hasn't seemed to make much difference.

Why not?
S: Well, people still look at it as a psychiatric disorder. Although, on the face of it, one can say this is a neurological disorder. People from the outside look at it as, "This person is acting crazy." So what came first, the chicken or the egg? It doesn't really make any difference, it seems, in how it's perceived, although I think that there's so much crazy behavior in this world now, that people allow for it more. And I think they're even a little more sensitive toward accepting craziness, and crazy behavior. People have had more exposure to that kind of thing.

Yes. I've even noticed some people in the group, who obviously have broken through denial enough to come to the group, who still seem to have a problem with their gut-level acceptance of the fact that there is really a disease process going on. I wonder if you've observed what sort of psychological factors feed into the denial?
J: I think it's when it first starts, when they're thinking, "This person's just trying to be mean to me. What's happened to his personality? Why's he picking on me like this?" It's much easier to handle it that way, it seems. As opposed to something happening to this person that there's no control over.
S: I think there's a lot of factors. One is that most of us in this culture are into denial anyway, about a lot of things that don't fit into our perspective, or the perspective that we want to have about life. We're very skilled at that. So I think there's the stigma of mental illness, and craziness, but there's also, I think, and it may be stronger than that, the unwillingness to give up what one had before.

And the implications of accepting that?
J: You can pretty well be sure what a certain person's going to bring up at each meeting. If you try to talk to them about

other things, it's "Yes, yes, but . . ." Boy, we're going to get back to whatever this is. Somehow or other, it's awful, but I can deal with this *one thing*. I can talk to you about it.

Some of the other things the caregiver could worry about, that maybe she can't deal with, she's going to put them away or ignore them. Maybe that's some of those traits the patient always had, and maybe this new one she talks about so much is one he didn't. I don't know why they zero in on a certain one, but it's a coping mechanism. I don't know what it is that they're doing. Some of these other things are so scary, you can't talk about what's down the line.

s: That's right. If I accept that my spouse, or my parent, is no longer going to be there for me, then what does that mean? What are the implications of that? If it's the spouse, there's a lot of implications. I won't have a partner anymore; a sexual partner as well as a companion, an adult that I can talk to. The role changes. Your spouse, companion, lover, and maybe provider, is no longer doing those things for you.

So, the relationship changes. I think most people, many people, would rather believe that it's a brain tumor or something. It's much easier if it's that kind of thing that causes this bizarre behavior, and it won't be a long-term thing, because with all the education that's been going on, we all know now that the implication of Alzheimer's is a long life with years of caretaking and deterioration.

For me, people would say, "Well, what does it matter what your mother has?" And I said I needed to know, because then I could stop looking. For me, it was a matter of ruling out everything until nothing else was left, and then I could say, "Okay, it's Alzheimer's." But until then, I didn't know that it wasn't something that could be fixed.

Can you make any comparisons between the way people who have had a loving and mutually supportive relationship with the patient, and those who haven't, cope with the demands of caregiving? What's easier, or harder, in terms of those two cases?

J: Well, I know that for the people who have had a shorter

or less involved relationship, there's a lot more bitterness. There's resentfulness. "I didn't expect this to happen to me, and I'm not going to do it." What I've seen often is a second marriage, and maybe they've had five, six, seven really nice years, and all of a sudden this thing is going downhill very fast, and they're extremely bitter. "Why should I be saddled with this, what have I gotten out of it?" Where, had there been years and years of marriage, it's "I've invested so much in this marriage, and this relationship." There's anger, but not that resentment.

s: I think it's much harder if you have not had a good relationship with that person. There have been several people who have come into the group who have had a terrible relationship with their spouse, and they're not all second marriages, either. Sometimes they're first marriages. There's a real resentment there, an implication that "We didn't have a good relationship and now I'm stuck taking care of you, you bastard."

Versus someone who had a good relationship who is really grieving with the loss. You grieve the loss of not being able to partake of all those dreams you had. We all dream that we're going to retire, and travel, and do whatever we're going to do, and here this is short-circuited. So there is that loss: not having the opportunity any longer to achieve those dreams that you've had, and most of us in this culture work toward retirement for thirty years.

So this is the case of the loving relationship that you're addressing?

s: Yes. And so there's that grieving and that sadness, but there's not all of that other stuff. They seem to be able to manage much better.

As opposed to the difficult relationship that is characterized by . . .

s: Resentment. There's a little bit of resentment sometimes in loving relationships, because, gosh, we don't get to do the things that we'd planned. But there's that love there that seems to compensate for it. In a relationship where there isn't any love, it's a duty, and I have to do it, and damn you. There is that that seems to speak real loudly.

J: That's what I see. And I see a lot of resentment in relationships that are not strong. In a good relationship the anger is not anger at the person, but anger that this situation happened. But in the other it's resentment against that person. That's the difference. It's a fine difference, but you understand what I'm saying.

Yes. Do you ever see a case where the people have not had such a great relationship, where they've lived parallel lives, and the caregiver is able to call upon her sense of personal identity as a dutiful person, and get some satisfaction out of doing the right thing toward the impaired spouse? Have you ever seen cases like that, or is it just total, unmitigated resentment?

S: I don't think anything's so black and white. I'm sure that there are cases in between, and I'm thinking of one lady like that who's been in our group. You don't always know about relationships, so I can't really say that it's one way or another. And what I know about life is that there is lots of gray in between. So I guess the question there would be, does that make it better? Does it matter?

What I'm trying to understand is how people find meaning in this experience for themselves. Someone who's loved the patient very much may find that meaning in continuing to give conscientious care, whereas somebody in a more difficult relationship is still able to find meaning in terms of their own identity. Someone who says, "I'm a person who tries to do the right thing and fulfill my obligations."

S: I guess one of the problems, now that you restate it . . . I'm thinking that maybe there could be someone who loves the person, but their relationship has been really tenuous, or up and down for years and years, but that's not to preclude them loving the person. I'm thinking, too, of my relationship with my mother, which was one in which I really didn't feel that she was an affectionate person. And that was something I had been wanting.

And so my relationship with her was a really difficult one, even though I did love her. I found myself trying to be the parent to her that she was not to me, and that I wished she had been. So I experienced it, and was able to analyze it. It never occurred to me that that would happen with unfinished business. So even though you love someone, there could be a real difficult relationship, and that's exactly where you start. With the relationship in caretaking, it starts at the place where you left off. It doesn't become better simply because you have become a caretaker.

So perhaps it's even harder because there's not only the anger at not getting what you needed, but also at seeing the deterioration of someone you love, which is a day-to-day reminder that you never will get what you needed from this loved one.

In my case, it's kind of interesting, because my mother, when she literally lost her mind and her memory, was then able to be very childlike and say, "I love you." The big joke was that she had to lose her mind to say, "I love you." For both of us, that was very freeing, although for her, it was on an unconscious level.

This leads into my next question. When we make the statement, "It's not him, it's the disease," what about the people who become confused who had unpleasant personalities already? For example, if they were suspicious, or miserly, or self-centered before the onset, is it really accurate to view all of their behavior through the filter of the disease idea? What are the benefits of looking at it in that way, as though all of their behavior is a manifestation of the disease?

s: Well, if it's a new behavior, I think it's fairly safe to say that it's because of the disease process, and that's real clear. That makes a lot of sense. If it's more of the same old stuff, what usually happens is that it becomes more embedded.

If it's behaviors that they had before, the plus is that they'll forget. They'll forget that they were tight or thrifty. They'll even forget what money is, and so it won't matter in the end.

J: The disease is certainly not going to help, but you can't blame everything on that. We used to try to say to the people in the group who would tell us, "He does this and he does that," we would say, "Try not to take it personally." We tried to help them distance themselves, and not internalize everything.

That is something that is very difficult for caregivers in the beginning, when the behavior is a magnified version of something the person has done all along, in terms of the caregiver trying to deal with her own feelings of being irritated by it. In a way it must almost be easier when the person gets worse.

J: That's right. Absolutely. There's a time element in there when it's impossible, when there's that overlap of the old person and the disease, and I think people just kind of muddle their way through. They're just trying to take one hour at a time, much less one day at a time. And they get so involved in getting through there, that sometimes some of these changes are not even quite seen.

S: Well, I think we need to think in terms of real specific behaviors. If we're talking about managing behaviors that are things like "You stole my money," those kinds of things are usually really new, even if that person was tight with money before. I think we need to be real specific about what kinds of behavior, and how they are demonstrated, and whether or not they are occurring because of the disease. Some typical kinds of behaviors that happen with wandering, and running away, and getting mad at the caretaker when you tell them to do something and they don't want to do it.

All of those are pretty typical. Those are kinds of behaviors that I think we can say are part of the disease. They're not trying to bug you, per se. I think what we caretakers don't understand sometimes is that we're often the key in managing behaviors. By what we do, and the way we react verbally and physically, we can escalate behaviors or calm people down.

J: The first thing I learned in doing counseling is that the only person you can change is yourself. You can't change the other person, but by the way you change yourself, you can change what happens, change the interaction.

S: Actually, you can stimulate assaultive behaviors, when the person hasn't been particularly negative before, just in what you say. And it's hard to read someone with Alzheimer's. The body language is oftentimes such that you get double messages.

That's a very important ability that skillful caregivers develop: the ability to have empathy for the patient. Some people seem to be able to develop that quickly, and others never do.

J: Never have. They absolutely don't have the capacity. Some people know how to read other people and some people don't. Ever.

I'd like you to address something that seems to be very common, which is the way that patients often seem to exhibit a rapid decline after any kind of a trauma or relocation. How does this fit in with the biological disease model?

S: It fits in because of failing memory, and short-term memory loss. And it makes sense in that if you have a routine that you do every day, and there are no changes, it's much easier to continue to do things on a normal level, given the tremendous memory loss and confusion.

When your whole world changes drastically, when you go on a trip, or when you move to a new house, then you no longer have any crutches that you can hold on to. I think that's the problem. When a routine is changed, it throws the person with dementia off track.

J: As you know, they travel along on their plateaus, and then something happens. Often it's a short hospitalization, a major change, or a move of some kind, and then they go down another degree and level off. I don't know enough about the physical part of it to know why this is so. I just know that many many times, it happens.

How would you respond to the analogy that dementia patients are like children, in terms of the ideal of continuing to respect them as adults?

S: I think that there's a real difference between expectations of behaviors, and tasks that you want them to do, and respecting them as adults. I think it's important to know that you need to keep your expectations of them appropriate. Usually we don't, so we get into trouble. In fact, that's one of the biggest causes of assaultive behavior and catastrophic reactions.

Our expectations are not always appropriate. They're too high for this particular level that the person is on. Where we get into trouble is that we need not to treat them as children, but to respect them as adults. It's not always easy when this person is drooling, and when you're in the role of taking care of this person. It feels very parental, the role that you're in. It's a difficult one, a real difficult one.

J: I think that's one of the problems. I hate to generalize, but as an example, you will see so often in nursing homes that people treat the residents like children. Even if somebody's acting like a child, you should treat him with dignity. But it's, "Now, now dearie, don't do that, or we won't have dessert." That sort of thing. Ooh, demeaning!

And I'm sure that it is very hard sometimes, but I think that you need to treat people who are behaving in a childish way with as much dignity as you can. There's so little dignity left in the life of the person who has Alzheimer's. But I think they deserve every amount that you can give them.

We have an ideal that the patient should be encouraged to do as much as he still can, but then there's the practical issue of the caregiver avoiding additional stress to herself by just taking over more of the necessary tasks. It's easier for caregivers to do things themselves. What are some of your views on that? And I'll just ask the next question, too, while I'm at it: how can you give an incompetent person any autonomy?

J: I think it's the same thing you run into with your kids. Some people really want to help their children grow, and will put up with the mess, or disarray, or whatever it is, in order to do that. I think other people can't handle that, and so therefore they take away this element of the patient being able to do things for himself, because they don't like all the mess.

I'm not a perfectionist at all, never have been, and I'm extremely happy that I was not born one. I think that people who are have a very, very hard time. Think how hard it would be to let somebody do something for himself if you could do it in a much faster, easier way. I think what they're doing is the way they want their life to work, the way they want everything to be, but I think they're doing a great disservice to the patient.

s: Besides doing for someone else because it's easier, or letting them do it because that's one way of them remaining autonomous for as long as they can; it also keeps them less dependent for longer, and less of a burden on you.

But there's something else in there, and it's real insidious. We want to do for our loved one what we can. And veiled in that is the fact that we think we're doing them a service by taking care of them in this way. We think of taking care of people as some kind of outward physical behavior.

And so we end up doing that without being aware that perhaps it's more detrimental than allowing them to do for themselves. And that's something we don't think of. It has to do with wanting to do all we can for the person we love, without considering whether we want them to remain autonomous or independent, or that it's easier to do it ourselves.

J: I think that patients should be allowed to do everything they can, and I know it takes tremendous patience, but there's not one element of this disease that doesn't take tremendous patience.

The question is, in what ways can a caregiver allow the person any autonomy? Because at some point, that takeover has to happen.

J: Yes, it has to happen. I remember one young woman telling us that she had somebody come in and help her with a couple of rooms in her house and fix them so that her mother couldn't hurt herself. She had a couple of rooms, and her mother could do anything she wanted in there, and it didn't mess up the rest of the house. It was her mother's domain and her mother knew it was, and she just said, "That's okay. If I have to go in once in a while and hose it out, at least I can allow her some functioning."

We read and hear a lot about "reality orientation." What is your opinion of this? Do you think that there's a point when efforts at reality orientation become more stressful than helpful, and if so, how can you know when that point's been reached?

J: I guess people need to be aware that this disease just continues and continues. The person continues to deteriorate with this. I don't know how people would be able to sense when it was, if they weren't sensitive toward people anyway.

A certain amount of reality orientation is fine, but my own feeling is that it's overdone a tremendous amount. I think it is, in nursing homes. They get everybody in a big room and they write "Today is Monday." The date and the day of the week and all this. I'm retired now and I'll get up sometimes and think, "I don't know what day it is." And unless it's a day that I have a big appointment and I have to be somewhere, it doesn't matter.

S: One of the things we tell people in the group: if the Alzheimer's patient is always right, that means that you don't resist them, because it never works, and that's the reality for the caretaker. And as soon as they can realize that, it'll be a lot less stressful.

It used to be in the early days, the early eighties, that we pushed reality on Alzheimer's patients, or patients that were demented. And actually, that was to suit *us*. We used to try to keep them as normal as possible. And I think part of that was we didn't want to let go of that partner, of who they were before, and the roles that they filled, and the needs they filled for us. But I think another part of that is that we want them to look as okay in public as we can make them, and what we're finding out is that that's more stressful to them, trying to maintain that facade.

A really good example is, I used to struggle with my mother so much because she would get dressed in the morning, and she would put her clothes, her pants, and her blouse on over her pajamas, and I would come in and say, "Mom, you've gotta take off your pajamas."

And there would be a struggle, because she would say, "No! No! Leave me alone!" This whole thing. And you can just picture what happened. But I wouldn't stop. I was undaunted, and somehow, an hour later, she would be without pajamas, in her regular clothes, and both of us would be angry.

And exhausted.

s: And exhausted. And of course she forgot it, but I didn't. I can remember one time talking about that at the group, and someone said, "Well, why don't you just let her wear her pajamas underneath?" And I said, "Oh! That never occurred to me!"

You know, we want them to look as normal as possible, and we have certain ways that we think normalcy looks like, and someone said, "Are you going to take her to the doctor, or out someplace?" And I said, "No." Then we all laughed. The same thing if she wants to wear her clothes to bed at night. Sure, wear your clothes to bed at night. We'll wait until tomorrow morning to fight about taking them off.

Did you find that you were able to get her to remove her clothes pretty easily when you needed to?

s: Yes. Pretty much. I think the secret is, make your work as light as possible. She's already dressed, and she feels good about dressing herself, and she happens to have her nightgown underneath, or her pajamas, and you're not going out, and it doesn't matter anyway, so why keep this appearance of normalcy?

I think you're getting into something that's part of the personality of the caregiver. Some people have an easy time letting the effort at normalcy go, and other people are firmly identified with the patient being squared away and dressed nicely. It's an example of a personality trait that would make it easier, or harder, to deal with this. Somebody who's really bothered by mismatched clothing, or somebody who can say, "We're not going anywhere. It doesn't matter. It's not important."

s: Well, yes. That's a good point. And I think you look at your charge, and if they look well kept, then it looks like you're doing a good job. It makes it easier, because you actually can see something. It's like cleaning house. If your house is a mess, you clean it, and you have visual feedback that, yes, I spent a couple of hours, and it really made a difference, and I like that.

It's the power of reinforcement. The person that you're taking care of can act as crazy as they want but, you know, let's try to keep them dressed, and looking good, and looking clean and well cared for, because at least we can achieve that. Some of the time.

When the patient is a parent, there's a built-in reciprocity issue; i.e., "My mother took care of me when I was a kid." You've already said that sometimes that sense of across-the-board reciprocity isn't as strong as it could be. Would you like to add any more to that idea?

s: Oh yes. I think the parent/child relationship produces a lot more guilt, whether it's been a good relationship or not. Obviously, either a good or bad relationship fills some kind of a need in both people, but I think there's this thing of "She took care of me," or "He took care of me," and I found myself thinking that the least I can do is take care of this person at home for a few years.

In fact, it goes like this: "Well, they took care of me for seventeen years. The least I can do is take care of her for two or three or four years."

J: "The decent thing to do would be to take my mother into my home." With the spouse, the spouse is already there.

S: And so, it was devastating when I finally had to make the decision to place her in a residential care home, and even worse when she had to go to a skilled nursing facility after she broke her hip, because there was always that: "The *least* you could have done . . ." But I think that whole thing makes it really harder.

J: What kind of a daughter am I, that wouldn't take care of her own mother or her own father? There's a whole element of guilt in there, and I have seen people take care of a parent when they really never had a good relationship with that parent. Maybe really, if they'd be honest, didn't like that parent, although nobody ever wants to say, "I don't like my mother," or, "I don't like my father." It takes a pretty mature person to be able to handle saying that, but I find that there's some kind of hidden guilt in there. "I'm gonna do it! I'm gonna do it!" But there's a tremendous amount of guilt.

S: I don't know about reciprocity, from the perspective of a spouse. I would guess that if it's been a good relationship where the spouse provided for thirty years, or twenty years, and provided well, that there might be that same thing working.

The idea of reciprocity in the people I've talked to who really did seem to have a good relationship was "I know if I was sick, my husband would be taking care of me." And it's a belief based on the way the marriage was up to that point. Not everybody has that, but that seems to be, in terms of the whole issue of reciprocity, how I've seen it expressed in marriages.

Moving into more of the practical issues, do you feel that physicians' awareness of memory-impairing illnesses has improved in recent years?

S: On a scale of one to ten? In the last ten years?

Yes.

S: I think it's probably to a five.

Okay. From what?

S: From a zero. I think it's a direct result of everything we've done in this county to educate the doctors, but many of them are still uninformed. I still hear doctors say, "Well, memory loss is part of the aging process." Severe memory loss is *never* part of the aging process, and if it's there, then they need to investigate what's causing it.

J: Doctors have improved in recent years, but they still have a long way to go. I know there are many of them who will send a caregiver to our group, so I know the word has gotten out. I don't know how much they are doing themselves, but at least they know that this is something, and it's prevalent, and people need help that are dealing with it, and the doctors know *they're* not competent to deal with it. It's a much more difficult situation to be a caregiver for a demented person than most people realized. I think things have improved. I think it has enormous possibilities of improving more.

Let me ask you this: in terms of your work with caregivers, what sorts of things would cause you to really wonder about a physician, or cause you to encourage a caregiver to look elsewhere for medical help?

S: If they're not getting their needs met, medically or personally, I would encourage them to see someone else. And if their needs are being met medically, and not personally, if they can live with that, then that's their choice.

We have a new lady in the group who has a doctor that I feel is real incompetent. He's terrible. I don't tell that person that they have a terrible doctor, because they need to believe in the doctor that they have. But I will often be real attentive to what's happening with that person, and will, maybe down the line, suggest that they see a neurologist, or that kind of thing.

J: I think a doctor will sometimes close the door and say, "There's nothing that can be done. This is Alzheimer's." It's important not to mislead people, or make them think this person can get better, but when they're going to a doctor for help and the doctor is just saying, "Forget it," that's bad.

I had a terrible experience in which a doctor told a woman who thought her mother had Alzheimer's that there was absolutely nothing anybody could do. I would never say, "He's wrong." I said to her, "If it would make you feel better, maybe it would be worth your while to have a second opinion."

I don't know what she told him, but he called me and said, "I'm the one who's trained in medicine, and I don't want you giving out any information, blah blah blah. Do you know how you undermined the relationship between me and my patient?" He just carried on. It was terrible.

When he finally stopped for a breath, I said, "Believe me, it was not my intent to undermine you in any way. It was my intent to have this person be reassured by a second opinion, and I thought all doctors felt that way." And I hung up the phone.

Moving into the area of you as support group facilitators: in terms of the support group, do you notice any differences in people's ability, or willingness, to open up and share their problems with others, in terms of their age group, or other personal traits?

J: Absolutely. Probably the person it's hardest for is an older man. This is a man who has been taught all of his life to be strong, to stand on his own two feet, not to be a crybaby, not to look for help. You can do it yourself, and if you can't you just grit your teeth and bear it. Now we're saying, "Come on in," absolutely the opposite, and "It's going to help you." It's very very difficult for him to do.

One of the things that's been started is a men's support group, and they seem to be a lot more comfortable in that. They don't even mind if a woman is the facilitator, but they're more comfortable around other men. We have had, from time to time, a man who would hang in there for quite a while, and they seem to get quite a lot out of it, because they certainly get a lot of strokes and a lot of support. If they realized how much support they're going to get, they probably would stay longer.

s: Actually, people who are older have been raised in an environment where you don't tell your neighbors what's happening. You keep secrets, and personal things stay in the family. But I came from a generation like that, too, and I never complied with that, so I think the answer is that it probably is both training and personality, and it has to do with trust. Whether or not people can be open has everything to do with trust.

I think, in the support group, that after a while a person can't help but trust. For some people, it takes longer, and that has to do with their history, and how their family system worked. So I'm not sure that it has anything to do with what generation they came from.

How do people overcome a lifetime of conditioning that valiant suffering is a virtue? Some people have been trained that self-sacrifice and martyrdom are good things. Their concept of a highly developed person is somebody who bears what she has to bear and doesn't complain. This may have worked fine for them all their lives, but now they're in a situation where this illness may have gone on for years, and it's getting worse and worse, and the "strong" routine is not working anymore. What finally helps a person get past that and start to see the possibility of a different kind of response to problems?

s: Well, I think through reframing the problem, or manipulating the end result. If we can sell those people on really thinking about the question that we ask them, "So what happens if your health goes down the toilet? Who's going to take care of your loved one?"

So you're still appealing to that in them, to that wanting to be the Rock of Gibraltar.

s: That's why I say manipulation, or trickery. But once they start to begin to take care of themselves and it feels pretty good, then they get hooked, and they see that they can succeed at that. Then they can continue with it. It's a starting place for them.

J: I think sometimes if someone is hurting enough that they'll listen a lot more. It's as if this strong, independent person has come to the end of something at that point. The point when you feel like it's going to all break and fall apart. Life events will bring them to it, and hopefully they will be able to hear things that will be able to help them.

Let's move on to the whole issue of nursing home placement. That seems to be the hardest thing that people go through, the process of coming to the decision about when it's time to do that. What are some of the most common events, or conditions, in your experience, that cause people to start thinking about nursing home placement?

S: I think it boils down to the fact that they can no longer physically take care of them, and they don't have money. And/or they don't have the money to get somebody to come in and take care of them. It's always either or both of those things.

In other words, practical considerations become compelling?

S: Right.

Is it more or less common, in your experience, that nursing home placements happen in crisis situations? So many people promise themselves never to place the patient, and so they don't go out and look or explore, and then their hand is forced.

J: It's awfully hard. Awfully hard. And see, once again you're seeing the denial. "I've finally accepted that this person has a disease, but I will never, never, never place this person in a nursing home."

I think that it's something the caregiver has been considering for some time, but it's always in the future. It's down the line. It's down the line, and then some crisis will come and it's not down the line. Here it is.

S: Actually, I think there are more decisions for nursing home placement when it's not a crisis. Also, as a caretaker there are so *many* crises. Sometimes it seems like a continual crisis.

J: I know that sometimes they're placed without crisis, but generally I think that the precipitating event feels like a crisis at that moment. Why it happens right then.

Maybe a crisis is just the last straw.

S: But it's usually also a medical crisis that kind of puts people over the edge, I think. Or the person they're caring for goes to another stage in their deterioration, and becomes incontinent or, like my mother, she broke her hip.

In the last ten years we've been trying to educate people to go look at residential care homes, go look at skilled nursing facilities, so that you have the data. Collect the information ahead of time because when the time comes, and you're in a crisis, that's not the time to be looking around.

And I think people are doing that more. I think it's always another event that causes people to place someone, but it's not necessarily a crisis. Like I said, it's hard to tell when you're dealing with someone with Alzheimer's. Everything seems like a crisis sometimes.

Right. Now, once the decision's been made, what is your opinion about trying to prepare the patient for the move, and should he or she be told ahead of time that they're going in?

J: I don't think so. You certainly could tell them, but that's about it. They're not going to retain it. Unless it's very helpful to *you* to talk about it, because I don't think they retain enough of it. The process should be described to them, what's going to happen, and I think if it's at all possible you stay with them, go with them, take them, and help them settle.

Sometimes the nursing home will tell the family it's best not to see the person for several days to allow them to have this adjustment. I've heard of several places that feel that way, and then others that say, "Don't leave them alone. Don't make them feel deserted." To me it would be very interesting to see if any studies have been done on this. Which is better? Who's in charge of letting who go?

S: That's a difficult one. I think that's a very personal kind of decision that needs to be made according to the people involved. It depends on where the person is that's going to be placed, in terms of their cognitive abilities. If they even know.

It has to do with the person who's placing them, and their family, and what they're feeling. It's been interesting to me to know that when I placed my mother in a residential care home I was saying, "Oh, my mother would like this," or, "My mother wouldn't like that." I knew at the time I was really trying to find her a place that I would feel comfortable with. And so it's almost always, whether it's conscious or not, the family finding a place that's going to make them feel better.

Is that an impossibility?

S: Well, we have only so many choices. Look at the plusses and minuses, and pick the one that has the most plusses.

Yes. It is always interesting to watch people in the support group developing assertiveness in advocating for their relative in the nursing home. Yet some people remain passive, and perceive themselves as unable to make changes. Some of them have never before had to face situations where assertiveness was so vital. What do you see as blocks to the development of assertiveness? Are there any hidden payoffs in passivity?

J: See, I truly believe the weak run the world. I think the weak get the strong to do what they want, because they can't do it themselves. I've always felt that's one of the best manipulations there is, being weak and letting somebody else do it. And that's a neat way to get out of stuff.

The difference is, some people have only been meek because they've never really had to do anything else up until now. But some people are just passive because that's the way their personality is: passive. I think some people are born with the ability to be assertive, and it's just never, ever been tapped, and some people are just never, ever going to have it.

s: I would say, "Yes, there are payoffs in passivity." I think passivity is trained, too. That learned helplessness that we have as kids. The payoff is that someone can always take care of you. However, when you have to take care of someone who can no longer take care of you, that adjustment to the reality that you're going to have to be independent is a very difficult one.

I think that whether a person learns to assert themselves has to do with self-esteem. Anybody can learn to assert themselves and to feel good about themselves as long as they're willing to take the steps that they need to take. Certainly, for someone who's never made waves, it's going to be difficult for them to start making waves.

That's why it's important to have someone like Aileen, who's willing to go with them to show them that their making waves is going to be okay, and then next time they'll venture out a little more. And it will be effective. Or, even if it's not effective, assertiveness is about maintaining, or developing, if you don't have it, your self-respect.

Personal integrity?

s: Right. In that, if you don't get things done, if all your objectives aren't met, at least you have that self-respect. You feel good about standing up for what you believe, because assertiveness certainly doesn't guarantee success in everything you ask for. That's only part of it, and it's nice when that happens, but that self-respect is really important. If a person has low self-esteem to begin with, that's certainly going to add to their self-esteem. All those little successes build up the self-esteem.

Okay. We know that retaliation against a nursing home resident for a caregiver's complaints is illegal, but in a practical sense, isn't it a genuine concern? If not overt retaliation, then an atmosphere of resentment that could make the care more cold-hearted? How would you reassure caregivers on this issue?

s: I had that experience with my mother, and then I filed a complaint with state licensing against her nursing home, and that nursing home is the place that I think is the best in town. So where can you go besides that?

But the truth was that although my mother was on Medicaid, I expected that she'd be taken care of properly, and there was what seemed like a burn on her lip. And nobody knew who fed her, nobody knew how it happened, and the director of nurses tried to tell me it was herpes and that I brought it in, when I've never had herpes.

It was that kind of not taking responsibility that really pushed me. And I was willing to take the risk. I went through the steps. I went through the administrator, and then I went to the ombudsman, and then I went to state licensing and didn't win.

What were you hoping to get, some statement of accountability from them?

s: Yes. That's exactly what I wanted, and I wouldn't have done that if they had just said, "Yes, so-and-so was negligent, and that person doesn't work here anymore," or *something*.

What was the outcome of your action?

s: The outcome was that they didn't mess with me anymore. And I was real clear that I didn't want to cause them any problem. What I was concerned about was the best care that my mother could get, whether she's on Medicaid or not. I made them very aware that it was illegal to . . .

Retaliate?

s: Retaliate with my mother. And I was there often enough so that I would know about it. And, in fact, as president of the family council, I knew a lot of stuff.

*How would you reassure caregivers about this fear of re-
taliation?*

J: I know it's an important issue, and I think one of the
very first things you have to let people know is that everyone
has the right to have an advocate, and that there's nothing
more important than to be an advocate for someone who
truly in no way is capable of doing it for himself.

s: I would tell them that it's a normal kind of fear, and that
even if it's against the law, it's something that they're really
going to have to just see, that it's going to be okay. Within
that whole struggle, they'll begin to feel like they have more
power when they're advocating for their loved ones. I think
you validate that that's a real worry.

*It really is. We hear it over and over again. People are
really frightened about it.*

s: Yes. And the only way to overcome it is with a sense of
some kind of power. And the only way to get that is to take
the risk and do what you need to do, because the bottom line
is, if you don't, then nothing's going to change for your family member.

Or anybody else.
s: Or anybody else.

*In terms of death and bereavement, do you notice any
difference between people in different age groups in terms of
their willingness to face, accept, and make preparations for
the death of the patient? Have you noticed any factors besides
age that seem to influence this?*

s: An interesting question. There are some people who
seem to handle bereavement better than others. And endings.
Age-wise, I'm thinking that older people have more losses
by the time they're in their eighties, but that doesn't necessarily mean that they're going to handle them better. I think
it has a lot to do with personality as well as life experiences,
and I think it certainly depends on what the relationship was
like, and I think it also makes a difference when you're deal-

ing with a degenerative process over years versus a sudden death.

Because there is so much anticipatory grief that's done with demented patients, you can see what Aileen was talking about, that she grieved so much during the years that Louie was alive, and then you wonder why there aren't very many tears afterwards. And yet, someone else might also grieve during the years that their spouse is alive, and then have lots of tears afterwards.

I think we have a couple of examples in our support group right now whose husbands have died. One of them, whose husband died five months ago, still gets teary-eyed, but she's really gone on with her life in so many ways. And then we have the other lady who is trying to go on with her life, but is still very attached to her husband. It's been difficult for her to let go.

Both of those things are okay, since we all have our own process. So, I don't know. It depends on the relationship, the caregiver's personality, and maybe, or maybe not, on life experiences.

I think what I was wondering about is the fact that some people seem to have a very hard time dealing with the concept of death in general, aside from their relationship. To them, it's almost a prurient thing, say, to mention preparatory funeral arrangements, or even mention the "D" word. It feels inappropriate to them because, for whatever reason, you just don't talk about death as a thing that happens. You kind of push it into the background.

J: Absolutely. It's like the "C" word that cancer was, you know. One of the words that, when I was raised, was a four-letter word. I think most people are in denial about death, which amazes me. No, it doesn't amaze me. I've never been frightened of death. I've been fortunate. But I think a lot of people are very afraid. I don't think you can go on living right unless you can face the fact that you're going to die, and face the fact that it's going to happen, that it's part of the cycle, and you go on until the cycle ends.

I think that some couples, if they made decisions before this illness became apparent, or before it became incapacitating, if they had already decided that "This is what we're going to do with everything," then it is all right. But I think once this comes in, the caregiver feels awful, and feels a terrible guilt about trying to make arrangements for death. It's as if they've gone too long, and now they're hastening this thing, and the patient has no input into it.

S: It always amazes me when I meet people in their seventies and eighties who are afraid of dying and don't want to talk about it. It's important to get those things taken care of ahead of time.

It just so happens that finances really help us to open up that area in that, in order to split assets, and spend down your mate's portion, that one of the things you can do is to pay for funeral arrangements and buy a plot and all of that. It makes sense to do that. It's much more prudent, and it kind of desensitizes people. It kind of forces people to deal with it, and they save some of their own money.

J: I think for those who really haven't done that it's very difficult, and I think that's why they deny, too. It's like, "I just can't think of that, too." I've known people, it's not uncommon at all, who wouldn't talk about life insurance. "We just can't talk about it. We can't do that."

S: But I think, by planning for those kinds of things, it brings up the whole issue of life, and the fragility of life, although we're really resilient. Human beings are really resilient. But it reflects the insecurity that people feel about death, and it challenges their belief system, and brings out that part of them which may not have been explored at all during their lifetime, which may have been seventy years or so, and that's the spiritual part.

And regardless of whether they go to a church, or belong to a church, we all have that spiritual part that connects with the Earth, and with nature, and it's not necessary to be religiously oriented.

I am so amazed, so often, to meet people in their seventies that are still void in that area. And it's been my observation, and it's only been my observation, I've not read it anywhere, that those people who deal poorly with death, or the impending death of a family member, or themselves, are those people who have not attended to their spiritual needs.

Respond to the statement, "God doesn't give us any more than we can handle."

J: I have a very hard time with that one. I was left a widow with three little kids at thirty-six. And people would say to me, "Oh, it's good you're so strong, because you wouldn't get any more than you can handle." God doesn't have anything to do with it! And I thought, if that's so, boy, then the only thing I would say to everybody is, "Be weak. Be as weak as you can and you won't get any problems." Why am I so lucky that I was strong? It's not how much we have to handle, or anything. I think we're dealt a hand of cards, and then we have to do the best we can with it.

People say, "Oh, how could you continue?" I didn't think I had any choice about continuing. There wasn't any question in my mind. It was up to me to do the best I could, to raise my children the best way I could. I couldn't be a mother and a father. I never tried to be. I could be mother, and that's all I could be. We don't have father, and that's sad, but that's the way it is. And let's see what we can do. Here we are, kids. Let's see what we can do.

How about you, Sharon? Do you think God doesn't give you any more than you can handle?

S: Well, as a caretaker, I used to think that that was trash! I thought that God and I just had an open, running disagreement about how much I could handle. And so, I never felt that we agreed, and that was okay, because my beliefs didn't seem to have any impact on what was dished out. So, I don't think that people respond well to that, particularly, even if they have a spiritual attitude, as I did.

I think they respond more to being asked about their feelings of hopelessness, and have you ever felt that way before, and they say, "Yes." And then we say, "When was that?"

And then we ask them, "Well, how did you overcome that? How did you get past that feeling of hopelessness?" And then they'll tell you.

You mean, you're calling on them to remember strengths they've shown in the past?

S: That's right, but without actually saying, "Well, you must have had *some* times when you utilized your strength." Instead, it's an exploratory process where they come up with the insights, and when they tell you how they overcame it you say, "Gosh, you have a lot of strength there. You have a lot of skills. Those are the things that are going to get you through *this* time, as well." And they go, "Hmm."

J: You talk to people about their coping skills and ask, "What has helped you the most in life? Is it working now?" And if it's not, then maybe we need to explore some other ways for you, or some new skills, that kind of thing. And if we do it together, it becomes a lot more palatable than if I tell you what those skills are.

S: And you talk about the other things they've had to overcome in life, and they talk about disabilities and unemployment and what they've gone through, and they see that they have more skills than they were aware of. And I think that works better. People don't want coined slogans. And it feels very much like a judgment, as well.

In other words, if you perceive yourself as not handling it well that it's a failure, in a way?

S: Well, most of us feel like a failure as caretakers, anyway. Anybody taking care of somebody that's demented never does anything right.

Feelings of failure are inherent in the situation?

S: That's right. And it's only until someone helps you to conjure up the successes you've had in the past in dealing with life and coping that you begin to see that you're not a complete failure, that you do have some strengths, and you do have some coping skills, which then really work on your self-esteem, to increase it.

Having to take over care for a person who's demented, and watching him get worse, and feeling like your own life is being sucked into it is, thankfully, really above and beyond what most of us are called upon to deal with in life. Do you think that handling all that requires a level of development that some people aren't capable of?

S: I think that's always true of everything in life. And I think it has to do with how people make choices. We can either be guided out of guilt, anger, resentment, reciprocity, or other unconscious motives, or we can make a decision that it's going to be tough, but this is the situation, and do it.

And again, it's not black and white, because there's a little bit of all that other stuff working in with the more altruistic kind of motives. And I think it gets to the point where you realistically have to look at the situation and say, "Are the ramifications too much for me at this time, keeping this person at home?"

People don't want platitudes when they're having to deal with coal mines. And that's life in general. You add taking care of someone who's demented, and it's a bit much. Anyway, we all handle our stressors differently.

Well, I'd just like to ask both of you now if there is anything you'd like to offer as a closing thought to people who may find themselves in this situation?

J: I think it's terribly important for people to get involved with some other people who are facing the same thing, even if it's not an organized group. People that you've run into at the nursing home, or wherever it is. At least get together with other people and talk, because it's very hard for anyone to understand what you're going through, and the only way they're going to understand is to respond to something similar.

I think it's terribly important not to feel alone, that there's a telephone number of somebody you can call, there's somebody out there who understands when you're just overwhelmed. I think the other thing we've mentioned is respite. I think it's terribly important, as far as it's at all possible, for someone to have some part of their existence be normal during this time.

If it means one afternoon a week, if it's one morning a week, if it's every other weekend, whatever it is that can be worked out. At least then you have those little islands in between that are calm and sane and you can do the normal things that other people do. Because, at least from what I see, people get so wrapped up in it that they've lost the whole idea of what living is about. It's so all-consuming that they lose any of the sanity or semblance of normalcy of life, and I think it's terribly important.

S: I think that it's really important to remember that the person who's demented is still a human being, and they need to be respected no matter whether they're incontinent or not, and no matter whether or not their behavior is bizarre, and we know that, if cognizant, they would be embarrassed by that behavior.

I wanted to say one thing about the quality of life as we judge it for our family members, and everybody has their own idea about quality of life. We might say that this person has no quality of life if they're demented, and I disagree with that. It took me a lot of years to really come up with some kind of belief about that, and for me it happened when my mother was in the nursing home and was interacting with the staff there, and was interacting with me, and it became apparent as she deteriorated, I thought she still had a quality of life.

I came up with the definition for myself, and it may not work for other people, that quality of life continued as long as someone interacted with their environment. And as my mother gradually became more fragile and less cognizant, and stopped interacting, I could see the real change. And at that point, where she was actually in a fetal position, then I was able to decide that the quality of life for her was nil, because she stopped interacting with her environment.

We need to be careful when we make judgments about quality of life for people, and I think we need to look at them through their eyes. My mother was much happier than I was. It's real important to think about that. On the outside, it may look as though your family member doesn't know you, doesn't know who you are, or what relation you are to them. And that often happens that they don't know.

But on a deeper level, the spiritual level, that person has to know, if you come in to the room and their eyes light up. They don't have the words, they don't have the names or relationship titles, but when that eye-to-eye communication is that intense, somewhere deep within them they know, at some level.

I feel like my mother knew that until probably a month before she died. So that was the real recognition. I don't think it's true that just because someone has Alzheimer's disease that they don't know, down deep, on a feeling level, on a spiritual level. That's all.

LOVE AND OBLIGATION

One time, about two weeks before he died, I had him at Safeway. He got out, and that's a bad parking lot. I was frantic because I couldn't find him, and I ran to the phone and called the police and said, "Listen, if anybody reports him, tell whoever's got him to hold on to him. He's not harmful. I'll call you back in fifteen minutes. In the meantime, I will look here, again." So I looked desperately again and I called the police back, and they'd got a call and they said, "He's at a real estate school at so-and-so address." I finally found the place. It took me fifteen minutes. The lady came out with him. We stood on the sidewalk and talked for a bit. She said, "He came in, just came in and sat down in my chair. I was sitting at my desk ready to cry because they had raised my rent two hundred dollars on this office. I have a daughter to support. I'm hardly making ends meet as it is. I don't know what I'm going to do for two hundred dollars. Instead of going out to eat, I was sitting here lamenting this situation. He came in and I looked at him, and he kind of babbled at me a little bit, and he was so sweet looking." She said, "I thought he was an angel sent from heaven. I really thought God sent him to me to show me that I wasn't that bad off."

—Irene

This book exists because eight women were willing to give me a painfully honest account of their experiences. The recognition of that fact has nudged me toward greater honesty, also. My original intention was to avoid any further mention of my grandmother, and just let it be assumed that she died a long time ago. Since my fondest hope for this book is that it may provide some of its readers with a renewed faith in their own ability to meet the future as it comes, it feels like something of an unkindness to reveal that today, sixteen years later, my grandmother is still alive. But that is the truth.

Now ninety-two years old and living in a nursing home, she needs help eating. She has forgotten everything. Sometimes it seems that she has simply forgotten to die. It must be said that I have never been her caregiver. We live at opposite ends of the country. My contribution to her care has consisted of a willingness to listen when my parents have felt the need to talk, and that is the extent of it. The last time I saw her, she recognized me as someone she loved, but she could not remember my name.

What is the glue that holds a relationship together when one person in it has changed so drastically? I only know that every time my phone rings after nine o'clock at night, and every time I hear my father's voice on the other end of the line, whatever the hour, my heart gives a small jump of awareness that I may be about to hear that the end has finally come for her. This has been true for the last five or six years. That little jump of awareness is what defines my bond with her now.

Looking at the stories of Aileen, Angie, Bonnie, Edith, Helen, Irene, Mabel, and Mary provides us with a glimpse of the steadily increasing demands and responsibilities placed on caregivers; escalating responsibilities encompassing everything from lawn maintenance to life-and-death treatment decisions. It is this steady progression that tutors people in the ways of dealing effectively with medical personnel, assorted bureaucrats, and, ultimately, nursing home staff. It is this cruel training program that teaches caregivers how to speak for their impaired relatives, and for themselves.

Becoming an effective caregiver means giving up assumptions about how the social world should work, giving up expectations of emotional reciprocity from the person we're taking care of, and reevaluating the most basic issues of what is subject to personal control in life, and what is not.

The women profiled here have so much to teach us if we will only look at their lives and try to appreciate what has been required of them. Examining the traits of those who have coped successfully with the demands of caregiving provides us with a description of people who are not merely buffeted by events—people who have a strong faith in their own judgment, a firm grasp of reality, a deep and abiding respect for humanity, and a value system that cherishes love and honors obligation.

There are legions of people in the caregiving role right now. To a great extent, they are invisible. We don't see them, we don't think about them, and most of us would prefer not to contemplate the fact that we may join their ranks someday. Yet, inevitably, more and more of us will find ourselves doing just that in the years to come, whether we are prepared for it or not. One of the striking things about the support group is that there are always new people to take the places of those who have moved on; always new people for whom the conditions of life have become so unbearable that they are finally willing to walk into a room full of strangers and say, "I cannot do this all alone anymore."

Working to improve things for those who will follow them has become part of the healing process for some of the widowed caregivers. Fund-raising for medical research, reaching out to newcomers, and campaigning for health care policies that recognize the needs of families are all examples of the work that veteran caregivers have done.

Aileen: If they do find it's hereditary, I have two sons and three granddaughters. Anything I can do may someday help them. I'll give new people my time, anytime. Because I feel I had no place to go in the very beginning. Fourteen years ago there was no place to go.

Mary's husband, Ira, has been gone for a long time. I asked her what it is that has kept her working so tirelessly on others' behalf all these years, when she could have pursued other possibilities for herself. Her answer reflects her sense of the interconnectedness of her life with the lives of other people. It reflects an attitude that lies at the heart of caring, and of giving:

Mary: I can't change the world. I'm not in a position to change the world. There are very few people who are. But I can change my immediate environment. Some people feel that an individual cannot make a difference. I *have* made a difference, on a small scale, and only in individual instances, but I am capable of making a difference. Therefore, I'm willing to work at it. We're not going to find the perfect solution, because there probably isn't any. There are no perfect solutions, and there are no permanent solutions, but that doesn't excuse me from trying to exert some influence on creating temporary, better conditions. The end product is always changing. I guess it's just basic philosophy. Just a feeling that I've asked for help . . . Sometimes I've received it, and sometimes I didn't. I remember what it felt like not to.

APPENDIX A

※

Financial and Legal Considerations

Anyone caring for a dementia patient has two major areas of legal and financial concern. The first is to secure the ability to act as the person's representative in matters pertaining to his finances and his health care. The second is to determine how nursing home care, if it is eventually required, will be paid for without devastating the family finances.

It is not my intention to offer legal advice. I'm not a lawyer, and even if I were, any such advice would almost surely be out of date quickly. Laws relating to such things as the fine points of Medicaid eligibility, for example, are constantly changing and vary from state to state. There are, however, a few things that people should be aware of if they find themselves in the position of needing to manage someone else's affairs.

Powers of Attorney, and Conservatorship

Anyone, dementia patient or not, could suddenly become incapacitated as a result of an accident, stroke, or illness. Therefore, it's a good idea for *everyone* to think about who they would choose to have managing their affairs in case anything like that were to happen. A **regular**, or **conventional, power of attorney** is a document in which a person, the **principal**, names the individual, called the **agent** or the **attorney-in-fact**, who is being given the authority to act on his behalf. A regular power of attorney can be limited to very specific things such as writing checks to pay household bills, or it can enable the attorney-in-fact to do almost anything at all in the area of financial management.

The difference between a regular power of attorney and a **durable power of attorney** is that the regular power of attorney is no longer valid if the principal becomes incompetent, and the durable power of attorney remains in effect in such an event.

The laws of different states vary in terms of what makes a power of attorney a legal document. Since different states have different forms for this, and different requirements about witnesses and/or notarization, it may be worth paying a legal fee for the assurance that this document has been executed properly.

While it is up to each family to find out what the proper procedure is in its own state, every state will require that the maker of the power of attorney be competent and lucid at the time he signs the document. This can mean that he signed it in a "lucid moment." What that means, exactly, can be subject to interpretation, as in Mabel and Roy's case:

Mabel: Roy had been friends with this attorney's mother and father. When I took the attorney over to the nursing home to get the power of attorney signed, whether Roy recognized him or not, I don't know. But Roy patted him on the back and shook his hand. We had the supervisor of nurses and the administrator there, and they felt that Roy understood what the attorney was telling him. Actually, the law reads that you do not have to be rational twenty-four hours a day three hundred and sixty-five days a year. You just have to be rational at the time. We had two witnesses who thought he was acting normally. They didn't know anything about Alzheimer's.

The important point here is to get the power of attorney from the patient while he is still competent enough to sign it. Serious problems can result if the dementia patient becomes unable to sign anything legally and the well spouse has no power of attorney. Edith had some tense moments at the time she sold her and Richard's home:

Edith: He would sign things for the real estate agent, especially if she asked him to. She'd come out and say, "Richard, we have a paper here for you to sign." And he'd sit down and write his name. He never said anything like, "You can't sell that." I went ahead and got stuff ready, and got rid of stuff I had to get rid of. When the day came to sign the final papers and everything, they called us in to the title company, to exchange the money and everything. He said, "Well, I'm not signing any papers." I thought, oh no, if I take him in there and he doesn't sign, what am I going to do then? So I called the agent and told her, "I just told Richard we have to go into town this afternoon, and he won't go, says he's not going, not signing anything." She said, "I'll come out with the papers." She came in and said, "Hello, Richard, how are you today? I've got some papers here for you to sign. Will you sign them for me?" He said, "What are they?" And he sat down and signed them.

A word of caution is in order here. Many people assume that a durable power of attorney will automatically be recognized at the patient's bank, but this is not usually the case. I called several bank managers to ask about this, and all of them said that their banks used their own form for allowing a customer to authorize another person to have access to his or her account. Both the account owner and the designated person are required to come in to the bank to sign this form, called a **power of attorney card**. Here again, it is never too early to think ahead.

The degree to which a well spouse will have leeway to manage property legally in the absence of a durable power of attorney will depend on whether that property is held jointly or separately, and whether or not the couple resides in a community property state. Whatever the situation, a durable power of attorney is always a good idea.

For more detailed information on durable powers of attorney, see *The Power of Attorney Book*, by Denis Clifford, published by Nolo Press of Berkeley, California. This book contains the forms from all fifty states for a conventional power of attorney, a durable power of attorney for finances, and a durable power of attorney for health care. This book is updated often, so make sure that you have the most recent edition.

* * *

If the patient becomes frankly incompetent without executing a durable power of attorney, it may become necessary for someone else to be named his **conservator**, also known as a **fiduciary** or **guardian**. There are two kinds of conservators: one is responsible for financial matters, and the other deals with personal decisions, such as where the conserved person will live. One person can hold both of these positions, or they can be held by two different people.

Only one of the women I talked to took this step:

Angie: It was too late. He was too far into his illness to legally sign anything. It was too late for him to do anything at that point.

Both types of conservators are appointed by the court after a legal proceeding in which the patient is declared incompetent to handle his own affairs. The conservator must make periodic reports to the court, and all accounts must balance to the penny. Becoming appointed someone's conservator is not a simple matter. It requires legal representation, and can be very expensive and time-consuming. Also, the emotional aspects of the procedure, and all that it implies, are very unpleasant, at best.

The role of a conservator is different from that of someone holding a durable power of attorney. *A conservator is legally bound to make decisions in terms of what is best for the patient and the patient only*. In practical terms, this means that, normally, the person's holdings must be preserved for his care. The most important consequence of this is that the transfer of assets that can be done to help qualify a person for Medicaid financing of his nursing home care may become impossible. What is legally "best" for the patient is not always the same as what is financially "best" for his family.

Health Care Decisions

Mabel: I have things written up, as far as I'm concerned. And my daughter says, "If we're stuffing the Christmas turkey and you cut yourself, and you look like you're bleeding to death, I back off?" And I said, "You've got it, kid." At this stage, after all, I'm pushing eighty, and I do not choose to suffer anymore. I don't like pain.

Mary: Say I had a mild stroke. As long as I could recover from it, yes, treat me. Give my body a chance to recover. But beyond that, no prolonged intervention in any way. Just let the body do what the body does. It has its own wisdom.

Many states do not recognize a general durable power of attorney when health care decisions are involved. A **durable power of attorney for health care** names the person who will be responsible for making health care decisions on a patient's behalf. In most states, a durable power of attorney for health care is what's known as a **springing power of attorney**, which means that it only goes into effect at the point where the patient becomes incompetent to make his own decisions.

Generally speaking, a patient's ability to make health care decisions lasts longer than his ability to make other kinds of decisions. For example, someone who is no longer capable of reconciling a bank statement may be very clear about the fact that he does not wish to be fed through a tube.

A **living will**, also known in some states as a **natural death act directive**, is a document in which a person spells out, specifically, which treatments he does not wish to receive if he is terminally ill or irreversibly comatose. It is important to have this document in place so that an attending physician can, without fear of liability claims against him or her, respect the patient's wish not to be kept alive by artificial means. The person signing the living will may or may not designate another person to see that his wishes are carried out.

Not all states recognize the living will, but most of them do. Even if your state does not, it still makes sense to have one in the event that a judge is ever called upon to render a decision in a particular case. Thankfully, such cases are very rare; still, no family should have to go through a long, litigious ordeal to enable someone to die peacefully.

There are other differences among the states regarding living wills, too. Some states will not allow the withholding of nutrition and water from any patient, regardless of that patient's stated wishes. States have different rules about who may witness the signing of the living will and, in most places, it is unlawful for immediate family members, the patient's doctor, or anyone who stands to benefit financially from the person's estate to sign a living will.

You can receive one free copy of the forms necessary for a living will declaration to be valid in your state, and your state's durable power of attorney for health care form, by requesting them from:

> Choice in Dying
> 200 Varick Street, 10th floor
> New York, New York 10014
> (212) 366-5540

You should receive the material in two to four weeks from the time of your request.

Choosing an Attorney

People with responsibility for a demented person have a number of different reasons for consulting an attorney, ranging from a quick consultation about a durable power of attorney form, to making changes in a will, to seeking representation in a complicated conservatorship proceeding.

It always makes good sense to hire an attorney whose practice is focused in the area where you need help. You wouldn't hire a patent lawyer if you were seeking a divorce, or a family law attorney to structure a corporate merger. Attorneys who specialize in "probate law," or in "estate planning," deal with the sorts of problems that concern families of dementia patients. Some attorneys are beginning to identify themselves as specialists in "elder law."

In every state, there should be available an agency providing free legal consultation for people who are aged sixty and older. This service is mandated by the Older Americans Act. There may not be an office in each county (some rural counties won't have one), but there should be a statewide agency which will come into an area to provide such services. These services are funded by the area agencies on aging, but not necessarily administered by them. See Appendix B for a state-by-state listing of state agencies on aging for more information.

If you're selecting an attorney, it is important not to choose one from the phone book; a referral from a satisfied client is much better. One of the best sources for information about competent, sensitive professional people of all kinds is your local Alzheimer's support group, or a similar organization. You will find information on how to get in touch with such an organization in Appendix B. Your doctor or banker may also be able to recommend someone. The National Academy of Elder Law Attorneys stresses the importance of getting a local referral from a local source.

No matter who makes the referral, or how enthusiastically he or she recommends the person, you will need to be prepared to ask a prospective attorney some important questions. Just because someone else was satisfied with the advice she received does not mean that you will be; her needs may have been very different from yours.

Lawyers should offer a free initial consultation. If the lawyer you have in mind does not, keep looking. The time to get your questions answered is during the consultation. Here are some of the things you need to know:

1. Does the lawyer specialize in cases of this type? One of the women in this book got a divorce on the advice of a lawyer who was not a specialist in the area where she needed help. This lawyer, though well-meaning, was not well versed in the constantly changing rules and regulations about Medicaid eligibility:

Bonnie: It was a stupid move. It made a hardship on me later on with Social Security. I lost a few benefits because of it. My lawyer wasn't up to date.

2. How long has the lawyer been working in this area? You are attempting to determine how much experience the attorney has. Another way of establishing this would be to ask how many cases of this particular type the lawyer has handled.

3. How are fees determined? Some attorneys will charge a set fee for certain services such as writing up a simple will. Others do all of their work at an hourly rate. Depending on the service requested, an attorney may use either of these billing methods. How are telephone questions billed? Does the attorney charge in increments of one-tenth of an hour, or one-quarter of an hour?

   Hourly rates for work on your case that is done by office staffers who are not attorneys should be less than those charged for the attorney's time. Ask about this, and let the attorney know that you will expect an itemized list of all charges on the billing.

4. Agreements between you and an attorney regarding fee schedules and the nature of the work should be in writing. Don't trust your own memory. If you enter into an oral agreement, you're still accountable for paying all fees. A written agreement helps you to know where you stand.

5. What, exactly, will the lawyer need to do to resolve the case? How long does the lawyer expect the work to take? An estimate of the time involved is very important. Angie's conservatorship case dragged on for many months, and she ended up paying a fee far in excess of what she should have. Angie may have been able to protect herself better if she'd initially tried to pin the attorney down about the time she could expect her case to take. It's a mistake to give a lawyer free rein to run up an enormous fee. You

can ask to be notified if your bill is going over a certain amount, or if the work is turning out to be more extensive than what has been agreed upon.

6. Will billing be done at the conclusion of the work? Once per month? Angie received a phone call from her attorney months into her still-unsettled conservatorship case in which the attorney asked her to pay up what she already owed him. The amount came as a nasty surprise, and the work still wasn't complete.

7. What is your overall impression of this person? You are looking for a competent attorney, not a "buddy." In fact, you can rest assured that the meter will be running as you're making small talk. However, if you are severely put off by the person, it may prove hard to work together. Trust your instincts.

Once you have chosen an attorney, always be honest with him or her. There is no sense in paying a lot of money for representation based on half-truths or incomplete information. Another aspect of honesty is speaking up and asking for more clarification if you don't understand something the first time it's explained.

Remember that the attorney, like a housepainter or auto mechanic, is someone that you hire. The attorney works for you. If you're unhappy with the attorney for any reason, you can collect your papers and go elsewhere as long as the bill is paid.

Planning for Nursing Home Care

Nursing home care is extremely expensive. Depending upon where you live, nursing homes, as of this writing, charge in the neighborhood of two to four thousand dollars per month, and those charges are edging upward all the time.

Few people, in the course of their daily lives, ever give much thought to how they would finance nursing home care if called upon to do so. This is not surprising: many of us assert strongly that we simply would never put anyone in a nursing home in the first place, or that we ourselves would "rather die" than go into one. Confronted with the grim reality, families are often caught unaware of the serious financial repercussions that result when nursing home placement becomes necessary.

Elder Care: Choosing and Financing Long Term Care, by Joseph L. Matthews, published by Nolo Press of Berkeley, California, is a guidebook explaining different long-term care options that are available, and it also explains how to choose a facility, taking some of the practical considerations involved in that decision into account.

The following discussion outlines some of the options available for paying for long term care.

Medicare

Many people have the mistaken belief that Medicare, the government's health insurance program for citizens over the age of sixty-five, will pay for long-term care in a nursing home. Medicare will *not* pay for any care that is deemed to be primarily *custodial* in nature; "custodial" being defined as care, such as bathing, dressing, and assistance with moving about, that can be given by someone who is not a trained medical professional.

Some nursing home care is paid for by Medicare, but only for a very limited time period, and only after discharge from an acute-care hospital. (Short-term therapy for a broken hip would be an example of this.) The rules about what Medicare does and doesn't cover are complex, and you can find out more about the eligibility requirements by contacting your Social Security office. The main point to remember is that if you are facing placing someone in a nursing home for indefinite long-term care, *Medicare is not going to be a viable source of financing* for this.

Veterans' Benefits

If the patient is a veteran, by all means check with the Veterans Administration or the local Veterans Service Office to see what benefits he is entitled to, if any. In the past, any veteran could receive care at a VA hospital, but as budget cutbacks have been enacted, means tests have been instituted. Beds in VA hospitals are in short supply, and they are allocated on a space-available basis, with priority given to those with service-connected disabilities.

As far as nursing home care is concerned, some coverage may be provided for a veteran discharged into a nursing home directly from a VA hospital. However, Arthur R. Pell, author of *Making the Most of Medicare*, states, ". . . unless you have some type of service-connected disability for which you have previously been treated by the VA, it is very unlikely that you will be able to obtain admission to a VA nursing facility."

Don't assume, because the patient is a veteran, that VA benefits will pay for long-term care. They probably won't.

Long-term Care Insurance

Angie: I don't want my daughter to go through what I went through, if I can help it, and that's why I'm doing as much as I can now. I'm going to the extent that I can to protect her from that. I have taken out long-term care insurance on myself. I've learned that lesson, which Hugo and I should have been aware of, but somehow or other we don't think of that when we're well, and I wouldn't have thought of it until Hugo got sick.

Long-term care insurance is just what it sounds like: it's coverage you buy specifically to pay for long-term care. *Long-term care insurance is not the same thing as "Medigap" insurance*, in spite of what many people may have been led to believe. **Medigap** policies, sometimes called **supplemental Medicare plans**, are only intended to plug some of the holes, or gaps, in covered Medicare benefits. Any coverage for long-term care under such a policy would only supplement what is already covered under Medicare's limits. As stated earlier, those limits are too restrictive to cover openended long-term care.

Long-term care insurance is available to address the need for long-term care coverage. At the present time, very few people have bought this coverage. Long-term care insurance is expensive, and becomes more so the older you are. Coverage that is extensive enough to be really effective costs more than what many people can comfortably afford. Also, policies are often so restrictive that they're of dubious value.

Whether long-term care insurance makes sense for you depends on an assessment of your own finances in relation to the going rate for nursing home care in your area. Find out what the price range is, and ask yourself how long you would be able to pay those costs out-of-pocket.

If you decide to investigate buying a long-term care insurance policy, you will need to shop carefully. You will need to read the policy itself, and not simply take the salesperson's word for everything. Here are some of the things to check for:

1. Does the policy cover both skilled nursing care and custodial care? Check to see what levels of care the policy covers. **Custodial** care can be done by nonmedical people, and **skilled** care refers to nursing or rehabilitation services given by specially trained health care personnel. A desirable policy will cover both levels of care. Some policies include home care, and others will include it at an additional cost.

2. What is the daily benefit payment? Currently, long-term care insurance policies pay a set rate per day of nursing home care, called the **daily benefit**. Here again, it's important to know what the daily cost of nursing home care would be for you. The amount stated in the policy may sound like a lot, but if it only pays a fraction of the cost, you are not getting a good deal. On the other hand, a policy may not pay the full amount, but may still pay enough to make it worthwhile for you.

Some policies allow for inflation, and some don't. Mabel and her husband bought long-term care insurance at a time when even fewer people had it than do today. Her case illustrates how inflation can undermine a daily benefit payment:

Mabel: At the time I bought it, the convalescent hospital costs at that time happened to be about nine hundred dollars a month. By the time he went in to the convalescent hospital about six years later, they'd gone up by two hundred and fifteen.

3. Check for excluded conditions. These will be listed under **waivers**, **exclusions**, or **limitations**. Some insurance policies exclude coverage for the very conditions, Parkinson's disease and Alzheimer's disease, that often lead to nursing home placement. The laws from state to state vary on this. In California, for example, it is illegal to exclude dementing illnesses such as Alzheimer's disease from long-term care coverage.

An individual applicant with a **preexisting condition**, meaning a condition that was already in evidence when the policy was purchased, cannot expect immediate coverage for that condition from a new insurance policy. Generally, there will be a specified time period before coverage for that specific condition will begin. Some states have laws about how long waiting periods may be. The office of your state insurance commissioner can inform you about this.

4. What is the **duration of coverage**? This means the amount of time that the benefits will last. Some policies state this in terms of a cap on the total dollar amount that will be paid out. A desirable policy should provide, at a minimum, two years of coverage, and preferably four.

5. Is there a **prior hospitalization** requirement? It is not uncommon for a long-term care policy to require that a patient enter a nursing home or a custodial care setting directly from an acute care hospital. It is better to avoid a policy that requires this.

6. Is the policy renewable? *You definitely do not want one that is* **optionally renewable**, meaning that it is renewable at the company's option. You may have to wade deeply into the fine print to determine this. The term **conditionally renewable** means that the company cannot cancel you unless they cut all policyholders from the same geographical area. **A guaranteed renewable** policy is the best choice.

7. Find out when the policy begins paying. Not all policies pay from the first day of nursing home or custodial care. The period of time that must elapse before benefits begin is called the **elimination period**, or **benefit waiting period**. Generally, the longer the elimination period, the lower the premium. A policy that doesn't pay anything until the patient has been in a facility for a month will cost less than one that pays from the first day.

Paying Privately

Angie: I didn't know whether he was going to go on for one more day, or ten more years. That was the scary part about it. It's just a very frightening situation to know that you're taking care of him, spending everything you have. Then who's going to take care of *you*?

Bonnie: I tried to get him on Medicaid, but in order to spend down our assets, it terrified me, and I thought, there must be a better way that I can do this. There must be a way that I can borrow from the IRAs, and borrow from insurance, and do that. Which is what I did do. I paid for the whole thing. So I went through a lot, and borrowed things I'm still paying back. Had he lived longer, I don't know what would have happened. Because it wasn't really that long that he was in there. He was in there nine months.

Mabel: Roy and I were one of the few families that could afford Alzheimer's. There's very few that can.

With nursing home costs approaching three to four thousand dollars a month in some places, it's clear that for the vast majority of families, paying privately for nursing home care for an indefinite period of time would not be a viable option. A hundred thousand dollar nest egg could be eaten up in less than three years.

In spite of the hardship, many people are adverse to applying for public aid, and hold on for as long as they can.

> *Aileen:* To think that I would have to go on Medicaid, that was humiliating. Because that was my ethnic upbringing. You paid your way, and if you didn't have the money, you didn't buy it.

The only way a family can plan for financing indefinite long-term care privately is to plan on having a very large amount of money.

Medicaid

Medical benefits for low-income people are jointly funded by the federal and state governments under a program known as **Medicaid** (called **Medi-Cal** in California). The Medicaid program is the largest single payment source for nursing home care. Unlike Medicare, it does pay for custodial care in a skilled nursing facility or intermediate care facility (that is, one that offers medical care, but not on a twenty-four hour basis), but not in a residential care facility, otherwise known as a board-and-care home.

Medicaid is available to those individuals who are classified as **categorically needy**; that is, people who are already receiving Supplemental Security Income (SSI), or who are receiving Aid to Families with Dependent Children (AFDC). Some states, including California, recognize a **medically needy** classification. This label applies to people who are deemed by their state to have sufficient income to support themselves, but not enough to pay their high medical bills.

Medicaid eligibility is a complex subject, and it is far beyond the scope of this book to attempt a thorough coverage of it. However, it can be stated with confidence that if there is any possibility at all that you will need to place someone in a nursing home at any time in the future, it is imperative that you inform yourself about this subject as soon as you possibly can.

You can get basic information and an application from the welfare office, the social service office, or the human resources office (whatever it happens to be called where you live). Although Social Security has nothing to do with Medicaid, the people at the Social Security office will be able to refer you to the correct place for getting an application in your area. Your regional area agency (or council) on aging will also have information for you. For more specific help in planning ahead, contact a specialist in elder law, a legal services attorney, or a long-term care ombudsman for advice on a particular case.

In order to qualify for Medicaid, a person's assets and income are assessed to see if they are at or below the guidelines for eligibility. Generally speaking, the home of a nursing home resident is protected as long as the spouse is living in it. The house, a car, household furnishings, and a burial plot are **exempt assets** in most states, which means that they are not counted in the asset-limitation test for Medicaid eligibility.

No source of income, such as pensions or Social Security, is exempt from the income-limitation test.

Since the states administer the program, regulations about eligibility can vary. Some examples of things that are different from state to state include:

- the amount of assets the well spouse can keep
- the amount of monthly income the well spouse can keep
- the monthly personal allowance for the institutionalized person
- what exempt assets consist of

The current rules are intended to prevent the noninstitutionalized spouse, known as the **community spouse**, from becoming impoverished paying for nursing home care, but even so, people often must "spend down" their assets in order to qualify the institutionalized spouse for Medicaid.

No matter where you live, your financial affairs for a certain time period prior to the date of application will be reviewed. Currently, that time period is thirty months. This means that you cannot give everything away and be eligible for Medicaid the next day, and this is why it's so important to arm yourself with information before nursing home placement is imminent. **Asset transfers** that are executed well and timed properly can make the difference between getting the patient qualified for Medicaid when he needs it, and having him rejected.

Some people have heard that it is wise to get a divorce in order to preserve more assets for the community spouse. However, there are relatively few cases where this is a good idea, and those involve people who can probably afford to pay their own bills in the first place. Even in those cases where divorce makes financial sense, the emotional trauma can be considerable, and must be factored in to a determination of whether or not a divorce is really a desirable option.

> **Bonnie:** I wasn't shocked that people did this, but I also was a little bit . . . "Well, should I be doing this or shouldn't I be doing this?" I was careful of who I told, because I thought that people would be taken aback and think, "Why? What for? Will she really abandon him?" I didn't broadcast it around, I'll tell you that.

The system is not perfect. The experience of applying for Medicaid can be exasperating. In fact, Bonnie became so disenchanted with the whole process that she decided to keep paying the nursing home bills herself for as long as she could:

> **Bonnie:** This one young woman at Medicaid said, "Well, we have to assume that if he gets well, he'll want to come home and drive a car. And he'll want nice clothes. And if he likes to fish, he'll want to go fishing. So you can buy those things. Bring the receipts, so we can add them and spend down." I said, "The man is dying!"
> I suppose if he had lived much longer I probably would have gone back, and filled out those forms, and gone through that horrible experience again. I'd like to go shake up all those people at the Medicaid building. You know how the Three Stooges had

all those faces in a row where they went pop-pop-pop-pop-pop? Line 'em all up and go *whap*!

It is never too early to begin assembling all of your important records. This means *everything*. If you eventually need to apply for Medicaid for someone, you will be asked to produce verification of all assets, income, and expenses that you are claiming. You will need to prove your claim by producing things like stock certificates and bonds, if you have them. If you have trusts, or deeds of trust, you will have to produce the actual documents. You will need to bring any medical or life insurance policies, your Medicare card, social security card, bank statements, and a copy of your tax return. Start keeping careful records of your expenses, and hold on to all your receipts.

There is no benefit to be gained by approaching the application process with anything less than total honesty. **Income Eligibility Verification** systems, or IEVs, are computer systems that the states use to ferret out unreported assets by checking, for example, interest paid on bank accounts and income reported to the Social Security Administration.

Federal regulations mandate that any Medicaid application be acted upon within forty-five days, but efforts are made to expedite the procedure when nursing home care is involved. People who are denied benefits have the right to appeal that decision.

Planning for long-term care is thinking the unthinkable. Most of us hate to contemplate the idea of placing someone we love in a nursing home. We're convinced that it's just something we would never do. Thinking about nursing home placement in terms of how it will be paid for feels even worse; somehow it feels so terribly inappropriate to be worrying about money when someone we love is slipping away from us.

Unfortunately, the financial aspects of dementing illnesses must be faced and dealt with squarely. Failure to do so can have a ruinous impact on the rest of the well spouse's life.

There is not much that can be done to ease the many losses a dementia patient's wife experiences, but with some attention, good counsel, and planning, she can take steps to see that she will not be devastated in at least this one area.

Aileen: We saved our money for our golden years, which got tarnished. We were not that frugal, but we saved. And all that money went to the nursing home. When the young people say, "I bought this," I think, "Go ahead and enjoy it. You can always remember when you had it." My idea of money is different now. It really is. I really have a different outlook on money. Take time to do what you want to do. My neighbors, ever since Louie got sick, and they saw what happened, they go on a cruise every year.

APPENDIX B

Organizations and Agencies

Alzheimer's Disease

Alzheimer's Association
919 North Michigan Avenue
Chicago, Illinois 60601   (312) 335-8700
(formerly the Alzheimer's Disease and Related Disorders Association)

Sends informational booklets, promotes and funds research. *Alzheimer's Association Newsletter* is published quarterly.

Provides an information and referral service to link families with local chapters. Call 1-800-272-3900.

Alzheimer's Disease Education and Referral Center
P.O. Box 8250
Silver Spring, Maryland 20907-8250   (301) 495-3311

Established by the National Institute on Aging (NIA); distributes information to health professionals, patients, families, and the general public. Provides information on support groups. Issues ten publications on Alzheimer's disease and will provide one free copy of each one. NIA funds twenty Alzheimer's Centers at major medical institutions.

American Health Assistance Foundation
15825 Shady Grove Road, Suite 140
Rockville, Maryland 20850   1-800-437-2423

Funds scientific research on certain age-related and degenerative diseases, including Alzheimer's disease. Offers eleven publications on Alzheimer's disease.

Administers the Alzheimer's Family Relief Program, giving grants of up to five hundred dollars to help defray the costs of short-term

nursing care, respite care, medical supplies, personal hygiene supplies, and other costs directly related to the patient's condition. Financial and medical need must be documented. Call 1-800-227-7998 for
an application.

Parkinson's Disease

The American Parkinson Disease Association, Inc.
60 Bay Street
Staten Island, New York 10301   1-800-223-2732

Gives research fellowships and grants. Provides free publications on
coping with Parkinson's disease. Some Spanish titles available. Publishes a quarterly newsletter, *The American Parkinson Disease Association*, which reports on medical developments and topics of general
interest to Parkinsonians.

National Parkinson Foundation
1501 N.W. 9th Avenue
Bob Hope Rd.
Miami, Florida 33136   1-800-327-4545   in Florida 1-800-433-7022

A research center and clinic affiliated with the University of Miami
School of Medicine.
Gives information on support groups. Sends several free publications,
including a detailed handbook that will soon be available in Spanish.
Publishes a quarterly scientific newsletter called the *Parkinson Report*.

The Parkinson's Disease Foundation (PDF)
William Black Medical Research Building
Columbia Presbyterian Medical Center
650 West 168th Street
New York, New York 10032
1-800-457-6676   (212) 923-4700

Will send a list of support groups organized by zip code, and three
free publications, including one devoted to exercise. Promotes medical
research, and publishes a quarterly newsletter devoted to research, new
books, support groups, and general advice on coping with Parkinson's.

Parkinson's Educational Program
3900 Birch Street #105
Newport Beach, California 92660   (714) 250-2975   1-800-344-7872

Catalog of booklets, books, and videos on topics such as nutrition,
caregiving, and chronic-illness issues. Free materials on how to start

a support group. Newsletter, *PEP Exchange*, covers new developments in research, drugs, etc.

Stroke

National Stroke Association
300 East Hampden Avenue, Suite 240
Englewood, Colorado 80110-2654 1-800-STROKES (303) 762-9922

Local support group referrals, information, videos, and quarterly newsletter, *Be Stroke Smart*.

American Heart Association
1-800-242-8721
(or contact your local Heart Association office)

Callers will be connected automatically with local AHA chapters, which can refer them to local groups and educational services for stroke patients.

Other Diseases

National Organization for Rare Disorders
P.O. Box 8923
New Fairfield, Connecticut 06812-1783   1-800-999-NORD
(203) 746-6518

Provides information on rare disorders, publishes a newsletter, *Orphan Disease Update*, and lobbies for orphan drug research and national health insurance.

Home Care

Foundation for Hospice and Homecare
519 C Street NE
Washington, D.C. 20002-5809   (202) 547-6586

Primarily a professional organization, the foundation does offer a list of publications, videotapes, and training manuals on subjects of interest to caregivers in many different situations. Booklet, ''How to Select a Home Care Agency,'' gives addresses of state home health associations.

Nursing Home Issues

California Advocates for Nursing Home Reform
1610 Bush St.
San Francisco, California 94109 (415) 474-5171

Works for nursing home reform. Will send a booklet, "Long Term Care Insurance: A Consumer's Checklist."

Concerned Relatives of Nursing Home Patients
P.O. Box 18820
Cleveland, Ohio 44118-0820   (216) 321-0403

Organization works to improve care in nursing homes. Publishes an informational newsletter called *Insight*. Good booklet on choosing a nursing home.

General Information

American Association of Retired Persons
Program Resources
601 E St. NW
Washington, D.C. 20049   (202) 434-6090

Write for AARP's free sixty-four-page catalog of publications and audiovisual materials on a wide range of subjects including legal rights for elders, financial and retirement planning, Alzheimer's disease, home care, choosing a nursing home, making long-term care decisions, funeral planning, grief, and widowhood. Allow four to six weeks for delivery.

Children of Aging Parents
Woodbourne Office Campus   Suite 302A
1609 Woodbourne Rd.
Levittown, Pennsylvania 19057   (215) 945-6900

Serves as a national clearinghouse on issues concerning caregivers. Has publications list on topics such as caregiving, guilt, and evaluating nursing homes. Offers catalogs of home care equipment.

Health Care Financing Administration
HCFA Inquiries
6325 Security Blvd.
Baltimore, Maryland   1-800-638-6833
in Maryland: 1-800-492-6603

Answers questions and fields complaints about Medicare coverage or payment policies.

Older Women's League
National Office
666 Eleventh Street NW
Suite 700
Washington, D.C. 20001   (202) 783-6686

Will send a publications list of approximately fifty titles on topics of particular interest to older women, including caregiving, health care financing, nursing home reform, adult day care, and death and dying. Publishes position papers, and has offered congressional testimony on the problems of caregivers and other health-related issues. Has local chapters.

Choice in Dying
200 Varick Street 10th floor
New York, New York 10014   (215) 366-5540

Sends one free copy, in state-specific language, of both the living will form and a durable power of attorney for health care form. Also sends one copy of a living will form in general language not specific to a particular state.

State Agencies on Aging

Agencies on aging can refer seniors, and help them gain access, to a variety of services such as adult day care, financial management programs, legal advocacy, senior housing information, and the long-term care ombudsman. The state agencies can tell you where to go to find services locally.

Alabama
Commission on Aging
Second Floor
136 Catoma St.
Montgomery, Alabama 36130
(205) 261-5743

Alaska
Older Alaskans Commission
Department of Administration
Pouch C—Mail Station 0209
Juneau, Alaska 99811-0209
(907) 465-3250

Arizona
Aging and Adult Administration

Department of Economic
Security
1400 West Washington Street
Phoenix, Arizona 85007
(602) 255-4446
Information and referral 1-800-352-3792 in Phoenix: (602) 263-8856

Arkansas
Division of Aging and Adult
Services
Arkansas Department of Human
Services
1417 Donaghey Plaza South
7th and Main Streets

Little Rock, Arkansas 72201
(501) 682-2441

California
Department of Aging
1600 K Street
Sacramento, California 95814
(916) 322-5290
long-term care ombudsman hot
line 1-800-231-4024

Colorado
Aging and Adult Service
Department of Social Services
1575 Sherman Street, 10th Floor
Denver, Colorado 80203-1714
(303) 866-5931

Connecticut
Department on Aging
175 Main Street
Hartford, Connecticut 06106
(203) 566-3238
Information and referral 1-800-443-9946

Delaware
Division on Aging
Department of Health and Social
Services
1901 North DuPont Highway
New Castle, Delaware 19720
(302) 421-6791
Information and referral 1-800-223-9074

District of Columbia
Office on Aging
1424 K Street NW
2nd Floor
Washington, D.C. 20005
(202) 724-5626

Florida
Program Office of Aging and
Adult Services

Department of Health and
Rehabilitative Services
1317 Winewood Blvd.
Tallahassee, Florida 32301
(904) 488-8922
Information and referral 1-800-342-0825

Georgia
Office of Aging
878 Peachtree Street, NE
Room 632
Atlanta, Georgia 30309
(404) 894-5333

Hawaii
Executive Office on Aging
Office of the Governor
335 Merchant St.
Room 241
Honolulu, Hawaii 96813
(808) 548-2593

Idaho
Office on Aging
Room 114, Statehouse
Boise, Idaho 83720
(208) 334-3833
Information and referral (208)
378-0111

Illinois
Department on Aging
421 East Capitol Avenue
Springfield, Illinois 62701
(217) 785-2870
Information and referral 1-800-252-8966
Nursing home hot line 1-800-252-4343

Indiana
Division of Aging Services
Department of Human Services
251 North Illinois Street
P.O.Box 7083

Indianapolis, Indiana 46207-7083
(317) 232-7020
Information and referral 1-800-622-4972

Iowa
Department of Elder Affairs
Suite 236, Jewett Building
914 Grand Avenue
Des Moines, Iowa 50319
(515) 281-5187
Information and referral 1-800-532-3213

Kansas
Department on Aging
Docking State Office Building, 122-S
915 S.W. Harrison
Topeka, Kansas 66612-1500
(913) 296-4986
Information and referral 1-800-432-3535

Kentucky
Division of Aging Services
Cabinet for Human Resources
CHR Building—6th West
275 East Main Street
Frankfort, Kentucky 40621
(502) 564-6930
Long-term care ombudsman hot line 1-800-372-2991

Louisiana
Office of Elderly Affairs
P.O. Box 80374
Baton Rouge, Louisiana 70898
(504) 925-1700

Maine
Bureau of Maine's Elderly
Department of Human Services
State House, Station #11
Augusta, Maine 04333

(207) 289-2561

Maryland
Office on Aging
State Office Building
301 West Preston Street, Room 1004
Baltimore, Maryland 21201
(301) 225-1100
Information and referral 1-800-AGE-DIAL

Massachusetts
Executive Office of Elder Affairs
38 Chauncy Street
Boston, Massachusetts 02111
(617) 727-7750
Information and referral 1-800-882-2003

Michigan
Office of Services to the Aging
P.O. Box 30026
Lansing, Michigan 48909
(517) 373-8230

Minnesota
Board on Aging
4th Floor, Human Services Building
444 Lafayette Road
St. Paul, Minnesota 55155-3843
(612) 296-2770
Information and referral 1-800-652-9747

Mississippi
Council on Aging
301 West Pearl Street
Jackson, Mississippi 39203-3092
(601) 949-2070
Governor's service line 1-800-222-7622

Missouri
Division on Aging
Department of Social Services
P.O. Box 1337
2701 West Main Street
Jefferson City, Missouri 65102
(314) 751-3082
Information and referral 1-800-
235-5503
Elder abuse and neglect hot line
1-800-392-0210

Montana
Department of Family Services
48 North Last Chance Gulch
P.O. Box 8005
Helena, Montana 59604
(406) 444-5900
Information and referral 1-800-
332-2272

Nebraska
Department on Aging
P.O. Box 95044
301 Centennial Mall South
Lincoln, Nebraska 68509
(402) 471-2306

Nevada
Division for Aging Services
Department of Human
Resources
340 North 11th Street
Las Vegas, Nevada 89101
(702) 486-3545

New Hampshire
Division of Elderly and Adult
Services
6 Hazen Drive
Concord, New Hampshire
03301-6501
(603) 271-4680
Information and referral 1-800-
852-3345

New Jersey
Division on Aging
Department of Community
Affairs
CN807
South Broad and Front Streets
Trenton, New Jersey 08625-0807
(609) 292-4833
Information and referral 1-800-
792-8820

New Mexico
State Agency on Aging
224 East Palace Avenue, Fourth
Floor
La Villa Rivera Building
Santa Fe, New Mexico 87501
(505) 827-7640
Information and referral 1-800-
432-2080

New York
Office for the Aging
New York State Plaza
Agency Building #2
Albany, New York 12223
(518) 474-4425
Information and referral 1-800-
342-9871

North Carolina
Division of Aging
Kirby Building
1985 Umstead Drive
Raleigh, North Carolina 27603
(919) 733-3983
Information and referral 1-800-
662-7030

North Dakota
Aging Services
Department of Human Services
State Capitol Building
Bismarck, North Dakota 58505
(701) 224-2577

Information and referral 1-800-472-2622

Ohio
Department of Aging
50 West Broad Street
Columbus, Ohio 43266-0501
(614) 466-5500
Nursing home hot line 1-800-282-1206

Oklahoma
Aging Services Division
Department of Human Services
P.O. Box 25352
Oklahoma City, Oklahoma
73125
(405) 521-2281
Elder abuse hot line 1-800-522-3511

Oregon
Senior Services Division
313 Public Services Building
Salem, Oregon 97310
(503) 378-4728

Pennsylvania
Department of Aging
231 State Street
Harrisburg, Pennsylvania 17101-1195
(717) 783-1550
Alzheimer's hot line 1-800-225-7223

Rhode Island
Department of Elderly Affairs
79 Washington Street
Providence, Rhode Island 02903
(401) 277-2858
Information and referral 1-800-752-8088

South Carolina
Commission on Aging

Suite B-500
400 Arbor Lake Drive
Columbia, South Carolina
29223
(803) 735-0210

South Dakota
Office of Adult Services and
Aging
700 North Illinois Street
Kneip Building
Pierre, South Dakota 57501
(605) 773-3656
Information and referral (605)
975-2222

Tennessee
Commission on Aging
Suite 201
706 Church Street
Nashville, Tennessee 37219-5573
(615) 741-2056

Texas
Department on Aging
P.O. Box 12786 Capitol Station
1949 IH 35, South
Austin, Texas 78741-3702
(512) 444-2727
Information and referral 1-800-252-9240

Utah
Division of Aging and Adult
Services
Department of Social Services
120 North—200 West
Box 45500
Salt Lake City, Utah 84145-0500
(801) 538-3910

Vermont
Office on Aging
103 South Main Street

Waterbury, Vermont 05676
(802) 241-2400
Hot line for the elderly 1-800-642-5119

Virginia
Department for the Aging
700 Centre, 10th Floor
700 East Franklin Street
Richmond, Virginia 23219-2327
(804) 225-2271
Information and referral 1-800-55AGING
Nursing home complaints 1-800-552-3402

Washington
Aging and Adult Services Administration
Department of Social and Health Services
OB-44A
Olympia, Washington 98504
(206) 586-3768
Information and referral 1-800-422-3263
Nursing home complaints 1-800-562-6078

West Virginia
Commission on Aging
Holly Grove, State Capitol
Charleston, West Virginia 25305
(304) 348-3317
Information and referral 1-800-642-3671

Wisconsin
Bureau of Aging
Division of Community Services
One West Wilson Street, Room 480
Madison, Wisconsin 53702
(608) 266-2536
Long-term care ombudsman 1-800-242-1060

Wyoming
Commission on Aging
Hathaway Building, Room 139
Cheyenne, Wyoming 82002-0710
(307) 777-7986
Information and referral 1-800-442-2766

APPENDIX C

✿

Recommended Readings

There are a number of excellent books available on all aspects of coping with dementing, care-intensive illnesses, and it is worthwhile for caregivers to build a personal library of books that can be referred to over and over. The following books are ones that may be particularly helpful. Anyone exploring this subject is sure to find additional titles that will also prove to be of help.

Aronson, Miriam K., ed. *Understanding Alzheimer's Disease*. New York: Charles Scribner's Sons, 1988.

Published in conjunction with the Alzheimer's Disease and Related Disorders Association, this book is a compilation of chapters by different authors who address a wide range of topics, including a discussion of the disease itself, the role of a support group, psychological coping, legal and financial matters, and the outlook for future research directions and treatment possibilities.

Cohen, Donna, and Carl Eisdorfer. *The Loss of Self*. New York: W.W. Norton & Company, Inc., 1986.

An excellent guide to practical matters involved in caring for a dementia patient, this book is noteworthy for its treatment of the emotional issues surrounding the caregiving situation. The emotional connections that can exist between a demented person and the person taking care of him or her and the meaning a caregiver can derive from that are dealt with particularly sensitively.

"A key to coping successfully is to recognize that the caregiver role is impossible and then to try to do the best you can. Accepting the harsh reality is the first step."

Corbin, Juliet M., and Anselm Strauss. *Unending Work and Care: Managing Chronic Illness at Home*. San Francisco: Jossey Bass Publishers, 1988.

This book deals with the way a person's self-definition is altered by illness, and how that illness "renders life discontinuous." The book deals with the process of coming to terms with illness, delving deeply into issues involving caregivers, and the strains placed upon relationships when one partner becomes ill.

"Calling attention to the problems and how people react to them is not enough. If we want to ease the plight of spouses, indeed of any caretaker, caught up in the problems of living with and caring for a chronically ill person, we need a much deeper, more explicit, and systematic understanding of what happens in such situations."

Kleinman, Arthur. *The Illness Narratives: Suffering, Healing, and the Human Condition*. New York: Basic Books, Inc., 1986.

While not specifically concerned with dementing illnesses, this book explores the ways in which people accommodate themselves to the reality of serious illness in their lives, how their social worlds are disrupted by illness, and how they make sense of the experience.

"Change, caprice, and chaos, experienced in the body, challenge what order we are led to believe—need to believe—exists. Disability and death force us to reconsider our lives and our world. The possibility of human transformation, immanent or transcendent, sometimes begins with this disconcerting vision."

Mace, Nancy L., and Peter V. Rabins. *The 36-Hour Day*. Revised edition. New York: Warner Books, 1992.

Perhaps the best known and most widely read of all the guides for families of patients with dementing illnesses, this book offers a wealth of practical advice, based upon the idea that it is important both to simplify the tasks of daily life, and to view the behavior of patients in terms of their illness. The concept of developing empathy for the patient is stressed, along with the necessity of assessing his or her abilities realistically. The importance of respite for caregivers is also emphasized.

Powell, Lenore S., and Katie Courtice. *Alzheimer's Disease: A Guide for Families*. Reading, Massachusetts: Addison-Wesley Publishing Company, 1983.

A practical guide with good general advice about patient care, and topics like structuring the environment and choosing a nursing home. This book makes good use of illustrative vignettes, and deals sensitively with emotional issues of importance to caregivers, such as denial, anger, guilt, and depression. The importance of self care for caregivers is also stressed.

Safford, Florence. *Caring for the Mentally Impaired Elderly: A Family Guide*. New York: Henry Holt and Company, 1986.

This book gives good all-around coverage to many of the practical problems involved in dealing with a demented person. Of particular note are sections on the paradoxical effects of medications, and guidelines for "coping with the institution" when a relative is in a nursing home.

BIBLIOGRAPHY

Aronson, M. K., and R. Lipkowitz. "Senile Dementia, Alzheimer's Type: The Family and the Health Care Delivery System." *Journal of the American Geriatrics Society* 29 (1981): 568–571.

Aronson, M. K., J. Levin, and R. Lipkowitz. "A Community-Based Family/Patient Group Program for Alzheimer's Disease." *The Gerontologist* 24 (1984): 339–342.

Aronson, M. K., ed. *Understanding Alzheimer's Disease.* New York: Charles Scribner's Sons, 1988.

Bandura, A. "Self-Efficacy Mechanism in Human Agency." *American Psychologist* 37 (1982): 122–147.

Barnes, R. F., M. A. Raskind, M. Scott, and C. Murphy. "Problems of Families Caring for Alzheimer Patients: Use of a Support Group." *Journal of the American Geriatrics Society* 29 (1981): 80–85.

Bass, D. M., and L. S. Noelker. "The Influence of Family Caregivers on Elder's Use of In-Home Services: An Expanded Conceptual Framework." *Journal of Health and Social Behavior* 28 (1987): 184–196.

Bass, D. M. and K. Bowman. "The Transition from Caregiving to Bereavement: The Relationship of Care-Related Strain and Adjustment to Death." *The Gerontologist* 30 (1990): 35–42.

Boller, F. "Mental Status of Patients With Parkinson Disease." *Journal of Clinical Neuropsychology* 2 (1980): 157–172.

Brody, E. M., M. P. Lawton, and B. Liebowitz. "Senile Dementia: Public Policy and Adequate Institutional Care." *American Journal of Public Health* 74 (1984): 1381–1383.

Brody, E. M. "Parent Care as a Normative Family Stress." *The Gerontologist* 25 (1985): 19–29.

Budish, A. D. *Avoiding the Medicaid Trap.* New York: Henry Holt and Company, 1987.

Butler, R. N., and M. I. Lewis. *Aging and Mental Health.* St. Louis: The C. V. Mosby Company, 1982.

Calkins, K. "Shouldering a Burden." *Omega* 3 (1972): 23–36.

Cantor, M. H. "Strain Among Caregivers: A Study of Experience in the United States." *The Gerontologist* 23 (1983): 597–604.

Carstensen, L. L., and B. A. Edelstein, eds. *Handbook of Clinical Gerontology*. New York: Pergamon Press, 1987.

Cath, S. H. "The Geriatric Patient and His Family: The Institutionalization of a Parent—A Nadir of Life." *Journal of Geriatric Psychiatry* 5 (1972): 25–46.

Cavanaugh, J. C., N. J. Dunn, D. Mowery, C. Feller, G. Niederehe, E. Fruge, and D. Volpendesta. "Problem-Solving Strategies in Dementia Patient-Caregiver Dyads." *The Gerontologist* 29 (1989): 156–158.

Chenoweth, B., and B. Spencer. "Dementia: The Experience of Family Caregivers." *The Gerontologist* 26 (1986): 267–272.

Cohen, D., and C. Eisdorfer. *The Loss of Self*. New York: W. W. Norton, 1986.

Colerick, E. J., and L. K. George. "Predictors of Institutionalization Among Caregivers of Patients with Alzheimer's Disease." *Journal of the American Gerontological Society* 34 (1986): 493–498.

Corbin, J. M., and A. Strauss. *Unending Work and Care: Managing Chronic Illness at Home*. San Francisco: Jossey-Bass Publishers, 1988.

Coyne, A. C. "Information and Referral Service Usage Among Caregivers for Dementia Patients." *The Gerontologist* 31 (1991): 384–388.

Crossman, L., C. London, and C. Barry. "Older Women Caring for Disabled Spouses: A Model for Supportive Services." *The Gerontologist* 21 (1981): 464–470.

Deimling, G. T., and S. W. Poulshock. "The Transition from Family In-Home Care to Institutional Care." *Research on Aging* 7 (1985): 563–576.

Deimling, G. T., and D. M. Bass. "Symptoms of Mental Impairment Among Elderly Adults and Their Effects on Family Caregivers." *Journal of Gerontology* 41 (1986): 778–784.

Doty, P. "Family Care of the Elderly: The Role of Public Policy." *The Milbank Quarterly* 64 (1986): 34–75.

Dura, J. R., E. Haywood-Niler, and J. K. Kiecolt-Glaser. "Spousal Caregivers of Persons with Alzheimer's and Parkinson's Disease Dementia: A Preliminary Comparison." *The Gerontologist* 30 (1990): 332–336.

Fengler, A. P., and N. Goodrich. "Wives of Elderly Disabled Men: The Hidden Patients." *The Gerontologist* 19 (1979): 175–183.

Fitting, M., P. Rabins, M. J. Lucas, and J. Eastham. "Caregivers for Dementia Patients: A Comparison of Husbands and Wives." *The Gerontologist* 26 (1986): 248–252.

George, L. K., and L. P. Gwyther. "Caregiver Well-Being: A Multidimensional Examination of Family Caregivers of Demented Adults." *The Gerontologist* 26 (1986): 253–259.

Getzel, G. S. "Helping Elderly Couples in Crisis." *Social Casework: The Journal of Contemporary Social Work* 63 (1982): 515–521.

Gubrium, J. F. "Family Responsibility and Caregiving in the Qualitative Analysis of the Alzheimer's Disease Experience." *Journal of Marriage and the Family* 50 (1988): 197–207.

Gwyther, L. P., and M. A. Matteson. "Care for the Caregivers." *Journal of Gerontological Nursing* 9 (1983): 92–116.

Gwyther, L. P., and L. K. George. "Caregivers for Dementia Patients: Complex Determinants of Well-Being and Burden." *The Gerontologist* 26 (1986): 245–247.

Gwyther, L. P. "Letting Go: Separation-Individuation in a Wife of an Alzheimer's Patient." *The Gerontologist* 30 (1990): 698–702.

Haley, W. E. "A Family-Behavioral Approach to the Treatment of the Cognitively Impaired Elderly." *The Gerontologist* 23 (1983): 18–20.

Haley, W. E., S. L. Brown, and E. G. Levine. "Family Caregiver Appraisals of Patient Behavioral Disturbance in Senile Dementia." *Clinical Gerontologist* 6 (1987): 25–34.

Haley, W. E., E. G. Levine, L. Brown, J. W. Berry, and G. H. Hughes. "Psychological, Social, and Health Consequences of Caring for a Relative with Senile Dementia." *Journal of the American Geriatrics Society* 35 (1987): 405–411.

Hanks, R. "Theoretical Questions and Ethical Issues in a Family Caregiving Relationship." *The Journal of Applied Social Sciences* 13 (1988-89): 9–39.

Hasselkus, B. R. "Meaning in Family Caregiving: Perspectives on Caregiver/Professional Relationships." *The Gerontologist* 28 (1988): 686–691.

Hausman, C. P. "Short-Term Counseling Groups for People with Elderly Parents." *The Gerontologist* 19 (1979): 102–107.

Hayter, J. "Helping Families of Patients with Alzheimer's Disease." *Journal of Gerontological Nursing* 9 (1982): 81–86.

Horowitz, A. "Sons and Daughters as Caregivers to Older Parents: Differences in Role Performance and Consequences." *The Gerontologist* 25 (1985): 612–617.

Kiecolt-Glaser, J. K., C. S. Dyer, and E. C. Shuttleworth. "Upsetting Social Interactions and Distress Among Alzheimer's Disease Family Caregivers: A Replication and Extension." *American Journal of Community Psychology* 16 (1988): 825–837.

Kitwood, T. "Brain, Mind and Dementia: With Particular Reference to Alzheimer's Disease." *Ageing and Society* 9 (1989): 1–15.

Klein, R. F., A. Dean, and M. D. Bogdanoff. "The Impact of Illness Upon the Spouse." *Journal of Chronic Diseases* 20 (1987): 241–248.

Kleinman, A. *The Illness Narratives: Suffering, Healing, and the Human Condition.* New York: Basic Books, Inc., 1988.

Kovar, M., and T. Harris. "Who Will Care for the Old?" *American Demographics* (1986): 35–37.

LaBarge, E. "Counseling Patients with Senile Dementia and Their Families." *Personnel and Guidance Journal* 60 (1981): 139–143.

Lawton, M. P., E. M. Brody, and A. R. Saperstein. "A Controlled Study of Respite Service for Caregivers of Alzheimer's Patients." *The Gerontologist* 29 (1989): 8–16.

Lazarus, L. W., B. Stafford, K. Cooper, B. Cohler, and M. Dysken. "A Pilot Study of an Alzheimer's Patients' Relatives Discussion Group." *The Gerontologist* 21 (1981): 353–358.

Lezak, M. D. "Living with the Characterologically Altered Brain Injured Patient." *Journal of Clinical Psychiatry* 39 (1978): 592–598.

Litz, B. T., A. M. Zeiss, and H. D. Davies. "Sexual Concerns of Male Spouses of Female Alzheimer's Disease Patients." *The Gerontologist* 30 (1990): 113–116.

Mace, N. L., and P. V. Rabins. *The 36-Hour Day*. Baltimore: The Johns Hopkins University Press, 1981.

Middleton, L. *Alzheimer's Family Support Groups: A Manual for Group Facilitators*. Tampa: Suncoast Gerontology Center, University of South Florida, 1984.

Morycz, R. K. "An Exploration of Senile Dementia and Family Burden." *Clinical Social Work Journal* 8 (1980): 16–27.

Morycz, R. K. "Caregiving Strain and the Desire to Institutionalize Family Members with Alzheimer's Disease." *Research on Aging* 7 (1985): 329–361.

Motenko, A. K. "The Frustrations, Gratifications, and Well-Being of Dementia Caregivers." *The Gerontologist* 29 (1989): 166–172.

Niederehe, G., and E. Fruge. "Dementia and Family Dynamics: Clinical Research Issues." *Journal of Geriatric Psychiatry* 16 (1983): 21–55.

Noelker, L. S., and R. W. Wallace. "The Organization of Family Care for Impaired Elderly." *Journal of Family Issues* 6 (1985): 23–45.

Northouse, M. L. "Who Supports the Support System?" *Journal of Psychiatric Nursing* 18 (1980): 11–15.

O'Connor, K., and J. Prothero, eds. *The Alzheimer's Caregiver: Strategies for Support*. Seattle: University of Washington Press, 1987.

Olesen, V. L. "Caregiving, Ethical and Informal: Emerging Challenges in the Sociology of Health and Illness." *Journal of Health and Social Behavior* 30 (1989): 1–10.

Ory, M. G., T. F. Williams, M. Emr, B. Lebowitz, P. Rabins, J. Salloway, T. Sluss Radebaugh, E. Wolff, and S. Zarit. "Families, Informal Supports, and Alzheimer's Disease." *Research on Aging* 7 (1985): 623–644.

Pagel, M. D., J. Becker, and D. B. Coppel. "Loss of Control, Self-Blame, and Depression: An Investigation of Spouse Caregivers of Alzheimer's Disease Patients." *Journal of Abnormal Psychology* 94 (1985): 169–182.

Parsons, R. J., and E. O. Cox. "Family Mediation in Elderly Caregiving Decisions: An Empowerment Intervention." *Social Work* 34 (1989): 122–126.

Pearlin, L. I., and C. Schooler. "The Structure of Coping." *Journal of Health and Social Behavior* 19 (1978): 2–21.

Pearlin, L. I., J. T. Mullan, S. J. Semple, and M. M. Skaff. "Caregiving and the Stress Process: An Overview of Concepts and Their Measures." *The Gerontologist* 30 (1990): 583–591.

Pell, A. R. *Making the Most of Medicare: A Guide Through the Medicare Maze.* New York: Prentice Hall Press, 1987.

Poulshock, S. W., and G. T. Deimling. "Families Caring for Elders in Residence: Issues in the Measurement of Burden." *Journal of Gerontology* 39 (1984): 230–239.

Pratt, C. C., V. L. Schmall, S. Wright, and M. Cleland. "Burden and Coping Strategies of Caregivers to Alzheimer's Patients." *Family Relations* 34 (1985): 27–33.

Pruchno, R. A., and N. L. Resch. "Husbands and Wives as Caregivers: Antecedents of Depression and Burden." *The Gerontologist* 29 (1989): 159–164.

Quayhagen, M. P., and M. Quayhagen. "Alzheimer's Stress: Coping with the Caregiving Role." *The Gerontologist* 28 (1988): 391–396.

Quayhagen, M. P., and M. Quayhagen. "Differential Effects of Family-Based Strategies On Alzheimer's Disease." *The Gerontologist* 29 (1989): 150–155.

Rakowski, W., and N. M. Clarke. "Future Outlook, Caregiving, and Care-Receiving in the Family Context." *The Gerontologist* 25 (1985): 618–623.

Reifler, B. V., G. B. Cox, and R. J. Hanley. "Problems of Mentally Ill Elderly as Perceived by Patients, Families, and Clinicians." *The Gerontologist* 21 (1981): 165–169.

Reifler, B. V., and S. Wu. "Managing Families of the Demented Elderly." *The Journal of Family Practice* 14 (1982): 1051–1056.

Rodin, J. "Sense of Control: Potentials for Intervention." *Annals of the American Academy of Political and Social Science* 503 (1989): 29–42.

Scharlach, A., and C. Frenzel. "An Evaluation of Institution-Based Respite Care." *The Gerontologist* 26 (1986): 77–82.

Scott, J. P., K. A. Roberto, and J. T. Hutton. "Families of Alzheimer's Victims: Family Support to the Caregivers." *Journal of the American Geriatrics Society* 34 (1986): 348–354.

Shanas, E. "The Family as a Social Support System in Old Age." *The Gerontologist* 19 (1979): 169–174.

Smallegan, M. "There Was Nothing Else to Do: Needs for Care Before Nursing Home Admission." *The Gerontologist* 25 (1985): 364–369.

Soldo, B. J., and J. Myllyluoma. "Caregivers Who Live with Dependent Elderly." *The Gerontologist* 23 (1983): 605–611.

Sommers, T., and L. Shields. *Women Take Care: Consequences of Caregiving in Today's Society.* Gainesville, Florida: Triad Publishing, 1987.

Spence, A. P. *The Biology of Human Aging.* Englewood Cliffs, New Jersey: Prentice Hall, 1989.

Stoller, E. P. "Sources of Support for the Elderly During Illness." *Health and Social Work* 7 (1982): 111–122.

Stoller, E. P. "Elder-Caregiver Relationships in Shared Households." *Research on Aging* 7 (1985): 175–193.

Townsend, A. L., and S. W. Poulshock. "Intergenerational Perspectives on Impaired Elders' Support Networks.'' *Journal of Gerontology* 41 (1986): 101–109.

Ware, L. A., and M. Carper. "Living With Alzheimer Disease Patients: Family Stresses and Coping Mechanisms." *Psychotherapy: Theory, Research and Practice* 19 (1982): 472–481.

Waters, E. B., and J. Goodman. *Empowering Older Adults: Practical Strategies for Counselors*. San Francisco: Jossey-Bass Publishers, 1990.

Wasow, M. "Support Groups for Family Caregivers of Patients with Alzheimer's Disease." *Social Work* 31 (1986): 93–97.

Wiancko, D. C., L. D. Crinklaw, and C. D. Mora. "Nurses Can Learn from Wives of Impaired Spouses." *Journal of Gerontological Nursing* 12 (1986): 28–33.

Wright, S. D., D. A. Lund, M. A. Pett, and M. S. Caserta. "The Assessment of Support Group Experiences by Caregivers of Dementia Patients." *Clinical Gerontologist* 6 (1987): 35–59.

Zarit, S. H., K. E. Reever, and J. Bach-Peterson. "Relatives of the Impaired Elderly: Correlates of Feelings of Burden." *The Gerontologist* 20 (1980): 649–655.

Zarit, S. H., and J. M. Zarit. "Families under Stress: Interventions for Caregivers of Senile Dementia Patients." *Psychotherapy: Theory, Research, and Practice* 19 (1982): 461–471.

Zarit, S. H., and N. K. Orr. *Working with Families of Dementia Victims: A Treatment Manual*. Washington, D.C.: U. S. Department of Health and Human Services, 1983.

Zarit, S. H., N. K. Orr, and J. M. Zarit. *The Hidden Victims of Alzheimer's Disease: Families Under Stress*. New York: New York University Press, 1985.

Zarit, S. H., P. A. Todd, and J. M. Zarit. "Subjective Burden of Husbands and Wives as Caregivers: A Longitudinal Study." *The Gerontologist* 26 (1986): 260–266.

INDEX

ABOUT THE AUTHOR

Patricia Brown Coughlan has a B.A. in sociology from the University of California at Santa Cruz and an M.A. in Interdisciplinary Studies/Gerontology from Sonoma State University. In the mid-1980s, while she was employed by the editorial staff of *Redbook* magazine to read submissions to their "Young Mother's Story" feature, she developed a deep admiration for people who have managed to cope with serious crises of all different kinds in their lives. Her personal interest in Alzheimer's disease is rooted in the case of her grandmother, Carol Brown, who is now ninety-two years old and residing in a nursing home.

Ms. Coughlan is currently working on an interview project involving workers in long-term-care settings. She lives in Sebastopol, California, with her husband and their two children, and is a member of the Sonoma County Alzheimer's Task Force. *Facing Alzheimer's* is her first book.